Andrew Murray
and His Message

Andrew Murray

and

His Message

One of God's Choice Saints

W. M. Douglas

BAKER BOOK HOUSE
Grand Rapids, Michigan 49506

Reprinted 1981 by
Baker Book House Company
from the edition published by
Fleming H. Revell Company
ISBN: 0-8010-2908-2

First printing, March 1981
Second printing, September 1983

PHOTOLITHOPRINTED BY CUSHING - MALLOY, INC.
ANN ARBOR, MICHIGAN, UNITED STATES OF AMERICA

PREFACE

THE remarkable man whose Life Story is told in these pages, was called to his reward in 1917, and it may appear strange to some, that this record of his life should be written so long after his death. The explanation is simple.

What may be called the " Official Life " of the late Dr. Andrew Murray was written by Professor du Plessis of Stellenbosch some years since, and was published in both Dutch and English. The book was most ably written and the publishers spared no pains in producing a work of abiding importance. Professor du Plessis, however, writes from the standpoint of the Dutch Reformed Church of South Africa, and tells the story of her most remarkable son, whose life history was so intimately bound up with her own struggles and triumphs, and from that side little or nothing remains to be said. It is the interesting story of the wonderfully interesting activities of that Church from its first undertaking the direction of its own affairs, up to its present robust and vigorous and influential position, and in the midst of all this movement Andrew Murray was a central figure.

Now while this gives to Professor du Plessis' book an unique position, it necessarily meant the partial over-shadowing of the other side of Andrew Murray's life, in which he appears not at all as the Ecclesiastical Leader, but as the Spiritual Teacher of hundreds of thousands of God's children scattered throughout the world, who knew nothing about the Church difficulties or triumphs of South Africa, and who have no time, and perhaps no inclination, to enter into those details which are so full of interest to thousands in South Africa.

This book, therefore, is in no sense a competitor with Professor du Plessis' larger and fuller life. The aim of this work is to set forth the MIRACLE of Dr. Murray's Life. The word " miracle " is used in its primary meaning of that which transcends unaided natural powers and indicates the direct and personal operation of God. While the larger work does not exclude this aspect of Dr. Murray's life, this is an attempt to tell chiefly and as simply as possible, the wonderful way in which God wrought out in this man of iron will, of strong personality, of gifts for leadership and government possessed by few; the gentleness and humility of Christ, till he became loved and trusted as a true shepherd of souls, by thousands who never saw his face nor heard his voice. And while Andrew Murray's name will never be effaced from South African history, his lasting monument will be the many helpful books he has left behind him to carry on his witness to the reality of the Indwelling Christ in the hearts of His people through the power of the Holy Spirit.

Following the Story of his Life there is a short treatise, written by Rev. Walter Searle of the S.A. General Mission, who for many years was Dr. Murray's friend, and at one time his travelling companion, having been associated with him in some of his wonderful Convention experiences. Mr. Searle has responded to a request sent to him to compile a short bibliography of works which came from Dr. Murray's pen. It would have been impossible for him or anyone to cover the whole ground in the limited space he had for some hundreds of books and tracts stand to Dr. Murray's credit; but it would, indeed, be difficult to find any man more fitted than Mr. Searle to give such a summary as is here and now, in this volume, presented to the reader, in the hope that it may prove a guide to those who are led to undertake the study of some at least of Andrew Murray's writings.

Mr. Searle chooses as title for his treatise " Andrew Murray as revealed in his Writings." He will feel that he has had a rich reward, if even some, are led to seek to know that Saviour Who was such a reality to Dr. Murray, and Who so wonderfully impressed his own character on His servant, especially His characteristic humility.

One word more. Many cannot read Andrew Murray. The probable reason is they try to read him as they read ordinary writers. But Andrew Murray is not an ordinary writer. If instead of trying to run through a volume, readers would be content to read no more than they are able to digest, taking a little at a time, and meditating on, and praying over what they read, there would be few who could not receive help and blessing from the study of his writings. He is a safe leader, because he is Himself so sane and Scriptural. He claimed no inspiration or knowledge for himself which he did not believe God designed for all Believers who were willing to surrender themselves to the sure guidance of the Holy Spirit through the Word, who were humble enough to leave Him to decide the rate at which His work should be done, and who were conscious enough of their own helplessness and need to look only to God for Salvation.

The Book is prayerfully committed to the over-ruling grace of God the Holy Spirit, that through its testimony, glory may come to the Glorious Lord Jesus Christ.

CONTENTS

CHAPTER		PAGE
I	SEPHER TOLDOTH	11
	The Book of Generations, Gen. v, 1.	
II	STUDENT LIFE IN ABERDEEN . . .	25
	1838–1845.	
III	STUDENT YEARS IN HOLLAND . . .	34
	Mr. Murray's Circle of Friends—He Obtains Assurance of Salvation—1845–1848.	
IV	EARLY DAYS IN BLOEMFONTEIN . .	46
	1848–1853.	
V	HOW MR. MURRAY SPENT HIS VACATIONS IN THE TRANSVAAL	60
	1849–1852.	
VI	LATER YEARS IN BLOEMFONTEIN AND VISIT TO ENGLAND	72
	1853–1860.	
VII	REVIVAL AND MISSIONS	84
	Worcester 1860–1864.	
VIII	CAPE TOWN	100
	1864–1871.	
IX	ANDREW MURRAY AS PASTOR . . .	111
	Wellington 1871–1906.	
X	THE CHRISTIAN EDUCATIONALIST AND EVANGELIST	119
	Wellington 1871–1906	

CHAPTER   PAGE

XI   EUROPE AND AMERICA VISITED   . . 133

XII   SUNSHINE AND SHADOWS 145
      Jubilee—Retirement—1898–1905

XIII   CONVENTION SPEAKER AND LEADER   154

XIV   DIVINE HEALING   180
      Experience and Teaching

XV   A GLIMPSE INTO THE HOME LIFE . . 202
      Andrew Murray as revealed in his
      Correspondence.

XVI   STILL BRINGING FORTH FRUIT IN OLD
      AGE—FULL OF SAP (*Psalms* xcii. 14. *R.V.*) . 226
      Missionary Enthusiast—1905–1916

XVII   " HE FELL ASLEEP." *Acts* vii. 60,   . 238
      " IN SURE AND CERTAIN HOPE." 1 *Thes.* iv. 14

XVIII   " HE BEING DEAD YET SPEAKETH."
      Hebrew xi. 4.   245

XIX   ANDREW MURRAY'S PRAYER LIFE . . 261

XX   THE MAN AND HIS MESSAGE   . . . 265

XXI   THE ATTAINABILITY OF HOLINESS   . 286

XXII   THE NECESSITY OF THE PENTECOSTAL
      SPIRIT 308

Chapter I

SEPHER TOLDOTH

The Book of Generations, Gen. v, 1

To few men is it given to influence a whole generation as the late Andrew Murray has done, and the Africa that gave birth to him, the Africa of nearly a century ago, was one of the last places where search would have been made beforehand by worldly-wise men for such a man.

At one of the seaside resorts of this same Africa not long ago two men met. One was a bright young Christian who was ever on the look-out for an opportunity of speaking a word for his Lord. The other was an elderly man with a sad face, the expression of which also possibly told the story of ill-temper and unpleasantness of disposition. The younger man greeted the elder cheerily, and received a cold reply, which was followed immediately by the question " Where do you come from ? " " Oh," said he, " it does not matter where a person comes from, the great question is where one is going to." " Well," said the other testily, " where are you going then ? " " I am on my way to Heaven," was the reply, " and may I ask if you are on the same journey ? " The elder man sadly confessed he did not know the way, but that was soon set right and another soul was set free in the liberty of Christ.

Now while from the standpoint of the younger of these men the question of origin did not count, it is of the greatest importance in answering the question how came South Africa to produce such a son as Andrew Murray.

Parallel with the Coast line of South Africa and at varying distances from the sea, now nearer, now farther off, runs a ridge of mountains which forms a sort of wall, but when climbed, the traveller finds there is no corresponding descent on the Northern side, but from this

mountain wall lies a great tableland covering an area of
hundreds of square miles rising gradually from about
2,000 to upwards of 4,000 feet above sea level. It is
called the Karroo, which is a Hottentot word meaning
" dry." The rainfall is small and the general appearance
is that of a desert. It formed a great barrier to the early
Dutch settlers, and would have effectually restrained the
wanderings of any race less hardy and less resourceful
than they. But they made their way through it, and
found in it many choice places, where water flowed from
deep springs, and in these places farms were established
and families settled down. These hardy Voortrekkers
(pioneers) made their way in a North-easterly direction
from the Cape of Good Hope, and finally settled down in
what is now the Graaff Reinet District. The town of
Graaff Reinet from which the district takes its name nestles
in the midland Karroo among the spurs of the Sneeuwberg
or Snowmountain Range. From this point the great plain
slopes off gently towards Cape Town, which is about 500
miles to the South-west, and towards Port Elizabeth,
which lies about 180 miles to the South. The establishment of the town is connected with one of the earliest of
those movements northwards which characterise the
history of the sturdy Dutch settlers of the Cape. Graaff
Reinet was meant by them to be one of those free states
which it was ever their dream and desire to establish.
Situated in the midst of " a dry and thirsty land," it is
itself well watered by the Sundays River, which flows
through the small plain on which the town stands. It has
in after days well merited the name it often bears, " The
Gem of the Karroo."

The story of the town is bound up with that of the
struggles, and difficulties, and dangers, attendant on the
settlement of Europeans in the Eastern portion of the
present Province of the Cape of Good Hope, but no fact
in its stirring history is of greater importance than the
birth there, of that Andrew Murray, whose name became a

household word in the Churches of Christ throughout the world.

The more remote ancestors of the Murrays were associated with one of the early secession movements in connection with the Presbyterian Church of Scotland, generally known as "Auld Lichts" or "Old Light" Presbyterians. They were evidently a very Godly race. Of one of them it is told that when old and deaf he used to wander on the sheep hills, unconsciously praying aloud for his relatives and friends, and it was remarked that all those for whom he was heard to pray, became decided Christians.

The immediate ancestors of Andrew Murray, Senr., were farmers in Aberdeenshire, in Scotland. Both his father and grandfather bore the name of Andrew. The grand-father occupied the sheepfarm "Lofthills," near Aberdeen, which had been held by the family for several generations. He suffered serious financial loss in connection with the general distress that was afflicting Scotland in the early part of the 19th century. He died whilst still comparatively young, leaving a widow with two sons and two daughters. The night on which he died he prayed aloud for each of his children by name. John, then a boy about 12 years of age overheard his father's prayer, and the impression made on him was so great that he dedicated himself to the service of Christ, resolving to educate himself for the Ministry and also to assist his brother Andrew in his education. The mother was a woman of great beauty and loveableness, and lived to see her children grow up to manhood and womanhood, giving promise of useful and honourable lives. John became a Minister of one of the first churches erected in Aberdeen by the Free Church after the Disruption, and he died in a good old age much honoured and esteemed. Elizabeth, one of the daughters, married Mr. Robertson, a Congregational Minister, who, after her death, removed to Canada with his children, and they, like the Murrays in South Africa, became the progenitors of a large and remarkable family connection there. The most notable of their descendants was Charles W. Gordon, grandson of Elizabeth Robertson, who wrote under the *nom-de-plume* of Ralph Connor. The " Sky Pilot " and other popular books came from his pen. It is a striking evidence of the value of the parents' covenant with God for their children that after more than fifty years of silence between them, the first greeting from the Canadian branch of the family to South African branch was a child's photo bearing the text, " Know therefore that the Lord Thy God, He is God, the faithful God, which keepeth covenant and mercy with them that love Him and keep His commandments to a thousand generations." *Deut.* vii. 9. The promise which the South African branch annexed to itself is *Isaiah* lix. 21, " As for me this is my covenant with them saith the Lord, my Spirit that is upon thee and My words which I have put in thy mouth shall not depart out of thy mouth nor out of the mouth of thy seed nor out of the mouth of thy seed's seed saith the Lord from hence-forth and for ever."

Andrew was the favourite son of his mother, and he warmly returned her affection. In after years he cherished very tender recollections of her, and used to describe her beauty to his children. It was love to his mother and regard for her wishes that had kept him at home at the close of his College course when he received an offer to go to St. John's, Newfoundland. But later on there came another call that he felt unable to refuse, and this call came from South Africa. How strongly it was felt by Andrew Murray is evidenced by the fact that in spite of his tender love for his mother, he left her while she lay on what proved to be her death-bed, and she was not told of the far off destination for which he was leaving. His brother John accompanied him to the stage-coach, and while they waited for it on the road-side they committed one another to God's care and sang together the old hymn

" O God of Bethel," which became a family hymn in the widespread Murray households. He spent some months in Holland before actually sailing for South Africa, in order to learn Dutch.

The circumstances which led to this call can be briefly related. The Dutch East India Company had, in 1642, founded a settlement at the Cape of Good Hope with no idea of colonising the country, but for the sake of having a convenient port of call between Holland and the East for the refreshment of the crews and the obtaining of supplies. Gradually the population increased. Made up of sturdy Dutch burghers, who soon became impatient of the Company's rule, and pushed off inland, forming settlements where they could find favourable conditions. Wherever they went they carried with them their Bibles and their love for their Church, and gradually congregations were formed of these scattered communities. During the time when the Cape was held by the Dutch East India Company, a strong and flourishing Dutch Church had been established, modelled on the lines of and drawing the supply of its Ministers from the Church in Holland.

After the advent of the British, difficulties arose in supplying the pulpits and congregations which were scattered through the country long distances apart. From the beginning this Church was closely connected with the Government, and even after the British took possession of the Cape this connection continued. It was truly the National Church of the Country. When Lord Henry Somerset was Governor of the Cape, he requested the Rev. Dr. George Thom, who had come to South Africa in connection with the London Missionary Society, but was then Minister of the Dutch Church of Caledon, to see what could be done to procure a supply of suitable Ministers from Scotland. Dr. Thom was at that time on furlough, and, throwing himself heartily into the task, he went to Scotland and had considerable success. On January 8th, 1821, he was able to write from London to Lord Henry and tell him that "he had secured the services of the Rev. Andrew Murray, M.A., a clergyman of about 30 years of age, of established character and of good abilities." Mr. Murray was thus the first of a band of able Scotchmen who heard the cry for help and wholeheartedly responded. Dr. Thom also secured the services of six young men as teachers, among them were Messrs. Innes and Robertson, whose names afterwards became so well known. These six accompanied Mr. Murray and Dr. Thom on their eventful voyage to South Africa, which was nearly fatally terminated off Cape de Verde. In his diary, dated 25th April, 1822, Mr. Murray says : " The previous night the vessel was held up in order to avoid danger of running aground, but on this night Capt. Anderson thought that he might safely continue his course. Worship was conducted as usual, and a few minutes after all the passengers were surprised to feel the vessel give a sudden, forcible jolt against a rock. The Mate cried out : " Capt. Anderson, come, we are on land, breakers are close to our bows." The sailors were crying out, while the Mate cried : " Make no uproar, keep cool, let us prepare for meeting death like Scotchmen." Mr. Brown and Mr. Murray were able to assist the seamen to shorten the sails, the rest remained on the quarter-deck, Dr. Thom giving orders for having the boats in readiness. After engaging a few minutes in prayer to plead the promise of God, " Call on Me in the day of trouble, and I will deliver thee," he read Psalm 91. The Captain and Mate came into the cabin, the former appeared to be in a state of intoxication, perhaps through surprise being unable to say where we were or what was the matter, or whither we could turn for safety. At last the vessel was got off the rock which we afterwards found to be a long point of the island, where several large East India-men had been lost. Mr. Murray and his companions had no doubt in their minds that it was God's over-ruling power alone which saved them from utter destruction. Mr. Murray remained on deck through the night, in the course of it he had an opportunity to speak to most of the seamen one by one on spiritual and eternal subjects. They arrived in Cape Town in July, 1822, and in the "Government Gazette" of the first week of that month, a few days after they landed, the following notice appeared: "It has pleased His Excellency the Governor to appoint the Rev. Abraham Faure (then at Graaff Reinet) as Third Minister of Cape Town, and Rev. Andrew Murray as Minister of Graaff Reinet."

There was no insuperable difficulty in obtaining a supply of suitable Ministers from Scotland, for the only real difference between the two Churches was one of language. An incident which occurred a few years since will illustrate the wonderful oneness of the two great Presbyterian Churches, that of Scotland and the Dutch Reformed Church of South Africa.

At one of the Conferences of the Students' Christian Association, which was held not long since in one of Mr. Murray's old parishes, Worcester, a gentleman from Scotland was there as a visitor. He was invited by one of the Secretaries to attend with him the Morning Service at the Dutch Reformed Church. The Secretary was an English-speaking man, but understood Dutch. When the Service was over he asked his Scotch friend what he thought of it. "Well," said he, "I did not understand a single word from beginning to end, but I felt perfectly at home, I was back again in the church of my childhood. I understood the atmosphere, and I was at home."

Mr. Murray must soon have gained a mastery of Dutch, for the following year a traveller speaks of having attended his services in the church, and having heard him preach in Dutch to a large congregation.

Mr. Murray was back again in Cape Town two years later attending the First Synod of the Dutch Church, and he took an active part in its deliberations and served on the most important Committees, one of which had under consideration the founding of a Theological Seminary, a project which was carried out thirty years later when Andrew Murray's eldest son, John, became the first Professor. During this Synod, Andrew Murray, Senr., however busy he was with the affairs of the Church, had time to attend to an important personal matter, for during this period he came into touch with the remarkable woman who next year became his wife.

The interesting family record entitled " Unto Children's Children," which was published for private circulation only, and from which frequent quotations are made in these pages, describes this event and the settlement in Graaff Reinet as follows :—

" This time it was not a meeting of the Synod that brought him to Cape Town, he came to claim the treasure which he had discovered on his previous visit—the young lady whose fair face had captivated his heart and whom after much prayer he had asked to share his home and future labours. How happy he was in his choice there are many witnesses to testify, besides her own children who arise and call her blessed. She was only 16 when she was married, and has been described by a friend who entertained them for a few days on their inland journey, ' She looked lovely dressed according to the fashion of the time in pure white muslin.' Graaff Reinet was and still is one of the most important towns in the Cape province. The Congregation there was founded in 1790, between then and the appointment of Andrew Murray five ministers had held a pastorate covering a period of 29 years, that of Mr. Murray extended over 45 years. The church was built in 1822, the parsonage had been built previously ; it still stands to-day though now it is used as a boarding establishment for girls who are being trained as teachers. It was a large and commodious house, prepared beforehand for the large family which was now to fill it. About a year after his marriage, Mr. Murray received the offer of an appointment to Tulbagh, near Cape Town, but he refused to move. He cast in his lot so whole-heartedly with his people that his children cannot remember ever hearing him express the wish to visit his native land. How happy he was among his people only his children who grew up in the presence of that loving intercourse could testify. Earnest, affectionate, and sincere in all his relations, he never forfeited the respect and esteem accorded him by all. How often he was heard to say, ' The lines have fallen to me in pleasant places.' "

Many words of Scripture became engraven on the hearts of his children through hearing their father repeat them with great feeling and emphasis. The Word of Christ did indeed dwell in him richly.

Sunday evenings left memories never to be effaced, but just as sacred were the memories of the Friday evenings which Mr. Murray regularly devoted to praying for revival. His children never forgot how they sometimes stood outside his study door listening to his loud crying to God as he pleaded for an outpouring of the Holy Spirit.

He had warm sympathy with every good work, by whomsoever begun, or in whatever part of the world it occurred. In every good cause he took the lead. Long before slavery was abolished he espoused the cause of the slave. When, upon his marriage, as was then the custom, a female slave was given to the bride to accompany her to her new home, he gave her her liberty, before she set out with them.

Mr. Murray died in 1866, a few years after resigning his charge which he laid down in his 70th year.

How minister and people were bound together in love was beautifully illustrated by an incident which happened towards the close of his life. He was suffering from the effects of a cold, and on leaving a certain farm a young man who had waited on him very tenderly brought a hot brick and placed it below his feet in the cart, whereupon he turned to his travelling companion and said : " Ik woon in het midden myns volks." " I dwell among my own people." *II Kings*, iv. 13.

His parish covered some hundreds of square miles, he established many new congregations, in Aberdeen, Colesberg, Middleburg, Murraysburg, and in other places also, until these townships were supplied with their own ministers he remained their preacher and pastor. But at every farm-house along the road as he travelled, where he stopped for the night, he was asked to conduct a service, and he always insisted on all the servants and shepherds being called in, and weary though he was, he rejoiced at being able to break the Bread of Life to hungry souls. In visiting these various congregations, an important part of his work was Huis-bezoek, which generally means " Visitation of families in their homes," but as this was impossible under the circumstances, Mr. Murray arranged for the families or their representatives who were present at the services to meet him by themselves apart. They were admitted into the room in which, for the time being, he lived, and they were seriously and affectionately exhorted, advised, encouraged or rebuked as the case demanded. He truly was a workman who needed not to be ashamed.

Mrs. Murray proved an eminently suitable helpmeet for such a man. One of her daughters writes : " How can a child attempt to describe a mother, and especially such a mother. To us she never seemed at all like anyone else, she was just ' Mama.' She taught us to read until we were old enough to be sent to School, and the hymns and verses we learned at her knee have remained in the memory of a lifetime. We can still hear her voice prompting us, and the prayer—after more than sixty years we venture to give it from memory. It was this : ' O Lord God Who knowest all things, Thou seest by night as well as by day, forgive me, I pray Thee, for Christ's sake, whatsoever I have done amiss this day. Keep me safe through all this night. I desire to lie down under Thy care, and to abide for ever under Thy blessing, for Thou art the God of all Power and everlasting mercy. Amen.' "

What a companion that mother was to her girls and to her grown-up sons! If asked what was her chief characteristic, we should reply: "Contentment, habitual, unvarying contentment." She was happy in her husband, and in her children, and supremely happy in the love of God, Who had been so good to her. The peace of God kept her heart fixed, and every action, and almost every moment, expressed that restfulness. Rest in the midst of work! Communion with God was the secret of it. She never failed to take time for her private devotions. Children and servants knew that when her chamber door was shut she must not be disturbed. They hesitated to knock, even if it seemed necessary. One of her children remarked: "There is hardly a letter of hers in which she does not speak of God's goodness and love." Another daughter says: "Mama's letters are all love letters." She became the mother of a large family of sons and daughters, most of them becoming ministers or marrying ministers, and thus exerting a wide influence.

A notable visitor from across the sea, who had full opportunity for forming a correct judgment remarked upon the warm spiritual atmosphere he found everywhere in "the Murray belt," referring to the part of the country where the ministry of the Murrays was exercised. One daughter gave over 14 years to teaching, and led many of her pupils to Christ. One son became a farmer, and exercised a strong Christian influence where he lived. Graaff Reinet was on the high road to the interior, and the parsonage there became the hospitable home of many of the remarkable missionaries of those early days. The visits of Dr. Moffat and Dr. Livingstone, who afterwards became so famous, were never forgotten. One of the family remembers seeing Dr. Livingstone come hurriedly into the room late for breakfast, triumphantly exhibiting a large hatchet, just to his mind, which he had purchased at the store. Lively recollections are cherished of the earlier French missionaries, Pellissier, Roland, Casalis and others. When in 1874 a grandson of the Graaff Reinet parsonage, Rev. Charles Andrew Murray, went to Edinburgh, he called upon old Dr. Moffat, whose joy at seeing him was unfeigned. " If a stone from South Africa had been brought to me," he said, " I should have been glad, but a son—a son whose father and grandfather it was my privilege to know ! " And then, addressing other visitors in the room, he told them how missionaries used to be received at the Graaff Reinet parsonage and said : " Do you think those missionaries left without praying God to bless that house ? Do you doubt God heard those prayers ? "

In the publication already mentioned, the writer says concerning the family : " The chief characteristic of the household was reverence. We reverenced God and God's Day and God's Word. The wife reverenced the husband ; the children reverenced their parents ; the servants reverenced their master and mistress.

" The children were trained in the ways of the Lord, they were taught to render obedience in such a way that they never seemed to know it. The father's word was law ; from his decision there was no appeal. But in that household love was the bond of perfectness."

Into this family Andrew was born in 1828. He was the second son, John, the elder, having been born in 1826. The education of these boys now growing up so quickly was a serious matter. The educational advantages for which Graaff Reinet is remarkable to-day were then unknown, so after much thought and prayer it was decided to send the two elder boys, John, now aged 12, and Andrew, aged 10, to Scotland for education.   It was a daring experiment, and meant the severance of tender ties, but it was undertaken and carried through in the fear of God, and from the beginning had His blessing. Their uncle, Rev. John Murray, of Aberdeen, received them into his home.

One thing which made it possible to face such an expenditure was the fact that through the hospitality and great kindness shown by Mr. Murray to an English official

of the Indian Service when on a visit to South Africa, a
sense of gratitude was awakened which led him to make
an acknowledgment of his appreciation of this kindness
by sending Mr. Murray a substantial cheque which he used
towards the payment of the many expenses incurred by
this trip. The lads were accompanied by their parents
to Port Elizabeth, about 180 miles south of Graaff Reinet.
Here they were committed into the care of a Wesleyan
missionary, Rev. James Archibald, who, with his wife,
was going on a visit to England, and in due time, after
what seems to have been an uneventful voyage, they
reached England and made their way to Aberdeen.

In 1913 Andrew Murray, the second, wrote the following
memorandum addressed to the entire Murray family circle.
It forms a fitting close to this chapter on Origins.

"A godly parentage is a priceless boon. Its blessing
rests not only upon the children of the first generation,
but has often been traced in many successive generations.

"But its blessings will depend upon the keeping up of
the spirit of prayer, with that direct sense of belonging
to God.

"When God blessed Abram and his seed it was that
through them all the nations of the earth were to be
blessed. And so God still means a family which He blesses
to be the channel through which a neighbourhood or a
people shall learn to know Him.

"To belong to such a family implies high privilege, but
equally high responsibility. The spirit of the world is so
strong, the slackening of the spiritual life on the part of
the parents comes in so easily, that unless the charge God
has committed to us be jealously guarded, the inheritance
may easily become spent and lost. It is well for a family
that acknowledges what it owes to the prayers of ancestors."

After 100 years! Here is the record by one of the
family :

"A remarkable centenary gathering was held in Graff
Reinet from June 28th to July 4th, 1922. Two hundred

and twenty descendants out of four hundred and eighty six came to celebrate the landing of the first Andrew Murray on these shores. Two daughters and a daughter-in-law were present, who seemed almost as youthful as the youngest present, to whose initiative the meetings owed their success.

" Graff Reinet received and entertained them right royally, for almost ninety years some member of the Murray family had served the pulpit. For forty years Miss Murray had been teacher and principal of the Girls' High School.

" During the hundred years now ending, over fifty ministers have been connected with the family by birth or marriage, and about the same number of men and women have given the whole or part of their lives to work in the Foreign Mission Field. Some of the young men are now attending the Theological Seminary and others are expecting to enter it in due time, some are studying medicine in the hope of becoming Medical Missionaries. One young man was ordained as Missionary just about the time of the holding of this interesting gathering. Looking over the past one could only adore the goodness of the covenant-keeping God and entrust to the same God the keeping of the future generations."

CHAPTER II

STUDENT LIFE IN ABERDEEN

1838—1845

THE boys arrived in Aberdeen in the autumn of 1838 and became inmates of their Uncle John's home for the next seven years. The family consisted of an uncle and aunt, one son and three daughters. The uncle was one of the keenest of the Evangelical Ministers in Scotland, a man of ripe scholarship, a good preacher, who maintained a tender walk with God. Andrew Murray of Graaff Reinet, writing to his sons, refers to the trust and confidence he had in their uncle, his brother John : " I may tell you now that I write familiarly, that when I was somewhat about your age, I found myself embarrassed with some little difficulties ; I knew prayer was the way to relief in great matters, but I thought it would be dishonouring to the great God to go and speak to Him about my little things. I spoke to my brother (their uncle John) on the subject, who assured me I could not honour God more than by taking all my little needs to Him, if in an humble frame of mind, and with a desire to obtain His direction and assistance. This simple assurance from one on whose judgment I depended gave me great relief."

The Aunt was of a depressed temperament, and Mr. Murray's tenderness in after years towards doubting Christians seems to have been largely the result of noticing how his Uncle tried to comfort his wife.

All that centred round these experiences made a lasting impression on Andrew, who, with John, was on a last visit to Aberdeen at the time.

The years of the boys' stay were filled with hard study which began the day after they arrived. The following account by a cousin is interesting : " He, Andrew and his brother when they arrived after a miserable voyage, were suffering from the effects of the voyage, and I have always thought with pity of the dear little fellow being entered at the Grammar School the first morning after his arrival. But he was very happy there, and had a great teacher in Dr. Melvin, of whom Professor David Masson has written so graphically. I cannot tell you anything remarkable of his early days with us. He was a bright, lovable boy, extremely obliging, and devoted to his brother John, to whom he owed much. John was studious and thoughtful beyond his years, and seemed weighted with a sense of responsibility both on his own account and Andrews'. Strange to say, when both boys sat for the entrance examination at Marischal College, it was the younger boy, then only thirteen, who gained the bursary. One remarkable thing I can tell you which applies to both boys—with neither of them had their uncle or aunt even once to find fault during their seven years' stay in our house, and this was due, we believed, to incessant prayer for them in the Graaff Reinet home. We, the younger members of the family, looked on them as brothers, and were broken-hearted when they left us.''

Those were stirring times that the boys lived through in Scotland. Philanthropy, education, religion, were all claiming fresh attention, and politically the Chartists were active.

Under the inspiration of the great-hearted and saintly Dr. Chalmers, everything Evangelical received a new impulse. He was recognised as the greatest preacher of his time, and attracted multitudes of hearers, not a few of whom were savingly impressed, and became from that time leaders in all good works. His influence told powerfully on the Church. His aim was not just the erection of places of worship for such as might be attracted by the ministry of the Word, but he sought to provide an agency to carry the Gospel to the homes of those outside the churches, and to compel them to come in. Although he was a College Professor he set an example to others by house to house visitation and work in the Sabbath school.

Through Dr. McCrie's works on Knox and Melville a new patriotism had been kindled with a new love for the Church.

Dr. Andrew Thompson had awakened a new interest in the Bible as the only authoritative guide to what the Church ought to believe and do. To him is due the prevalence of the views long held in Scotland regarding the inspiration and the sole and supreme authority of the Scriptures as the rule of faith and morals.

This new life and energy came early into conflict with the prevalent Moderate School of thought. Among the younger Evangelicals were Dr. Candlish ; the saintly R. Murray McCheyne ; the two Bonars ; and A. N. Somerville. All these stirring events and remarkable men left their mark on the Murrays.

The following account of Dr. Chalmer's visit to Aberdeen after the Disruption will be of interest. " The free Church was then worshipping in a tent, which was enlarged to hold 2,000. Two hours before the time a message came, the tent was crowded, and three times as many were gathered round, while crowds were hastening to it. It was obvious that Dr. Chalmers would have to preach in the open air. In front of the house at Banchory Dr. Chalmers preached to a crowd variously estimated from 6,000 to 10,000, by whom he was completely heard." Although there is no express mention of the fact, it may be confidently supposed that John and Andrew were present at this great gathering.

It was Andrew's task to read aloud to his Uncle while he dined, and by this wise arrangement many a thought of Dr. Chalmers, Dr. Candlish, Hugh Miller and other Christian leaders was sown in fertile soil of his keen young mind. How he must have been thrilled at the accounts of ministers preaching on the bare hill side, or by the sea shore within high water mark, baptised by the spray of the incoming tide. During all that Summer there was scarcely a rainy or inclement Sabbath.

During these years a great spiritual awakening passed

over Scotland very similar to what had stirred America under Finney. The much used man of God was Rev. William C. Burns, who was destined to exercise a great influence over both the lads, but especially over the younger brother, Andrew. Mr. Burns is thus described by his biographer. " Young, inexperienced, measured, and slow of speech, gifted with no peculiar charm of poetry, or sentiment, or natural eloquence, or winning sweetness, he bore so manifestly the seal of a Divine Commission, and carried about with him, withal, such an awe of the Divine presence and majesty, as to disarm criticism, and constrain even careless hearts to receive him as a messenger of God. If his words were sometimes few, naked, unadorned, they were full of weight and power, and went home as arrows directed by a sure aim, to the heart and consciences of his hearers."

He spent very much time in prayer and fasting, and carried with him a sense of the presence of God. John was deeply impressed by a new conception of the holiness of God through an opening prayer by Mr. Burns beginning " Holy, holy, holy, Lord God of Hosts." Mr. Burns feared much, lest he should preach himself and not Christ, a fear which also haunted Andrew Murray.

Mr. Burns spent some time with Rev. John Murray during his visit to Aberdeen, and was thus brought into close touch with the brothers John and Andrew. Andrew had the privilege now and then of carrying his Bible and cloak for him as they went to meetings together. His tireless energy, his deep voice, earnest manner, and pointed appeals made a lasting impression on him, as did the scenes he witnessed in the services.

The following letter from Mr. Burns to John is characteristic of the man :

" DEAR FRIEND—I was happy to receive your interesting letter, and I have been attempting in the all prevailing name of Jesus to commend your soul in its present affecting case to the infinitely merciful and gracious Jehovah. Do not, I beseech you, give way to the secret thought that you are excusable in remaining in your present unrenewed state, or that there really is the smallest possible hope of your being saved unless you are really born of the Holy Spirit, and reconciled to the Holy Jehovah by the atoning blood of His only begotten Son. Search your heart, my dear fellow-sinner, and I am sure that you will find something which you are refusing to let go at the command of God, and look upon this secret reserve in your surrender to Him, as the reason, on account of which, He seems for a time to overlook your case. He is a God of infinite holiness and cannot look upon iniquity. If we regard iniquity in our heart the Lord will not hear us. But if you are coming in sincerity of heart to Him through Jesus Christ you will find Him to be a God of infinite mercy and loving kindness, delighting in mercy and having no pleasure in the death of the sinner. Do not doubt, as your own wicked heart, under the power of Satan, would tempt you to do, that there is mercy for you if you will not willingly harden your heart against Jehovah's voice of authority and love. He will make Himself known to you in good time. Wait on Him. I can testify this to you from my own experience. Often do I think God has forgotten me, but I find afterwards He answers prayers which I have forgotten. Oh, dear friend, be not tempted to put off to a more convenient season your entire consecration to Emmanuel. You are enjoying in Jehovah's infinite and most undeserved mercy a convenient season at present ; oh, improve it, lest the great God should be provoked and swear in His wrath ' You shall not enter into my rest.' I will continue to pray for you, and I have hope in the Lord that I may be heard for His own glory. Jesus service and His presence are indeed sweet.

I am, dear John,

Your affect. friend in the Lord Jesus,

WM. C. BURNS.

P.S. Show this to Andrew whom it may also suit. I got his letter and shall answer it afterwards if the Lord will. Write me again.''

Some extracts from letters from and to the father will show the affectionate relationship existing between them :

The first is from the Father :

" I like your desire after information, but I confess some of your queries could not be answered in a single letter, e.g., ' Describe the constitution of the D.R. Church in South Africa ' is, in a letter, no easy task. The Church is Presbyterian, has its Sessions, Presbyteries and Synod. New laws are about to be submitted to the first meeting of Synod in November next, in which it is proposed to have a General Assembly as the highest court of appeal in Spiritual things. The present Governor, Sir George Napier, has expressed himself inclined to give more latitude in this respect. You must know when I came here we had no church courts ; we have, as yet, no tithes, or other sources of income for our churches, and draw our salaries from the Colonial Treasury, which the Governor could not, but a British minister might, at once, withdraw from our whole church.

As to the case of intrusion at Somerset, or any other vacant church you suppose, I need hardly say what a Presbytery would be bound to do—for this reason, that a congregation would never dream of seriously opposing a man the Governor nominated : such would be thought open rebellion in this Colony. I may, however, mention that the majority of ministers and elders in last Synod carried a proposal of giving congregations a right to call their own ministers, subject to the approval of the Governor, every Governor has consulted more or less the feelings of the people. Sir George Grey intended giving Somerset to Dr. Roux or Mr. Borcherds, but on the memorials of churchwardens he gave the living to Mr. Pears, and sent Mr. Roux to Albany, where Mr. Pears was. . . . ''

Another letter :

" In short I am fully of Aunt's opinion. I should not like after going from Graaff Reinet to Aberdeen and to College, to learn a business or trade I could have learned as well at the Cape of Good Hope. I should never wish you to think of the law, as our Bench and Bar and notaries are of such principles and morals, that I should tremble for any contact with them. Should you feel inclined to turn your attention to theology or medicine or mercantile pursuits, I have no doubt there will always be openings at the Cape, as well as at other places. If I were in your circumstances, I should cast an eye toward the Indian Missions, there is something there worthy the ambition of great minds. But even promoting the moral and religious improvement of the rising generation under Dr. Innes is something more worthy of having obtained a liberal education then turning the attention to any common handicraft."

1840. " Nothing could afford me greater delight than to hear of those revivals of religion in the West of Scotland to which Andrew alluded in your letter. It affords me joy to hear of any number of souls brought to Christ anywhere, and it would increase the joy to think my dear boys, that you, though young, begin to take some interest in these things."

1843. " It is now time that I come to some of John's questions. The emancipated slaves cannot become small farmers here as farms are become scarce and very dear. One in Uitvlugt, purchased some time ago for 5,000 rix dollars (or £375) was wanted as a site for building a church. The people offered 1,600 rix dollars for it but in vain."

To their Parents, dated " Aberdeen, 11th April, 1844 :

" My Dear Papa and Mama—We received yours of October 30th about the beginning of February, and as we had written a little before, we delayed answering it till we should see what our success might be at the end of the session. That success, however, has been very small : John has gotten the seventh prize in Mathematics.

The Rev. MacDonald of Blairgowrie has been here lately, collecting for a scheme for building five hundred schools, giving £100 to each, which will not in all places wholly build the school. At a public meeting he held here £1,942 was subscribed, and at a second meeting the amount announced as having been collected in three days was £3,533 to be paid in five years by instalments. He requires £50,000 and wants yet about £10,000, which will soon be raised as he is a very good beggar.

The attendance at the Free Churches in Aberdeen, according to a report made by a magistrate, is about five times greater than that at the Established Churches, and two of the Established Churches in which ministers are about to be settled average an attendance of only thirteen. There is still considerable distress produced by a refusal of sites in some districts. The Duke of Sutherland, however, has given sites."

From the Father :—

" MY DEAR ANDREW—I have been favoured this morning with yours of September 7th, and am surprised at having received it so soon. It must have come by steamer . . . I have now to congratulate you on your choice of a profession and rejoice that the Lord has been pleased to incline your heart the way He has done. I trust however, my dear boy, that you have given your heart to Jesus Christ to be His now and for ever, to follow Him through good and through bad report.

The service in the Church of South Africa does not promise you much wealth or ease in this world, but a field of usefulness as extensive as you could desire among a kind and indulgent people. I may now mention for your encouragement, that I have for upwards of twenty-two years enjoyed much happiness in the work, and, I humbly trust, through the blessing of God to have some success

in the same.   You will also do well to remember that not
a few pious students in divinity have been taken away
before entering their work, but where God has seen it was
in their hearts to help to build Him a house, He has taken
the will for the deed, and has taken them to Himself.   If
we seek to be prepared for death that will be the best
preparation for usefulness in this life.   I have not space
to explain myself fully, but when you show this to Uncle
he will do so *viva voce.*"

The day was drawing near when the loving desires and
prayers of this father should be fulfilled.   Even at this
time the Holy Spirit was powerfully preparing both the
sons for the reception of His fuller grace and gifts.

After nearly seven years devotion to their studies both
brothers graduated in the Aberdeen University, taking
their M.A. degree.   John took his degree with honours.
The notice runs as follows :—

" On Friday, the 4th of April (1845), the degree of
M.A. was conferred on several candidates after exam-
ination in the Evidences of Christianity ; Natural History ;
Mathematics ; Natural Philosophy ; and Moral Philos-
ophy ; and Logic, among whom were John Murray and
Andrew Murray."

As they had both been led to dedicate their lives and
powers to the Ministry of the Word in South Africa in the
Dutch Reformed Church and as during their long residence
in Aberdeen they had well nigh forgotten the Dutch they
had acquired in childhood, it was decided that they
should take their Divinity Course in Holland, and so
towards Holland they turned their steps, leaving Aberdeen
in June, 1845, for Utrecht, where in due course they arrived,
strangers among strangers, but they were safely and
surely directed by the gracious over-ruling care of the
God of Covenant Grace.   They were to be made the centre
of a spiritual movement in connection with student life
in Holland, the results of which did not soon pass away.

CHAPTER III

STUDENT YEARS IN HOLLAND—
MR. MURRAY'S CIRCLE OF FRIENDS
HE OBTAINS ASSURANCE OF SALVATION
1845—1848

FROM the warm religious atmosphere of Scotland the Murrays now passed in to the cold formality and deadness of Holland. While in London on the way thither they spent a Sabbath with Mr. Nesbit, and heard Rev. J. Hamilton preach a sermon, in which he made use of an illustration drawn from the plant called " The Devil's Bit," to enforce the warning against beginning any work with enthusiasm and then growing weary before it is finished. Andrew took the warning to himself, recognising his own weakness, and steadily cultivated the power of perseverance which afterwards distinguished him. The following letter from his father shows how clearly he foresaw the difficulties they would encounter in Holland : " It afforded your mother, myself and friends, sincere pleasure to learn from your Uncle's letter that you both seem disposed to devote yourselves to the service of the sanctuary. As to John's former conscientious scruples or rather fears of entering on the preparation for so sacred an office, I expressed my views so fully in my former letters that I need not state them now again. Since you have made up your minds for this blessed service, oh ! let me entreat you to lead watchful and prayerful lives, that you may be preserved from error in sentiment and from every deviation from the becoming line of conduct. You may soon hear sentiments broached among the students, and even by professors, on theological subjects which may startle you, but be cautious in receiving them, by whatever names or number of names they may be supported. Try to act like the noble Bereans (*Act*. xvii. 11). By studying your

Bibles and your own hearts, I doubt not, under the guidance of the blessed Spirit, you will be led into all truth. One of the temptations you will be exposed to through companionship is the use of " Holland's " (*alias* gin) and water, and smoking tobacco or cigars. Do resist both these abominable customs. If necessary at any time, entertain your friends with tea or coffee which are both excellent in Holland. Do not be afraid to be singular in such things.

Whatever books may be recommended to you, be sure not to neglect the study of the Holy Scriptures. This must be a daily exercise and attended to with humility and much prayer for the guidance of the Holy Spirit."

They carried a letter of introduction to Dr. Cappadose, one of the leaders of a small but earnest circle of Evangelical Christians, and he invited them to attend some meetings for Bible Study. They thus became acquainted with some students with whom a lasting friendship was established. One of these friends later on thus described how they first met :—

" A Fair was being held in Utrecht and it was an excessively busy time. Yet Utrecht was lonely for us, for the members of our circle were for the most part absent from town. In a house at the extremity of the new canal, near the plantation, Dr. Cappadose was to give a Bible Reading. I set out for the meeting from my home in Booth Street. When I reached St. Jans Churchyard I saw two youths, in somewhat strange garb, walking ahead of me. They appeared cheerful and unassuming. Had they come to Utrecht for the Fair ? No, they walked straight on across the little Stammerers' Bridge, behind St. Peter's, along the new canal, yes, to the very end, and actually entered the house to which I also was going. I found, P. A. van Toorenbergen talking to them in Latin. He introduced me to them, they were John and Andrew Murray, newly arrived from Aberdeen, in order to study here and become ministers at the Cape. What a surprise !

Not frequenters of the Fair, but Cape brethren with Scotch blood. From that evening we became friends and brothers."

" We met again for tea the following Sunday at the rooms of P. A. van Toorenbergen. Discussion was carried on in Latin, for the Murrays spoke only English and very imperfect Dutch. The reading and discussion of a portion of Scripture was in Latin as well as the prayer. But whether Cicero or Professor Boumans would have found our Latin classically pure, or even intelligible or endurable is open to question. But it was sufficient, we understood one another."

This meeting was held in connection with a Society which had been established by some earnest students some time previously, the declared object of which was : " To promote the study of subjects required for the ministerial calling." It was from its members the Murrays received such a cordial welcome.

Both from motives of economy and for the sake of good example the members of this Society resolved from the outset to avoid the use of wine and spirituous liquors at their gatherings. This decision exposed them to the scorn and ridicule of their fellow students, who dubbed them " the Chocolate Club " and the " Prayer Club," so strong was the feeling against them, that men refused to sit next them at lectures, or to rub shoulders with them on coming out of class.

There was also, as might be expected, a zealous missionary spirit among the members of the Society, and the Murrays were instrumental in the establishment of a Missionary Band which met twice a month, and proved to be a plant of vigorous growth, for only recently has it been incorporated in the Netherlands Christian Students' Association. This Band flourished when in the Netherlands no other Society for Missions except the Rotterdam Missionary Society was in existence. From interest in foreign missions interest in home missions was awakened.

This Band prepared the way also for the work which Utrecht is now doing on a larger scale and with rich blessing.

It was here in Holland that Andrew Murray entered into the assurance of Salvation. He conveys this great news to his parents thus :—

" UTRECHT,

" 14th November, 1845.

" MY DEAR PARENTS,

" It was with very great pleasure that I to-day (after being out of town three days) received yours of the 15th of August, containing the announcement of the birth of another brother. And equal, I am sure, will be your delight when I tell you that I can communicate to you *far gladder tidings, over which angels have rejoiced, that your son has been born again.* It would be difficult for me to express what I feel in writing to you on the subject. Always hitherto in my letters, and even yet in my conversation, there has been and is a reticence in speaking about these things, and even now I hardly know how I shall write.

" When I look back to see how I have been brought to where I now am, I must acknowledge that : ' He hath brought the blind by a way that he knew not, and led him in a path he hath not known.' For the last two or three years there has been a process going on, a continual interchange of seasons of seriousness and then of forgetfulness, and then again seriousness soon after. In this state I came here, and as you may well conceive there was little seriousness amid the bustle of coming away. After leaving, however, there was an interval of seriousness, during the three days at sea, our departure from Aberdeen —the voyage—the recollections of the past, were all calculated to lead one to reflect. But after I came to Holland I think I was led to pray in earnest, more I cannot tell, for I know it not, but ' Whereas I was blind, now I see.' I was long troubled with the idea that I must have some deep sight of my sins before I could be converted, and though I cannot yet say that I have had anything of that deep special sight into the guilt of sin which many people appear to have, yet I trust, and at present feel, as if I could say, I am confident that as a sinner I have been led to cast myself on Christ.

" What can I say now my dear Parents but call on you to praise the Lord with me ? ' Bless the Lord, O my soul, and all that is within me bless His holy name. Bless the Lord, O my soul, and forget not all His benefits. Who forgiveth all thine iniquities Who healeth all thy diseases Who redeemeth thy life from destruction, Who crowneth thee with loving kindness and tender mercy.' At present I am in a peaceful state. I cannot say that I have any seasons of special joy, but I think I enjoy a true confidence in God. Short, however, as my experience is, I cannot say that it is always thus. Already have I felt my sins separating between me and my God, and then the miserable consequences, a sort of fear, and the wretched feeling of being held back in prayer by sin."

" November 24th. In taking up my pen again, I have to lament my inability to write on the great subject. Though I can say that my heart at present is warm, yet whenever I begin to write or speak I fail. I sometimes think how glorious it will be when it shall be impossible to do anything but ascribe praise to ' Him that hath loved us and washed us from our sins in His blood and hath made us kings and priests unto God.' There certainly must be a great change in us before we are ready to do that."

On the eve of his 18th birthday he writes : " To-morrow will close a year which is certainly the most eventful in my life, a year in which I have been made to experience most abundantly that God is good to the soul that seeketh Him. And oh ! what goodness it is when He Himself implants in us the desire of seeking while we are still enemies. I rather think when I last wrote I gave an account of what I believed was my conversion, and, God be thanked, I still believe that it was His work. Since then I cannot say I have had as much enjoyment as before it, but still there has been much joy in the Lord, though alas! there has also been much sin. But through grace I have always been enabled to trust in Him who has begun the good work in me, and to believe He will perform what He has, out of His free love before I was born, begun. Oh that I might receive grace to walk more holily before Him.

"John has written both in this and former letters very fully as to public matters here. I shall try and tell something about domestic affairs. In the last letter Papa says that he proposes sending two bills about £60 each a year. We had calculated that we would need very nearly that a year, on an average. I may state our principal expenses. House rent with service—two very large nice rooms at a cheap rate £15 a year. Dinner about 7d. each day, £17 a year. Clothes—we are not very sure how much they will amount to. During the past year we spent about £10, but we shall not need much for a considerable time to come. Bread—nearly 10s. a month. Books —we are not sure, perhaps £15 a year, too. And then innumerable sums which mount up—tea, sugar, lights, etc. At present we have no college fees. These will all have to be paid together at the end of the course.

"As to our external circumstances here, they are very much the same. We still associate only with our own circle of students. If you see the number of the Free Church Missionary Record for April you will see mention made of them and us. At present we meet every Friday evening for work from 5½ till 10, and then sup together from 10—12, very plainly of course, bread and butter, cheese, and some sort of coffee. On Wednesdays we meet in a church for oratory, when one delivers a sermon, another speaks extempore and a third reads a piece of poetry, all of course to accustom us a little to the work in which we expect and hope to be engaged.   On Sabbath evenings, we meet together for reading, singing and prayer, when one generally speaks on a chapter.   We have also begun a missionary society to meet twice a month for communicating missionary intelligence and prayer for the extension of the Kingdom of our God and His Christ ; so that on the first Monday of the month we shall have the pleasant feeling of being engaged about the same time as you and thousands of God's children throughout the whole world in supplicating for an outpouring of God's Spirit on the world.   Most of us also generally spend the Sabbath afternoon in visiting the wretched districts of the town and speaking to the people about their souls, and in teaching a few children in our rooms.   Oh that all this may not remain there and go no further but may God grant His abundant blessing on our work and on our own souls.

" There is a plan that I have to propose to Papa.   I cannot say that I am sure that it will meet with his approbation, but I mention it thus early that he may think about it and shall write more fully about it afterwards, and then he will be kind enough to give me an answer. In about two years from this date, which is all the time that it will be necessary for us to stay here, I shall be just twenty years old.   The lectures here are such that it is almost impossible to get any good from them.   What would Papa say to my, or perhaps both of us, then going to Germany ?   It would likely be to Halle, where there are a great many excellent (both in head and heart) professors, at the head of whom stands Tholuck, a pious man, professor of exegesis, who is the leader of those who at the present time oppose the German neology—at least as to what concerns the New Testament.   From living being cheaper in Germany than here, the expenses of the journey would be compensated for by the difference in the living.   About the same time the Cape students at Barmen would be going there so that perhaps we would be able to live still cheaper. The reason I have spoken of myself alone is that from the want of ministers at the Cape it would perhaps be necessary for John to come home immediately, and he would then be just about the age at which he could be ordained, while I think it very unlikely that in this stiff country where everything must happen according to rule, they would ordain me so young, little more than twenty. It would, however, be of course a very great advantage for him too. You will say, my dear Father, that is looking far forward. May God guide us in all our steps, and give us grace to do whatsoever our hand finds to do with all our might."

From one of John's letters we have the following :

" But about this country (Holland) I am sure if people in general and the ministers of South Africa knew of the doctrines taught here at Leyden and at Groningen particularly ; of the contempt with which the most influential ministers (as those of large towns) talk of Dort orthodoxy ; of their alteration of the words of the formulary ; for instance that of baptism, they would have done with the relations they maintain with this country. Above all, I forgot to mention the scandalous morals of the theological students. I solemnly assure you, the name of God is profaned in the theological classrooms, even by orthodox and respectable students ; nor do they lose character by being intoxicated now and then on some festive occasion, provided only it does not take place immediately before the candidates' examination. And in this I do not take notice of grosser offences of which a few are guilty, who though destitute of character and notorious, still become ministers when they are ready."

At the same time Andrew writes :—" I rather think I told you of a missionary society we had established, to read together a few missionary periodicals in English and German. We are now going to publish a missionary periodical in Dutch—sixteen pages monthly—consisting of extracts regarding the progress of God's work throughout the whole world. The reason that we—there are eight of us—are doing this is that Holland is lamentably deficient in interest in missionary work, and the two existing periodicals are spiritless, and confine themselves to rather small fields. I hope that the Lord will direct us in the management of it and give His blessing."

In the next letter he writes :—" You can conceive how anxiously we are waiting for the letters from home which shall decide the question as to my next year. Although I still feel the necessity of staying, yet I am prepared for whatever shall be good, trusting that that gracious Father will guide us now, as He has hitherto so kindly led us, and believing that He knows what is best for His Church in that part of the vineyard where I desire to labour. My desire is to place myself in His hands and He can use even me although I have not had the advantage of an additional year's stay in Europe—perhaps even better than if I had such additional stock of human wisdom, which so often proves nothing else than an obstruction in God's way.

I say it is my wish to do this, for alas ! the general state of my mind is not so much a faith resting in God's leadings, but a certain indifference and contentedness as to the future, resulting from my natural character. What a blessed thing it would be if we could commit ourselves and all our cares to Him in that active living faith that is really concerned about the future. I . . . Oh ! how different is that faith which arises from a soul really concerned about its own interest and God's glory, that sees and feels human aid insufficient and failing, and flees to Him who is the strong Refuge. I am sure we have often been reaping the fruits of your believing prayers, whilst we were still unacquainted with true prayer and I trust we may still go on to experience what a blessing praying parents are. I must reproach myself too, that I feel this so little and that I so little seek in prayer those blessings for you which we have so often received from you through this means. The Lord teach us to pray, and oh ! although I do not pray for it as I ought, may He grant you a rich answer to the many prayers you have offered for us in an abundant blessing to your own souls."

The two Murrays, during the long vacation, made a walking tour among friends living on the Rhine which they much enjoyed, and there met Pastor Blumhardt, a minister whose remarkable work for demon-possessed souls and healing of the sick by faith led to the beginning of a great revival in the Rhenish provinces.

In reply to a letter written during this tour his friend writes :—" You say that you pray for little but deeper sense of sin because you see no preciousness in Christ. But why must God give you a sight of the preciousness of Christ through a sense of sin ? Is He not able to do this by a view of your privileges given for Christ's sake ? O the sight of sin is so fearful. The Lord grant you and me a sight of the preciousness of Christ by any means He will."

Notwithstanding all Andrew's fears that he would not be ordained, the two brothers were ordained together at the Hague, on Andrew's 20th Birthday in 1848, and at once they began to make preparation for their return to their far away home in South Africa.

The leave taking in Holland was of a striking character and it was evident that the two young men had made for themselves a circle of warm and attached friends. One of these has left on record the doings of what he describes as " that eventful day." The extract is from the letter of one of their friends to the lady to whom he was engaged and it was written the day after their departure, while all was fresh in mind and heart. He says :—

" We felt the need of uniting once more in prayer and praise . . . We met—fifteen of us . . . to show forth the Lord's death . . . and to declare our expectation of His return. John Murray led our devotions . . . After prayer and the reading of a beautiful portion of the formula for the Lord's Supper we again raised our voices in confession and prayer. Once again John Murray led us in prayer and then we partook of the elements . . . John read *Psalm* ciii. and *Col*. iii. After a prayer of thanksgiving and united commendation of one another to God's love and faithfulness we sang *Psalm* cxxxiii. and received the benediction from our leader.

" At 7 o'clock we met again in a roomy apartment in my father's house . . . I opened the gathering with prayer and song and read a portion of *Romans* xvi. . . . We then had opportunity for conversation . . . they stood there one of them closely surrounded by half our number, and the other by the other half. At 9 o'clock we had supper, Andrew asking the blessing on our meal. At 10 o'clock we sang together portions of *Psalm* cxvi. after which I read *Ephesians* i. and ii. and spoke a few words on the passage. We then knelt down and I had the privilege of leading in prayer in which I expressed the gratitude which filled our hearts for the inexpressibly precious blessings we had enjoyed, especially during the past three years ; and also for the blessings of this last day when we were able to commend our beloved friends to the love of our God with whom is no variableness or shadow of turning. We then united in singing *Psalm* cxxxiv. standing close round John and Andrew. We wept and embraced the brothers so dearly beloved. John then extended his hands over our heads : ' The grace of our Lord Jesus Christ the love of God and the communion of the Holy Ghost be with you all.—Amen.'

" At the front door stood a faithful housemaid who always attended on us when meetings were held at my home. On leaving, the brothers put a gratuity in her hand. ' But, gentlemen,' she remonstrated, ' am I the only one from whom you part this evening as a stranger ? ' ' No, no,' they replied, ' we look upon you as no stranger and part from you as a sister.' ' Well then, a sister receives no tip ' she said, and the money glided back into the hands of the friendly brothers. Outside a carriage was waiting to take them to Vreeswijk. It was half past ten. We went outside to refresh our spirits in the silent and beautiful night."

What an insight this incident gives into the hold these men had on the affection and esteem of their fellow students, and how prophetic it all was of the important positions to be taken by them in the coming days. It was a notable close of a notable student career—and bore in some respects a striking resemblance to the experience of two brothers, John and Charles Wesley, at Oxford—of whom probably the Murrays at that time knew nothing.

From Holland they made their way to Aberdeen for a farewell visit to their Uncle and Aunt there. A letter still extant describes the joy of the Uncle's family and congregation when the two young men preached there. It says, " The family and congregation were divided in opinion as to which of the " twa laddies " was the grander preacher.

And so they set out for home, leaving behind them in Scotland and Holland relations and friends whose loving interest in them never ceased and never grew less.

Chapter IV

EARLY DAYS IN BLOEMFONTEIN
1848—1853

In the Scotch manse, under the scholarly and benevolent guidance of the Uncle, the boys were trained to take a keen interest in the questions of the day, and this resulted in a mental alertness which enabled them easily to recognise the significance of the times, and to mould current events for spiritual ends, and made them also a power for good in their country.

During their ten years absence, South Africa had been steadily, if slowly advancing. Steam communication had been started, shortening the voyage considerably, and bringing mails more often. Education had been taken under the fostering care of the Government. The South African College had found a permament home, and a Normal School for the training of Teachers had been established. Dr. Innes had been appointed the first Superintendent General of Education. Important steps had been taken towards the formation of an Elective Assembly, which afterwards developed into a true Parliament. The seventh Kaffir war had been successfully ended, holding out prospects of a permanent peace. The Orange River Sovereignty with an area of fifty thousand square miles had just been annexed. Road making, too, was receiving a good deal of attention, and this meant increased facilities for travelling, but no railways were as yet in existence.

Travelling was still often difficult and dangerous. Many roads were mere tracks across the veld, or open country, made by travellers, and wagons carrying merchandise from the coast to the inland villages. Bridges were few, sometimes ponts or a kind of floating bridge was found, but usually a river was forded wherever a suitable place (a drift it was called) could be found.

During the rainy season the roads became deeply rutted and furrowed, churned into mud, making traffic difficult, and at times impossible, wagon axles got broken, or the wagon would become embedded in the mud. Sometimes torrential rain upstream, would send down the generally dry water course, a sheer wall of water seven feet high, or a steadily rising flood which would in either case carry all before it. Sometimes rivers would continue in flood for several days, and it might be weeks, and then the only course open to travellers was to wait with patience till the water was abated. Farms were few, and scattered over wide stretches of country, lying fifteen, twenty, or more miles apart, and ofter a hundred or more miles from the village which was usually built at some central spot around a church.

Owing to these great distances it became customary for the more distant farmers to come to church only at the quarterly Sacramental service. This visit entailed often an absence from home of two weeks or more. The services usually lasted from Friday evening till Monday morning. During that time the minister would have six or seven or even as many as nine services. The young people would have to be examined for confirmation, and church discipline administered. Marriages would have to be solemnized for a number of couples. At the same time all the necessary supplies for the next three months would be obtained at the shops, or stores, as they are called, before the farmers started for their far off homes. All this time, the people would for the most part live in their roomy wagons and tents, though some who were able to afford it would have what were called " church houses," built specially for these occasions and being locked up the rest of the year.

After the Communion services were over the village would sink back into its usual monotonous condition. Now began the minister's hard work of pastoral visitation. This often took him away from his home for a fortnight at a time, all of which would be spent in riding or driving over all kinds of roads in all kinds of weather. Usually the Sunday was spent at some outstation where a service had been previously arranged for. Some of these congregations covered an area of seven or eight thousand square miles or even more, and much of the travelling had to be done by ox-wagon, the average rate of which was about two miles per hour or even less. Two miles per hour might be regarded as express speed.

The ministers who served these Dutch farmers secured a unique position amongst them. They represented all that was best in the civilization and culture of the unknown but revered European countries. They had crossed the ocean and studied in foreign lands, of which they had much to tell. The larger knowledge of men gave them a wisdom which often helped the farmer in difficult situations. The contrast between them, and the often inferior schoolmaster, who was the only other outsider they came into contact with, greatly increased their respect for them. The Church had been fortunate in securing for her service several men of sterling piety and character which gave an added prestige to her position.

Such was the time, and such the conditions which the young men were called to meet on their return from Europe. How they were welcomed by relations and friends in Cape Town, Andrew's letter will show. It is evident that it was no small disappointment not to be met in Cape Town by their parents, but already we trace that spirit of loving acceptance of God's dispensations which was such a life long habit, his humility also is manifested in this, his first letter written after his return to the homeland.

" CAPETOWN,
" 15th November, 1848.

" MY DEAREST PARENTS—

" You will perhaps just at this moment have received the letter John sent off last week, and be rejoicing in the mercy of the Lord, Who brought us hitherto. Oh ! that I felt more what it is that we have enjoyed at the Lord's hands during the past ten years, which He has thus crowned with His goodness in granting us the long looked for consummation of our hopes. And, it is certainly for good that some time will elapse before we meet, although it was a disappointment to us not to find you here, as we had been delighting ourselves with the thought of meeting you all here.

" We have, of course, not yet made any plan as to coming home. The letter we hope to receive from Papa next week will certainly contain directions for us how to act. As to one of us staying at Wynberg, I think I could agree to it, were it necessary, but I hardly see the need of it ; and without a very pressing need of duty, I think it would be almost doing violence to your—and especially to Mama's feelings. Should Papa, however, in his letter say that this appears to be a call of God, I think either of us is ready to stay. I almost suppose it would fall to my share, as John is likely to be placed long before me.

" Papa certainly knows already that we heard from Mr. Faure that John will most likely be called to Burgersdorp, while I shall have to act as assistant until I am twenty-two ; so I am indulging in the pleasant prospect of spending at least a year at home before taking sole charge of a parish. I do trust and pray that the Lord will prepare us for all He has prepared for us, whether that be meeting or separation. . . .

" I cannot say with what kindness we have been received here, not only by our dear Grandparents and relations, but also by other friends. Especially is the interest which the people of God take in us quite humbling, when I think how little they really know what I am. Oh ! that my soul were really brought to a sense of its own littleness by the overwhelming load of God's mercies.

" Uncle William won't be in Town till Saturday night ; we both long very much to see him. On Sabbath John is to preach in the morning at Wynberg, and on Sabbath week for Dr. Heyns in the Town Church. I am to officiate there this Sabbath for Mr. Faure, and will likely in the afternoon or evening, have to occupy the pulpit of St. Stephen's. The reason for my preaching first in the Reformed Church is that my voice is stronger than that of John, and he would like me to try it first. My text is : " We preach Christ crucified." *I Cor.* i. 23. May it be true ! But I feel it very difficult not to preach myself, by attending too much to the beauty of thought and language and feeling too little that God alone can teach me to preach."

It is easy to imagine what a deep joy it must have been to the grandparents, Mrs. Murray's father and mother, to see their two grandsons so full of enthusiasm for the calling which was to be their life-work, especially as the great needs of the country were considered, and also in view of the fact that some ministers had already brought with them from Holland a taint of rationalism, and it was felt these young men would greatly strengthen the hands of the orthodox and spiritually minded in the Church.

To reach Graaff Reinet, the home of the Murrays, they might either go by sea to Port Elizabeth or take the five hundred miles journey overland by horse or ox-wagon, lasting about ten days. The land journey from Port Elizabeth was considerably shorter and they apparently went by that road when they returned from Europe.

There were great rejoicings in the Graaff Reinet parsonage on their arrival. The father and mother daily rejoiced in the answers to their prayers as they marked the genuine piety and simplicity and unworldliness of the sons. In these two elder brothers, the sisters and brothers who followed them found much happy companion-ship, and the foundations were laid of that mutual admiration and affection which ever afterwards distinguished them. Andrew was so boyish, so merry, so full of fun, that one of the younger ones asked with some surprise if he really had to go into the pulpit to preach. The two sons seem to have brought a heavenly influence with them, for the sister writes, " When our hearts were heavy, now that the time for parting drew near, Andrew said, ' What ! would you have us make a little heaven here for ourselves and never want to leave it for another ? ' "

While his two sons were with him in Graaff Reinet the father would often ask one or other of them to preach for him, and the Sexton always wanted to be told which of them was to preach for, said he, " If it is Mr. Andrew I must remove the lamps, for in his fiery zeal they will be in his way." This characteristic marked his preaching till the end.

About the year 1904, he was invited to preach the annual sermon in connection with the Christian Endeavour Convention, which was meeting that year in Capetown. Two elderly men were present, one of them had known the preacher for only ten or twelve years and he remarked to the other, after the service, on the vigour and power with which the aged preacher delivered his message. " Yes," said the other, " but if you had heard him fifty years ago, as I have, you would have said he was indeed vigorous in those days."

Some of his hearers at a Convention of the Students' Christian Association held in Cradock some years later noticed with interest the clouds of dust which rose from the pulpit cushion when he began his sermon, but ere it was finished the dusting had been completed. Yet he was never violent or unrestrained, but just glowing with intensity.

At the first communion served by father and sons, before dispensing the elements and giving the customary address, Andrew rose, closed his eyes and seemed lost in meditation and prayer. An almost painful silence filled the building, and a deep hush of solemnity fell upon the great assembly. When he spoke the words were so evidently sincere, so intense, so uplifting that many of the older people could scarce restrain their tears.

Andrew was not permitted to remain long in Graaff Reinet, although too young to be appointed to a charge in Cape Colony, there was nothing to prevent the Governor appointing him to a charge in the New Orange River Sovereignty, and this is what he did.

After the English took possession of the Cape the Dutch Reformed Church became the custodian of the Dutch language, and all the highest ideals of the newly acquired people, especially when, after 1820 when English became the official language. The ministers of this Church were partly Hollanders, partly South Africans trained in Holland, and partly like Mr. Murray's father, Scotchmen, who identified themselves very closely with their parishioners.

In 1836 there was a great emigration to the country beyond the Orange River. Before that date people for one reason or another had been moving across the river in small companies. The people on the borders of the Colony were very widely scattered. It was difficult to attend church at all, or to communicate with Government. Those who had grievances had much time for brooding over them, and many felt they had just cause for grievance. Those who lived nearer Cape Town began to agitate for responsible government, while those further off thought emigration was the only cure for their troubles, so in 1836 the discontented Boers went in search of a land out of reach of the Government centre at Cape Town. The fighting spirit of their Batavian ancestors, developed by centuries of struggling with the elements and human beings for a bare existence, and the pioneering impulse which came from their seafaring forefathers was strong in these men. Numbers of them crossed the Orange River, led by some of the ablest and best men in the country, who left the choicest lands in South Africa to set up an independent government somewhere—anywhere, in the interior. It was the same spirit that in later times led to smaller emigrations from the Transvaal Republic itself.

The country north of the Orange River had but recently been devastated by the savage hordes of Moselekatse, a Matabele despot, who kept the few natives who remained in a state of continual dread. More than one party of the emigrants had been murdered by his troops, until finally, in a nine days engagement with the settlers he was so defeated that he retired beyond the Lompopo and founded a capital on the site of the present town of Bulawayo. The farmers claimed all the country he had ruled, as theirs by conquest, and founded a republic with Winburg, a small village in O.R.C., as the capital. There were, however, constant disputes between the emigrants and the remnants of native tribes, so in 1848 the country was annexed to the Colony, and called The Orange River Sovereignty, and those who were still discontented crossed the Vaal river and founded the Transvaal.

Such was the country and such the people to whom Mr. Murray senior brought his son as minister. Many of the emigrants were known to him and had been his parishioners in Graaff Reinet. Four times, as Mr. Murray inducted his son into as many different congregations, he gave him the charge of David, " And thou Solomon my son, know thou the God of thy father, and serve Him with a perfect heart and a willing mind," (*I Chron.* xxviii. 9), while the son took the words " We preach Christ crucified . . . Christ the power of God and the wisdom of God," (*I Cor.* i. 23) as his first text to the new charges. In these verses we have the keynote of his life.

We can imagine what it cost the father to leave his young son thus, barely yet in manhood's years, and we do not wonder that at parting from him he took hold of the hands of the two elders and placing his son's in them, he said, " Deal gently with the young man." It was no easy task to which he had come, 12,000 souls scattered over a vast area, a wild country, full of wild animals and yet wilder men, turbulent emigrants, and cruel heathen.

Here he learnt to exercise that living faith which ever characterised him. In his ceaseless travelling, under the uncertain conditions of the country, he constantly says, " I must have plenty of time to make arrangements," for there was no regular means of communication with the North, and use had to be made of any apportunity which presented itself, and even with the South the only communication was by an irregular post. At the close of his journeys he is full of gratitude for God's care. When, later on, he used to say to one of his own children, " My child, make a friend of God if you desire to carry out your plans," he was but passing on the lesson he himself had learnt so well. The following incident will show how real were his dangers. He had made arrangements for Sacramental Services at a place about 70 miles from Bloemfontein. The road to it lay across a wolf-infested plain, and it was at a time when they were very fierce. After fording the river he off-saddled, the grazing horse hearing a pack of wolves approaching, ran off. Mr. Murray took up his pack and carrying it on his shoulders walked some twelve or fifteen miles to the nearest house. The surprised farmer on seeing him said, " How did you do it ? " The calm answer came, " I knew I was in the path of duty so prayed to God to keep me, and walked straight on, the wolves snapped at me but did not touch me." This same calm trust was shown on another occasion when he was returning home, and had to travel over a steep mountain pass which was dangerous when a strong south-east wind blew. He slept at a farm at the foot of the mountain. The next morning a furious gale was blowing, and the farmer was much troubled on Mr. Murray's account. Mr. Murray, however, cheered him by saying, " Don't fret, Uncle Jacob, I have planned to dine with you, it will be all right after dinner." By noon the gale ceased and the journey was safely taken at the time arranged for.

He learned to take things as they came, cheerily. He

writes :—" I had purposed giving you some account of my last journey, as that would give you an idea of what a minister's life here is better than any general description. I might have told you of a drive of 70 miles through a country in which we found only five inhabited farms along the road, a service at the farm appointed (as a church place) sometimes a house, sometimes a church made of tents and wagons, and sometimes in the open air, once even in the moonlight, with candles lighted only during the singing. I might have told the story of the birth of a new village from the sermon in which the minister urges the people to pay a good price for the plots for the benefit of the church, down to all the minor questions in which the minister must take a lead in giving a decision. You might have accompanied us (in thought) to another village, when our first incident of any interest was the fording of a full river, our horses being exchanged for oxen, and ourselves cooped up in the very top of the wagon for fear of getting wet. But that would have been followed by an account of moonlight travelling till midnight, a Dutch gentleman reciting poetry to keep himself awake, and all the pleasures attendant on the bivouac in the open air. And much more which might have showed you that if we sometimes miss the comfort of more advanced civilisation, our circumstances still have their peculiar pleasures."

Writing to his father on the fourth anniversary of his induction to his first congregation in the Sovereignty, he says :—" Personally I have much cause for gratitude nor only for external mercies, but for what I have experienced of the grace of God. I often spend happy days in the assurance of God's love and presence and when I look back upon what I was when I became a minister and the dangers I had to encounter, I can observe most distinctly how the Lord has been caring for me. I feel indeed it was not my own watchfulness or faithfulness, for alas what was I when I settled here, yes, what am I still ?   I can truly say ' He has led the blind by a way they knew not.'   But alas ! when I look at my people, my peace forsakes me and doubt and darkness take possession of my mind. I know not what to think. The thought of my own want of entire devotion and especially of believing, pleading prayer, of a thousand neglected opportunities of God's free grace in giving His Spirit and the right of withholding it, of my people's personal accountabilities in refusing my message, these thoughts meet in such different shapes that I get quite bewildered. *Perhaps that is just what God intends*, for then I am obliged simply to flee to the Master I serve, and to seek for grace for a new and more entire surrender to His work. Oh ! to feel aright—I am His. Oh ! I have thought could His name be stamped with burning irons on me to remind me more that I am His property—I would willingly bear it—could the mark of His right to me, be cut in the living flesh, I would not shrink from the agony, to be but more impressed with the conviction that I am not my own. And yet, when believing prayer for the Holy Spirit to set the mark upon me, and stamp me with the impress of Jesus' holiness, is the available means of attaining my wish, how often does the flesh refuse ?—Oh ! that the coming year of my ministry may see me more and more a minister of the Spirit."

By a visitor to Bloemfontein he is described as " a zealous young minister in a difficult position, which he has filled with great discretion." He did what he could ; Sunday schools, Bible classes and Temperance work all claimed his attention. The characteristic of his ministry at this period was his burning love for souls and his intense earnestness. People flocked to hear this wonderful Boy Preacher, and years afterwards when he travelled through the Transvaal or Orange Free State many came to him saying, " I was brought to the Lord under your preaching." There were Church Sessions to be presided over, Discipline to be administered, Confirmation Services to be held, Baptisms to be administered, sometimes from 50 to over 100 children were presented, and the names of all carefully registered ; Marriages had to be solemnised, and private exhortations had to be given. It was a heavy burden, especially, as he felt so keenly the spiritual issues. When preaching, so absorbed was he in his message, that should he by his violent gestures knock down Bible and reading desk of the impromptu pulpit, he would not notice it. Solemn were the Confirmation Services when, after teaching, pleading, preaching sermons, which might be well described by the words " Knowing the terror of the Lord we persuade men " by loving words, before the final Confirmation Promise was made, he would lift his hand, and with deep emotion would adjure them not to reject the Saviour, saying, " if you do and promise falsely to be true to Christ, this hand will witness against you in the day of judgment."

Before following Andrew Murray to his new charge in Worcester, it would be well to take a glance at the work he undertook in his vacation weeks in the Transvaal. The Government by which he had been appointed to the Orange Free State would not permit him to spend his time in the Transvaal, but during his vacation weeks he had the right to go where he liked, and he went into the Transvaal on long and trying tours.

It was here also there was awakened within him that sense of the importance of having true Christian Teachers to care for the children, which never left him. The following incident, interesting in itself, is important also as giving a concrete illustration of the soundness of Mr. Murray's conclusions.

" In Mr. Murray's congregation in Bloemfontein was a youth, R.F., who held an appointment in the Civil Service. He was one of a large family of children, and his parents were thankful that he was so well provided for and had every prospect of promotion. But to their surprise and disappointment he decided to throw up his work and become a farm teacher. This was considered such a poor calling in those days that no young man dreamt of taking it up. But R.F. had become a Christian, and as he listened to the passionate appeals of Mr. Murray for the education of the children of the land, he decided to dedicate his life to that work. He had no opportunity to be trained for a teacher, but Mr. Murray gave him much practical advice, and lent him books, and as often as he came to town he visited Mr. Murray for further help. On Sundays he would hold a service for the adults as well as for the children. After a few years R.F. married an earnest Christian woman, and Mr. Murray sent this youthful couple out to start the first farm-boarding-school in the Orange Free State. It proved to be a great success and blessing to the Country. Years later, when R.F. was at the head of a much larger farm boarding-school, Mr. Murray came to examine the school work, and expressed his pleasure with what had been accomplished, and then he asked, " How many of these children are converted ? ". R.F. could not tell, for his religious teaching had not been personal. But the question took deep hold of him and he promised Mr. Murray that he would deal with the children personally, and he did so. All through his later life he worked faithfully for the salvation of his scholars. He then taught them the necessity of prayer in private, and in small prayer circles. Among the many who were won for Christ through his teaching and labours are Clergymen, Teachers and earnest Christian Workers. Through Mr. Murray's influence and teaching he became a man of much power in prayer.

He started circles for Bible study and prayer among the people, where possible. He spent much time in private prayer, and had a long list of names of institutions and people for whom he prayed regularly. When he was too old and weak to attend any place of worship, he spent several hours a day in Bible-reading and prayer. This is but one case, illustrative of the many who were taught and inspired by Mr. Murray. At a gathering of ministers who were invited to meet Mr. Murray on his last visit to Johannesburg near the end of his life, the Bishop of Pretoria who was present, said, " Almost all I know about prayer I have learned from our venerable guest." He too was but one of many in all walks of life, who feel the same sense of gratitude to God for this ministry of His servant.

Chapter V

HOW MR. MURRAY SPENT HIS VACATIONS IN THE TRANSVAAL
1849—1852

BEYOND the Vaal river were 7,000 emigrants who for twelve long years wandered hither and thither looking for a fixed abode. Hundreds of children had grown up with no more education than was implied by reading an easy chapter in the family Bible, usually an annotated copy of that edition of the Bible sanctioned by the Dutch States General, with notes that were reverenced almost as much as the text itself.

Although Mr. Murray bore a heavy burden in his fifty thousand square mile parish, with its twelve thousand souls, those scattered farmers further north weighed heavily upon his heart. At the close of his first year of service in 1849, he decided to spend his six weeks holiday on a visit to as many as he could reach. It was a difficult task to undertake as the arrangements had to be made long beforehand, to let the different leaders know of his coming, to enable them to get things in order for the visit, to make the necessary appointments for services, and to give due notice to the widely separated people. The journey was undertaken during the rainy season over a sparsely inhabited country, with no roads, only tracks. He was often ten, twelve, fourteen hours in the saddle, with services of all kinds thrown in, until he reached the preaching place with its strenuous labours. Early on the tour he caught what seemed at first to be a chill, but which proved to be a fever, but although so unwell, he went through all the appointed services until he reached the border town of Potchefstroom. There a particularly large gathering was awaiting him, as the Raad or Council was soon to be held, and Party feeling was running high and strong. He preached on Friday and Saturday, and writes :—" On Sabbath I dispensed the Sacrament and had far too many communicants, though I tried as *faithfully* as possible *to set forth* what *Ps.* xxxii. 4 represents as the way to God. What they wish for is a scolding, and if that but produced good effects I would willingly scold, but I sometimes feel sad at the thought that the blessed Gospel of God's love should be degraded into nothing else than a schoolmaster to drive and threaten." On Monday there was much contention and strife, so he preached twice on *I John,* iv. 7, and *Phil.* i. 27. Many professed thankfulness for the message and determined to live in peace.

The Deacon who was accompanying him and who, apparently suffered as he did, died when he reached his home. Mr. Murray writes, " Many people say Deacon Coetzee succumbed to Delagoa Bay fever to which so many have succumbed in the low-lying parts. As I was unwell at the same time, and exhibited the same symptoms, the report was spread that I was suffering from the same disease. On my arrival at Winburg I found the people so alarmed that they almost persuaded me that I had it." He was ill for some time there, " Though I could not see any danger myself, yet I could not help thinking of death, but through God's goodness its fear was taken away."

The story of his severe illness is thus told by his eldest daughter :—" During his journey in the Transvaal he contracted fever, and lay for six weeks very near death, for hospital he had a tent and the vestry of a church, and was there kindly and faithfully nursed back to life by the old Dutch ladies who loved, yea almost worshipped him. But the sickness told on him. Instead of a strong, healthy, rosy-faced man of six feet high, he seemed to have shrunk into a bag of mere skin and bones, and looked more like a living skeleton than anything else.

" When he returned to Bloemfontein and saw the kindly Doctor there, he said, ' I fear you will never preach

again, but must be content to spend your life on a sofa.'
But God had much work still for him to do."

The Boers beyond the Vaal regarded the Church of the
Colony with suspicion. The chief objection lay in the
fact that the ministers were appointed and salaried by
the Government though a certain amount of freedom was
allowed in the acceptance or refusal of calls. The
importance of this first visit was that it allayed suspicion,
and led to expressions of confidence in the Dutch Reformed
Church at the Cape and created a desire to remain in
corporate ecclesiastical communion with that body. It
knitted their hearts in a peculiar manner to the earnest
Gospel preacher who was so unwearied in his services.

He writes : " You may imagine how very strange and
varied my feelings were on crossing Vaal River again. I
had passed over it hardly knowing whither I went and
what might happen, and when I looked back at the Lord's
leading over the way, all the strength and assistance I
had enjoyed, the blessing of which I had been the unworthy
channel to not a few, I trust, and the measure of comfort
with which He had enabled me to do the work : and when
I then thought on the little progress I myself had made in
grace, on the want of true love to my fellow-sinners, on
the hardness and indifference of my wicked heart, on the
absence of that true heavenly-mindedness in which an
ambassador of Christ ought to live, on all the pride and
self-sufficiency with which I had taken to myself the
glory which belongs to God alone—surely I had reason
to glory and rejoice in God, and to weep in the dust at
my own wickedness. How fatherly have not the dealings
of my Covenant God been with me, how unchildlike my
behaviour towards Him. Oh ! bless the Lord with me,
my dearest father, and praise God for all His loving kindness and long-suffering, praying that the Lord Himself
would pardon and renew me, that I may be truly fitted
to glorify Him."

In spite of the experiences of the first tour, the end of

1850 saw Mr. Murray taking a second tour of ten weeks across the Vaal River. On this tour he writes : " I was enabled to set forth Christ for the free acceptance of a simple faith with almost more plainness and earnestness than elsewhere. I did not, however, feel that reliance on God which I wished. I saw clearly that faith is a fight, and at moments I laid hold on the Lord, but alas ! I am so little accustomed to crucify the flesh and really to believe, that I found it hard work, which will require much more strenuous effort, and more wrestling with God in private, than I have hitherto given. It requires a person of much more spirituality and habitual intercourse with God and heaven than I have, to travel this way, as there is very seldom the regular opportunity for private devotion ; and there is really nothing that can be a substitute for intercourse with God." He was very particular about Baptism. At one place the emigrants had made a camp for safety, as there was fighting between them and the Kaffirs. Here the parents wanted him to baptise the children, but he writes : " I refused, I felt that they were wholly unprepared for the administration of such a holy ordinance, drinking and cursing having been too much the order of the day."

Among the emigrants there were many who took with them the old family Bible with marginal references issued by the States General of Holland. In this there was a map showing that Palestine could be reached by land from Africa. Some of these emigrants decided to make Jerusalem their goal, hence were called " Jerusalem-pilgrims." These also read the marginal notes and found in them the enumeration of the ten kings in Europe, who represented the ten horns of the beast, one of whom was supposed by them to be the King of England. These people refused to come to church when Mr. Murray preached, the argument being that as he was a salaried servant of the British Sovereign, he was partaker of her sins. Speaking of one of them, Mr. Murray writes : " I hardly knew whether to weep or to smile at some of his explanations of the prophecies and of Revelations, all tending to confirm their hope of soon being called to Jerusalem." On his second tour as he approached the western boundary of the Transvaal, on the confines of the Kalahari Desert, he was met by a party of these pilgrims. These men detained Mr. Murray and his companions, saying they might not proceed farther until he had given an account of himself. In the course of the evening, the leader in whose name he had been stopped arrived, he begged Mr. Murray to consent to an examination, as many people were anxious to be present. About forty men stood round while Mr. Murray was urged to come out from under the Anti-Christ, as he could not be a true Minister until he had done so. His companions, finally becoming impatient saddled the horses, as Mr. Murray and friends rode off, the pilgrims called out : " If you cross the Marikawa River we will shoot you," to which his friends replied : " Well, we will shoot back," but they were allowed to proceed in peace. Of a second disputation he writes, " I need not repeat the nonsense, I may almost say blasphemy, which they uttered. I was very sorry to see them going on in fancied security and holiness on the way of destruction ; for literally they seek their salvation in their opposition to Anti-Christ. May the Lord have mercy upon them."

One day's work in his Transvaal tour is thus described : It was a ride from Marikwa to Klerksdorp. Mr. Murray says : " I rose at four o'clock and baptised some babies before starting, and at the next off-saddling baptised some more. My companion brought another man to make the return journey with him as it was right through a lion infested district. After a while the third horse became jaded, so there was nothing for it but for the two men to mount on one horse, while the other rider dragged the jaded horse which was urged on by the three riding together. It would not have done to leave it behind, as horses were scarce, and it would have been devoured by lions. At 4 o'clock we reached a farm where we left the man and horse. After a little refreshment we rode on and reached Klerksdorp just as the church was being lighted for the service I had appointed, which I took as soon as I had partaken of some refreshment."

This was his first visit to the North West and many begged him, with tears, to come again. In spite of the unhealthiness of the season, the lion and snake infested country he travelled through, Mr. Murray was brought home in the Providence of God in safety. The result of these visits was a unanimous call for him to become the pastor of the emigrants in the Transvaal. In 1852 Mr. Murray was able to visit them again with a colleague, and reached the most northerly outpost of civilisation, in spite of the prevalence of the yellow fever, and although his older friends begged him not to go as it was so deadly. But nothing would prevent the zealous young evangelist (Mr. Murray) and his friends, from keeping tryst. They found the fever had been very severe, out of 150 souls, 24 had died, 18 within a fortnight, but the protecting hand of God brought them safely home again.

This was Mr. Murray's last pastoral visit to the Transvaal emigrants as the following year a minister from Holland settled among them, and a little later, a second.

Matters were looking very black for the Sovereignty, the military force was not sufficient to maintain order, and both natives and emigrants were discontented. The latter called on Andries Pretorius, an outlaw, to come as a peacemaker, and he started to come, but Mr. Murray, fearing the results of such a step in the disturbed state of the country, met him at Potchefstroom in the Transvaal and persuaded him to turn back.

Mr. Murray writes to his father : "The British Commissioners have thought fit to think a good deal of my opinion on Transvaal matters, as well as on the state of things generally. You may be aware that Pretorius is pardoned. On the 16th instant it is intended to have a meeting a little beyond Sand River . . . Major Hogge has requested me to go as translator . . . I shall very likely go, as I feel that they might break upon some insignificant point, which a little explanation might rectify." This was the Sand River Convention which gave the Transvaal their independence.

Writing to his brother, he says : " The hurry of the different engagements in connection with our country prevents my writing you at length. You would hardly think me the man for drawing up a protest as I have been busily engaged in doing with Dr. Fraser. We are not without hope that the country may yet be saved —it appears to be an experiment of Government whether the majority will be delighted to accept their freedom . . . ' He that dwelleth in the secret place of the Most High shall abide under the shadow of the Almighty,' This I pray I may remember amid all this bustle. You will, I am sure, pray for me that I may be preserved, yea, even blessed in the midst of all that goes on. ' We have an abiding city.' "

How he worked, the following extracts show : " The English service has thrown a great deal of work upon me, my hearers all wish to be called upon, and I hardly feel comfort in preaching without trying to speak from house to house. Tho' alas ! the pointed, personal preaching of Christ in this way, has not yet been attained."

" Ministerial responsibilities begin to press increasingly heavily upon me. Oh ! how easy and content have I been living, while souls have been perishing. How little have I felt the compassion with which Christ was moved when *He wept* over sinners. Oh ! I feel it is not enough to be faithful in speaking the truth—the minister's spirit is something very different, love to souls so filling the heart that we cannot rest because of them, would lead us to be very different from what we are. While abundant in external labours, oh ! I have felt nothing of that ' zeal of Thine house hath consumed me.' I trust that the Lord is, however, leading me to more earnestness in prayer—though I feel if He keep me not my reluctant flesh is every moment ready to say ' It is enough.' I trust you do not cease to remember me in your intercessions."

Again : " Would that the spiritual prosperity of the Church were as encouraging as its numbers increase in my congregations. I begin to fear that the state of a great majority of members is much sadder than I at first realised, and I feel in some little measure that nothing but God's mighty Spirit is able to conquer the deep enmity of the unconverted heart. I rejoice at the proposal of a weekly concert of prayer throughout the Church."

" Most cordially," he writes later, " do I sympathise with Papa in the wishes he expresses for the Spirit being granted in connection with our preaching. And yet, I do not know what hampers me so dreadfully in striving to believe in prayer or even to pray earnestly. I fear it is because my religion is as yet very much a selfish thing. When I read Brainerd's Life, and see how he speaks of desiring nothing but the Glory of God, I think I see the reason I cannot plead and pray—my faith wants the true ground ' for Thy name's sake.' Was it not this that enabled Moses to prevail, when he fell down forty days and forty nights to plead for the rejected people. ' Yet they are Thy people and Thine inheritance.' "

" Did I really feel how worthy the Glory of God is to be the only object in life, then I would not need to force myself to pray. But alas ! if my own soul be safe—or if my ministry be blessed—or if our Church might be revived, is too much yet the only motive in prayer. . . . As yet my prayers are not such as will draw down blessing. But, it may be God will give it of His great mercy. And yet I will try and cry still, however guilty and vile the prayers may be—that is at least the postue, where ws can hope the Lord will teach us to pray. As regards myself, I trust the Lord is leading me in His own way, and teaching me much—may it but be to fit me for His Service. I often enjoy much peace and happiness, but lest I should be exalted, the thorn in the flesh and the messenger of Satan is not wanting, and that is the fearful outbreak of my pride and self-esteem. I trust all will do the soul good in the latter end."

" What an impression this whole scene ought to make upon me of the necessity of being in earnest—how soon the opportunity of quietly preaching the Gospel may be removed, how soon the world burnt up, as well as the Sovereignty abandoned."

" The Lord grant us mercy to be faithful."

" And does the want of the blessing really cause the idea seriously to arise of the propriety of relinquishing the ministry ? Would to God my light and classic spirit could be compelled to the same earnestness, so that it could feel thus. At moments I feel dissatisfied, then again very earnest, but still I fear there is at root a secret feeling that I could be worse, and that there are many a great deal worse. This has, I fear, been the baneful fruit of what I thought I hated, the name of being very diligent and earnest in the work of God—and yet my deceitful heart has not failed ' to appropriate a portion of the praise, for the satisfaction of its own vanity, and an opiate amid the consciousness of much that is wanting.'

" My secret self-complacency was somewhat unexpectedly disturbed last week—it was, perhaps, in answer to prayer. On a round of pastoral visitation, two different people reproached me with having neglected my congregation, one, a woman, who had four years lived within an hour of the village. Conscience told me I might have done more for them—and I found that my self-satisfied heart resented the wound that had been given to it. Thus I have learnt that an appearance of zeal will not appease the conscience whilst it can point to a thousand opportunities that have been neglected, to a thousand efforts that might easily have been made. And when this reflection extends to the whole ministry, to what has been and to what might have been, its character and spirit, it certainly would be no wonder if the heart were to shrink from the awful responsibility."

" May the Lord enable you to experience all the preciousness contained in His own covenant, and fit you for the new dedication of yourself and those He has given you. I remember you constantly in prayer, may you receive a full answer in rich blessing upon yourself and your people."

To his brother John, who was his neighbour and had promised to assist him with the Communion Services, he writes :

" Bloemfontein, 1854. My dearest Brother, a single line to tell you that I have intimated that you are expected here at our Communion and that it is on that account fixed for the 26th. The Lord come with you.

" This is the anniversary of my church having been opened. Another memento how time is passing. I sometimes feel inclined to rebel and murmur at seeing so little fruit. Why hath the Lord put me in the ministry —so unfit as I am—leaving me to wrestle with the awful work in my own impotence ? I feel it is sin. It is God, a Sovereign God, and He has a right to set us to labour and has power to give us the needful strength. But oh ! why can I not find the needful strength ? O that ' why ' sometimes distresses me sadly. I have found a little peace this evening in the thought, ' In due time we *shall* reap if we faint not—but still my soul is often sadly tossed about—and all the while cleaving to the dust."

Finally Mr. Murray and Dr. Fraser were deputed to plead the cause of the Sovereignty in England. To his brother he writes :

" There are some little difficulties in the way of Dr. Fraser going. I hope they will be overcome, as I would not feel the same liberty in going with anyone else. I see sometimes signs of serious feeling—a liking for religious conversation, and he says at least that the hope of profiting in a religious point of view has also weighed in inducing him to go in company with myself. The sense of responsibility in this view you can imagine does not weigh lightly with me."

" I can say I have felt very strongly the necessity of more prayer as the only channel for attaining more of the Spirit for ourselves, and each other, and the whole Church. And what is it that makes prayer so difficult even when we feel its necessity, and that makes us so soon desist, even when we kneel down with the fullest determination to implore God's blessings ? I begin to think the gift of secret pleading prayer is a higher attainment in religion than I have generally been inclined to suppose. It is the most spiritual act, in which the soul is deprived of every external support, and in it the soul's power of communion with the Eternal God is put to the test. I have thought much of the text mentioned in my last, ' If ye abide in Me, ye shall ask what ye will.' The real prayer of faith I fancied could be offered up whenever we chose to take up a promise and plead it, but I now find it to be a very difficult matter. Even when the desired blessing is earnestly longed for, an ordinary degree of spiritual religion will not reach up so high as to attain to it. It will require much holy acquaintance with God, as well as a strong and earnest struggling against the carnal and unholy state of our minds before we will be able to pray aright. I often secretly wonder at that word ' righteous ' in the expression of James, ' The effectual fervent prayer of a righteous man availeth much.' I think I now see somewhat of its force. A child cannot do the work of a man, so with prayer in the spiritual life —and a man can't accomplish his work if his strength is not daily maintained by eating. So it is only a daily living on Christ that can make us strong for the great work of interceding for sinners. I begin to think this is far too much lost sight of as the great duty of Christians in general, as well as of the ministers. It is indeed a great work, very heavy, when we feel it as we ought, and what folly to think of performing it by a single earnest prayer. Oh! my dear brother! let us pray that the Lord may shew us what the work is He has called us to, and may fit us for it. 'If ye abide in Me, ye shall (not may) ye *shall* ask what we will, and it shall be done unto you." Oh! for holier lives, more of the felt power of an indwelling Saviour, more living participation in the new life, and the power revealed in the resurrection of our Jesus."

Chapter VI

LATER YEARS IN BLOEMFONTEIN
AND VISIT TO ENGLAND.
1853—1860

THE decision of the British Government to withdraw
from the Sovereignty of the territory North of the Orange
River, was felt to be such a serious matter that an appeal
against this decision was drawn up by the inhabitants,
and Mr. Murray was requested to accompany Dr. Fraser,
a retired Army Surgeon who had settled in Bloemfontein,
to lay an appeal before the Privy Council in London.
The Mission, however, was unsuccessful.

Mr. Murray's relations to the movement are interestingly
revealed in a letter to his father on the subject. He writes :
" An opinion has been very generally expressed that I,
as Minister of Bloemfontein, ought to be one of the delegates
to England, and in the course of a short time I may receive
a request to that effect. You may imagine that there is
much that is pleasing to the flesh in the prospect, especially
if there is the possibility of doing the country any good.
My own health would also plead for my going. The
weakness in my back, legs and arms, with a sort of nervous
trembling in my hands, made me believe I would be better
for a rest, and I had resolved to ask for three months'
leave of absence during the heat of summer. This object
could now be attained by the voyage to Europe and back.
It is, of course, easy pleading where the judgment is no
longer impartial. I feel, however, there are very great
dangers connected with going on such a Mission. As
regards my people, a growing interest in their welfare
would not allow me to leave them the objects of so many
prayers without fears lest impressions already made
might be lost, lest promising blossoms should be destroyed.
I cannot conceal from myself the dangers I incur, of losing

amidst excitement and bustle, that measure of the quickening and enjoyment the Lord has been granting me. However much there is to attract on the one hand, I hardly think my fears will allow me to accept. However, I believe that if I go, my God will show me the way. You will not only give me advice, but on receipt of this will offer a special prayer that I may be directed aright. If I know my own heart I have but one wish, ' Lord what would Thou have me to do ? ' If I am permitted to go I shall be thankful. If I stay I trust I shall equally rejoice in His faithful loving kindness."

He ultimately decided to accept the appointment, and started for Europe with Dr. Fraser, whose companionship on the three months' voyage enabled him to obtain a wider outlook on many questions than he had hitherto had.

While in England he sought medical advice concerning the state of his health. The doctors returned a very grave verdict concerning him, and this resulted in his spending more than a year in Europe, leading to a much longer absence from Bloemfontein than he had anticipated.

In spite of the unsatisfactory state of his health, he often preached when requested to do so. In London his ministrations were so acceptable that he was asked to take charge for three months of Surrey Chapel, which Roland Hill had made famous, till Rev. Newman Hall should arrive. Though too unwell to accept this invitation he appreciated the honour of having been asked to fill such a pulpit.

From England he went to Holland, where he had a warm welcome from his old friends. The Baron van Boetzelaer cleared everything out of his conservatory and turning it into a place of meeting, filled it with his friends and retainers, that they might have the opportunity of hearing the Gospel from Andrew Murray.

He was busily engaged in Holland and in Rhineland, to which he went from Holland, seeking for possible ministers, teachers and even professors for South Africa. The professors were wanted for the much needed Theological Seminary which the Dutch Church was then seeking to found. In Scotland, also, he was busy on the same quest, but without success. Meanwhile, however, things had been moving in South Africa and his brother John had been spoken of as eminently suitable for the post of Professor. In writing to his brother he says : " You will undoubtedly have heard that your name has been mentioned in connection with the Theological Seminary. It may be premature to say so, but should you be called on to act as Professor, I do pray you may feel at liberty to accept it. In fact, I hardly see how you could decline."

Though the deputation to London had been unsuccessful, Mr. Murray had a very warm welcome at Bloemfontein on his return in 1855. He writes concerning it : I am quite ashamed at all the warmth of friendship with which I have been received, and I fit more easily into Bloem-fontein than I expected. I was very much fatigued when father was here, and could hardly enjoy his society."

While in Cape Town in connection with this journey to and from Europe, he, like his father before him, found in that city the amiable lady who was to be the long sharer of his joys and sorrows. The lady was Miss Rutherford, daughter of a devoted Christian, and highly-respected merchant, whose large-hearted hospitality brought him into contact with good men of all classes. He acted as agent for the French missionaries in Basutoland. When in 1848 owing to the Revolution in Paris, financial matters were very unsettled, and the missionaries had been without income, he told his clerk to write them out a cheque for £1,000. The clerk replied : " We shall be in financial straits ourselves if you withdraw that amount from the business, and you will suffer serious loss." " My business," replied he, " may suffer loss but never the Lord's, write the cheque." The Lord cared for his servant, and the business did not suffer. Mrs. Rutherford was an earnest, vigorous Christian, who had helped in establishing several schools for the poorer people, and in these schools she and her daughter delighted to give the Bible lessons. Miss Rutherford devoted herself also to the visitation of the poor and neglected. She was highly cultured, not only as a student of English, but also had a knowledge of Greek and Latin. She was an excellent musician, both as instrumentalist and singer. She proved herself a true helpmeet to her husband, and it was delightful to see her whole-hearted devotion to his work. In a letter written about this time Mr. Murray contrasts the work of a missionary with his own, giving an insight into the strenuous life they were leading at Bloemfontein. He says : " Our people are found scattered over the country at distances from the church varying from 6 to 60 miles ; none of them come every Sunday to church, this places us in a very disadvantageous position, we can do nothing in the way of exerting the influence of the regular continued use of the means of Grace. The same people come to church only once in a month, or once in six weeks. Hence the Sunday School can scarcely be said to exist. I can catechise all of those who happen to be present that day. Hence the intercourse of a minister with the people is limited. Those who attend church come on Saturday in their wagons and then crowds of visitors have to be received. During the rest of the week we do not see one of them, unless one goes out on pastoral visitation. This is one of our most laborious duties and necessitates the minister spending a considerable part of his time away from his home.

" I have spoken thus far of our people as a whole. We generally have in the villages a few individuals belonging to our Church, along with a few English-speaking people, of whom we have a good many here who attach themselves to our Church, and these always afford a field of labour, though somewhat limited in extent. That labour is from the character of our villages of a peculiarly difficult nature. People of different social standing are mixed together, and instead of want of society, there is a danger of too much *of a certain sort*. A minister if liked is considered public property and everybody's friend."

Andrew's brother John was keenly desirous that he should write for the people so as to help them in their want of the public means of grace, but Andrew himself was loath to do this, feeling his want of style. He writes to his brother concerning some booklets he had already issued : " I was glad to see the advertisement of my book ' Jesus, The Children's Friend.' I only wish my name had been left out of it. What do you think from your experience would be the time needed to regain the capital that has been laid out ? You have never yet let me know what the printer's bill comes to. I would be sorry if you should suffer the least inconvenience in making my money arrangements. Only let me know betimes, and I will manage it. You will be gratified to hear that Beelearts writes that he uses the Kinder Bybel (the Children's Bible) with much pleasure. He says it has caught the right tone. You can fancy how anxiously I look forward to my College prospects (he was to become Rector). I think of commencing about the middle of January with two teachers, one Dutch and one English, the whole thing is surrounded with special difficulties. I feel I have need of special faith in undertaking the work and in dealing hereafter with the individual boys. I began it with a strong desire that to some of them at least it may be made the means of salvation.

" About our teachers' scheme, Hofmeyr will have told you. I propose writing by this mail to secure, if possible, six more teachers, as I have hitherto done nothing for my own congregation. I am extremely anxious to avail myself of the Government allowance for itinerant school-masters. Religious education must, I think, become the watchword of our Church, before we can expect abiding fruit on our labours. God forbid that I should limit the Holy One of Israel, or reject the lesson He is teaching from America, but still I think that in the ordinary course of things, education is our hope. I have just received the first copy of ' Jesus, The Children's Friend.' I like it, but I am disappointed that it is not more simple. It is to myself intensely interesting as containing the expression of what filled my mind some time ago. There are passages that I hardly believe that I myself had written.

" Thanks for your last private note and the wish that I may soon be released from school duties. I hardly wish it. I feel deeply interested in the work, and do not think it will be too much for me as long as I have no direct instruction to give. It is an experiment to try what influence can be exerted upon the boys by daily inter-course. Will the result be more encouraging than preaching ? Pray for me that the Spirit of Faith and Love may possess me, that Wisdom and Diligence may be given me fron on High for the work. Emma and I are both surprised that things go on so smoothly. Our numbers to-day are 14, with a prospect of four more at the end of the month.

" Have you read ' English Hearts and Hands ? ' Such a simple narrative, it is worth gold in revealing the secret springs of persevering and successful labour in our Holy work. We need more of such love in all its forms, its largeness, its bright hopefulness, and we need more strong faith in the power of a love higher than our own."

In 1857 the Synod was held at Cape Town, whither Mr. and Mrs. Murray went, she to her parents to show them their first-born daughter. It was an important Synod, for there were far-reaching decisions taken ; one was the establishment of the Theological Seminary at Stellenbosch. Many of the older ministers were against it, as they were sure it would mean spiritual and intellectual loss. However, the proposal was carried, and the Rev. John Murray was appointed as one of the professors. This was a great loss to the younger brother, Andrew.

Their wide parishes adjoined one another, Andrew's being North of the Orange River and John's South, with its centre at Burghersdorp, and they usually arranged their work of pastoral visitation so as to meet on the confines of their adjoining parishes every three months, and his letters afterwards to his brother often expressed the longing he had for their old fellowship in prayer, but Andrew felt he was the man for the position of professor, and he encouraged him to accept it. The second proposal was that a forward step should be taken in regard to mission work. The Synod had already appointed a Missionary Committee, but the Senior Members of this Committee were cautious and not very enthusiastic, and the burden of the souls of the scattered white population was a heavy one, and ministers were scarce, one-third of the churches were without pastors. The younger men, especially John, Charles and Andrew Murray, had come into touch with the missionary work of the ministers in Scotland, and had learned what God was doing in other countries, and having also come into direct contact with thousands of unchristianised natives in the Free State and Transvaal they were ready for a forward movement. The proposal was finally endorsed by the Synod, and a new Committee was formed, of which Messrs. Murray, Neethling and Hofmeyr were members, with one older, a tried servant of the Church, perhaps with the idea of restraining the enthusiasm of the younger members. This was the dawning of a new area in the Dutch Reformed Church and the beginning of its now widespread and successful missionary work.

Across the Vaal matters were in a very perplexing state. The people were exceedingly fond of Mr. Murray. His singular unselfishness and loveableness united with a fearless courage in the case of danger when on the path of duty had won their hearts, so they gave him, as previously related, a unanimous call to become their minister. He was much inclined to accept this, but his father did not wish it, principally on account of his health. The following incident illustrates his telling way of dealing with people. Arriving one day at the drift (ford) of a river, he found a span of oxen with a wagon stuck in the mud on the river bank. The driver was lashing them furiously and cursing and swearing in a dreadful way. Mr. Murray alighted from his cart and asked the man why he swore so. He replied that oxen could never be driven without swearing. " Give me the whip," said Mr. Murray, and, lifting up his heart in prayer for help, he commenced to crack the whip and encourage the oxen, and in a little while under his gentle treatment he got the span and wagon out of the mud. He then returned the whip to the driver, and said : " Remember, now, you can drive oxen without swearing." The driver asked who he was. On hearing his name, he said : " I might have known it by his holy young face."

In 1858 the whole country was in a state of unrest, but that did not prevent Mr. Murray from his pastoral visitations. The Basuto and Koranna tribes were threatening to invade the territory occupied by Europeans, and it was in this threatened territory Mr. Murray's duties lay. Mrs. Murray writes : " My husband will not return till Thursday week. They have brought in reports of an attack made by the Korannas on Boshof, and though I do not believe them, such things unnerve me in some measure. I know the district of Winburg where Andrew is, is considered the most dangerous part of the country, and though he says he will always have an escort, the very fact of his travelling with arms in the cart, and an armed escort, is very dreadful to a simple woman like me, and the fact of Mr. Wilson's dreadful death haunts me."

After Mr. Murray refused the call to the Transvaal, a Hollander, The Rev. van der Hof arrived there, and began to persuade the newly settled Boers to refuse to acknowledge the authority of the Cape Synod. A number were persuaded to do so, and several other ministers came out from Holland to join Mr. van der Hof. This was a source of great grief to Mr. Murray. Soon afterwards another Hollander, the Rev. D. Postma, arrived. He was a member of the Separatist Reformed Church of Holland, and he found ample scope for his energies among a class of people called Doppers, who, while mixing with the members of the Dutch Reformed Church had conscientious scruples in regard to hymn singing. They resemble the Presbyterians who in Scotland took up the same attitude. The Republican Government of the Transvaal was much troubled by these religious dissentions. They felt they had already enough strife in the country. They therefore invited the ministers of the three sections to a Conference at Potchefstroom to see if the breach could be healed. But although it was hoped that something had been effected, shortly afterwards Mr. Postma came to Bloemfontein and started a Dopper Cause there. Mr. Murray thus refers to it : " It certainly does appear strange that after an apparent consent to measures for healing the breach across the Vaal, he should come here. I believe we have, as yet, very little idea of the influences of the movement on the Church of the Colony. I sometimes think it may do good that our monopoly is brought to an end. . . . As to myself, the words have sometimes occurred to me very strongly ' He will let out the vineyard to other husbandmen which will render him the fruit in due season.' We have never been able to reach the real stiff Dopper mind, our language was strange to it. These new ministrations possessing their confidence may reach hearts that appear to us quite closed to the Gospel. . . . I look upon the whole thing as the direct work of Providence, and though I would have been anxious to open our Church for these Psalm singing congregations and ministers, yet as no opportunity for acting in the matter has been afforded I am content."

Sir George Grey, then Governor of Cape Colony, was

anxious to render assistance to the new Republican Government of the Orange Free State, and offered a substantial sum towards the establishing of a college for the education and training of young men as teachers ; the Presbytery of the Dutch Reformed Church, to whom it was offered, would be the Board of Management, and control the Institution in accordance with the terms of a suitable Trust Deed. The Presbytery accepted the gift, and Mr. Murray became one of the most active members of Committee. Sir George Grey also promised £1,500 for the erection of a building to accommodate 30 boarders in connection with the Institution. Mr. Murray heartily entered into the matter, and as no headmaster could be found, he became the Rector, in addition to his other manifold duties, and he and his young wife commenced the work at once. She bravely took hold of the housekeeping and other responsibilities which fell to her care during her husband's prolonged absences. Writing to her while on a tour in Natal, Mr. Murray says, " Yesterday I celebrated the Lord's Supper for the third Sunday in succession. I spoke much on the Covenant—what God engages to do and what we engage. I have prayed that we may be able to realise with our Father that all that is solemnised and sanctified in this covenant relationship may be working still in us, especially in the prospect for the approaching year." Writing later from Durban, he says : " This evening I arrived here, to-morrow I go to see Mr. Lindley, how I hope and pray that you are well and happy, that you have been helped to consent to my long absence. How very often the only drawback to my happiness has been not having you with me. I did specially wish for you this afternoon, as I rode through the most splendid country imaginable, and this evening when I spent a most pleasant hour with the missionary's wife. I will tell you afterwards how she envies you the sphere of labour in the school, and how she says to us ' Fix your hearts on the conversion of those boys.' "

" I often ask myself why it is that I have so unexpectedly got this vacation just now. Oh may it indeed be a preparation for our work. My prayers rise daily for you, my precious darling, that you may be abundantly blessed in our separation, and that we may be enabled, when we meet, to live more and more for Him Who loved us. How little we have lived the real missionary life."

Just before Mr. Murray finally left the Free State, another instance of his tactful wisdom is given by a teacher then residing in Bloemfontein. He says : " In 1859 a new President was to be elected for the Free State. Party feeling ran very high and bloodshed was feared. Mr. Murray, seeing the danger of the people having too much time on their hands in which to discuss politics, invited them to a magic lantern entertainment. It was a novelty in those days. In his own inimitable way he kept them entertained all the evening, and we may be sure that many a wise counsel concerning current events was also given, bitterness was allayed, and the election passed off peaceably."

Calls from several churches came to Mr. Murray during his laborious life in the Free State, but they all fell on deaf ears. Among these were calls from Robertson, from Prince Albert, from his brother John's late charge, Burghersdorp, from Victoria West, from Pietermaritzburg, for he was recognised far and near as a man of great ability and devotion. All these calls were declined. When, however, the invitation came from Worcester, he felt drawn to consider it, and finally to accept it, after his eleven years of faithful toil in the Orange Free State, where he sowed the seed of which others have ever since been reaping the harvest. He never forgot his first love, and, when an old man of over 80, he preached for the last time in Bloemfontein it was pathetic to hear him say at the close of the Service : " I bid you farewell, my congregation," as if he realised it was his last farewell.

Writing of this period in her Father's life Miss Murray

says : " The photographs taken of him at this time represent him as a stern looking man, and his wife often speaks of his hard criticisms of and deep dissatisfaction with himself. He would say : ' My work seems vain, the people have no real consciousness of sin, no real dread of it ; there is so much frivolity and lightheartedness, they come so thoughtlessly before God and to His Table, with no real preparation and no deep heart-searching.' He himself was constantly probing his own heart and blaming himself because of the unreality and want of consecration in his hearers, though we know he was much respected and loved at Bloemfontein. His earnest prayers for Revival and true conviction of sin became a burden to him. But God was ever leading His servant on, and opening out to him the secret of a life of victory and peace, into the enjoyment of which he became the leader of many who never saw him. He was being fitted for a world-wide ministry.

CHAPTER VII

REVIVAL AND MISSIONS
Worcester
1860—1864

FROM the commencement of his Pastorate in 1822 in Graaff Reinet, Mr. Murray, senior, had devoted every Friday evening to praying for revival. He encouraged his faith by reading the account of God's wonderful works in the past. Later on, other ministers, like-minded, united with him in a concert of prayer for the same object. Thirty years they prayed and waited in faith, and then a glorious answer came.

God had all along been preparing Andrew Murray, junior, to be a polished shaft in His hands. Even so far back as in 1853 he wrote thus to his brother: " I am looking with great fear to our sacramental service on the 16th, as the 14th is the day appointed for a great meeting about the state of the country. Alas ! I can exercise so little faith in regard to my labour and my people. My own work loses much of the value it once, alas ! possessed in my own eyes, and I have not yet been able to take my Lord's strength instead of my own. My prayer for a revival in which I have been somewhat careless for a little time back, is so much hampered by the increasing sense of unfitness for the holy work of the Spirit's ministry, especially with the unfitness rendered doubly vile by the awful pride and self-complacency which have hitherto ruled in my heart. For the last six months I have been led to see this, and it appears now to be increasing daily. Resistance is ineffectual, its seat is too deep, its working too deceptive, mourning and prayer have done little, though I trust they will bring the answer in due time. Yea, I will even hope the increasing discovery of its presence and power may be the first fruits of an answer. Oh! to be one with Him who humbled Himself, and took upon Himself the form of a servant. Oh! to know Him in the likeness of His death and the fellowship of His sufferings, for *nothing but a crucified Jesus revealed in the soul can give a humble spirit.* Pray for me, my dear brother."

At Worcester God had raised up a band of Intercessors. For many years a worn footpath was visible by which one of these intercessors made his way to the hill-top overlooking the village, that he might the better pray for the place from that point of vantage. Mr. Murray's predecessor himself had prayed and worked faithfully during his pastorate. When the Theological Seminary at Stellenbosch was opened the professors and resident minister had been requested to arrange for a Conference of Ministers to consider important matters concerning the work of God. This Conference was arranged for at Worcester, and was the first of those gatherings of Ministers and Elders which have brought untold blessing to South Africa. Mr. Murray's arrival at Worcester synchronised with this first Conference, and it had been suggested that his induction should take place during its sessions. Mr. Murray writes concerning this. "I am still in doubt whether I can, and, in fact, whether it would be desirable to be inducted in connection with the Conference. I was indeed at first delighted with the idea of it, and with the hope of being present, but I do not know whether the excitement of such a Conference would be desirable when I was about to have my Spiritual vocation renewed, unless indeed we had faith to hope that it would be a time of God's mighty power. I feel much the prevalence and danger of carnal excitement and the heat of nature in Spiritual work."

The subjects to be discussed were the great church problems of the country, Missions, Education, Sanctification of the Lord's Day, Intemperance, the Christian Ministry, Public Press and Revival. Being so widely

separated from each other the Ministers at that time had
very little opportunity for fellowship, so they were glad
to unite for such a purpose. For some, it meant long
journeys and long absence from home, but a fairly large
and representative Conference was held. The subjects
for consideration were matters on which Mr. Murray had
thought long and deeply, his suggestions commended
themselves to his hearers. On his advice nothing was
said about the Public Press, but the matter was kept
in mind, and some years later a newspaper was started
with the purpose of cultivating a high moral tone in
politics. The most important decision arrived at by this
Conference was to send to Europe for Ministers, Missionaries
and Teachers to supply the clamant needs of the different
congregations. Dr. Robertson was deputed to go to
Scotland and Holland for them, and he returned with
eleven Ministers, two of whom were for Mission work.
He also procured some Teachers and a Catechist, all of
whom did good work.

Dr. Robertson spoke on the subject of revival, and Dr.
Adamson gave an account of what was happening in
America, where a remarkable outpouring of God's spirit
was being experienced, and he pointed out the conditions
of its reception. When Mr. Murray, Sr., attempted to
speak on this subject, his heart was too full, and he broke
down. These addresses made a deep impression on those
present and sent them home with the renewed sense of
responsibility and an earnest expectation that God was
about to visit His people. These expectations were
realised, first in the quickening of the life of believers,
which was manifested by increased attendances and
warmth of atmosphere in the meetings for prayer. Not
only in the villages but also on lonely farms the Spirit
of God was at work.

How the village of Worcester felt the rising tide of life
and power is well described by an eye-witness, who says :
" On a certain Sunday evening there were gathered in a

little hall, some 60 young people. I was the leader of the
meeting which commenced with a hymn followed by a
lesson from God's Word, and then I engaged in prayer.
After three or four others had given out a verse of hymn,
and offered prayer, a coloured girl about 15 years of age
who was in the service of a farmer at Hex River, rose at
the back of the hall and asked if she might give out a
hymn. At first I hesitated, not knowing what the members
of the meeting might feel about it, but after consideration
I agreed to her doing so. She gave out a verse and then
prayed in a moving way. While she was praying we heard
as it were a sound in the distance which came nearer and
nearer until the hall seemed to be shaken, and with one
or two exceptions the whole meeting began to pray, the
majority in ordinary voices, but some in whispers, never-
theless the noise made by the concourse was deafening.
Rev. Andrew Murray had been preaching that evening
in English, and when the service was over an Elder passing
the door of the hall heard the noise and looked in, and
then hastened to call Mr. Murray, presently returning with
him. Mr. Murray came forward to the table where I
knelt praying, and touching me, made me understand
that he wanted me to rise. He then asked me what had
happened, I related everything to him. He walked down
the hall for some distance and called out as loudly as he
could : " Silence," but the praying continued. In the
meantime I knelt down again, it seemed to me that if the
Lord was coming to bless us I should not be on my feet
but on my knees. Mr. Murray then called out : " I am
your minister, sent from God, silence," but there was no
cessation of the noise, no one heard him, but all continued
praying, and calling on God for mercy and pardon. Mr.
Murray then returned to me and told me to start a hymn.
I did so but the noise continued, the people went on
praying. Mr. Murray then said : " God is a God of order
and here everything is in disorder," and he left the hall.
After that, evening prayer-meetings were held daily. At

the beginning of the meetings there was generally great silence, but after the second or third prayer the whole hall was moved as before and everyone commenced praying. Sometimes the meetings continued till three in the morning, even then many wished to remain. As they returned homeward they sang through the streets. The little hall soon proved to be too small, we were compelled to move into the school building, and this was also filled, and scores and hundreds came in from the farms surrounding the town. On the first Saturday evening in the larger hall Mr. Murray was the leader. He read a portion of Scripture, made a few observations on it, and engaged in prayer, and then gave others an opportunity for prayer. During the prayer which followed his, I again heard the sound as it were in the distance, it drew nearer and nearer, and suddenly the whole gathering was praying. That evening a stranger had been standing at the door from the beginning of the meeting watching proceedings. When Mr. Murray called for silence, the stranger stepped up to him and said : " I think you are the minister of this congregation, be careful what you do, for the Spirit of God is at work here. I have just come from America and this is precisely what I witnessed there."

His father visited him at Worcester at this time and blessed God that he was allowed to be present at such meetings and to speak. He said : " Andrew, my son, I have longed for such times as these, which the Lord has let you have."

Mrs. Murray writing to her mother about the Revival says

" MY DEAREST MOTHER,

" We are having many visitors from the surrounding places who come to see us on account of the Revival Meetings and they go away blessed saying that half has never been told. It is a solemn thing to live in such a congregation at such a time. I feel sure the Lord is going to bless us even more, and yet there are heavy trials before us ; the work is deeply interesting and yet some things are painful. In the midst of an earnest address a man drove a dog into the church with a tin tied on to its tail and frightened the people. Andrew came down the aisle and prayed a most solemn, heart-searching prayer, that if the work was not of God, He Himself would put a stop to it. The people were terrified as the excitement was very intense and some even fainted. . . .

"The Prayer Meeting last night was very full and ten men decided for Christ, but fifty undecided left the building about 12 o'clock. We had no idea of the time. Two souls afterwards came through who were wrestling in agony for a time, but got into the light in their own houses. Some go through a fiery struggle. Two sisters have both passed through are now bright and rejoicing. . . ."

And again :—" Last night again the church was full and Andrew preached so powerfully and yet so simply on " the Lamb of God." He is so very discreet in dealing with souls, about twenty came forward, and others stayed behind to be talked to. We do feel and realise the power and presence of God so mightily. His Spirit is indeed poured out upon us.

" My little ones are very good so I am able to get out almost every night to the meetings.

" Andrew is very tired after the meetings but is generally able to sleep well and feels refreshed in the morning."

The fruits of the revival were seen in that congregation for many years. One of the immediate results, among others, was that fifty young men offered themselves for the ministry of the Word, when previously it was almost impossible to find men for the work.

This revival spread throughout the whole country, and both white and coloured people were richly blessed. Professor Hofmeyr wrote concerning it, " We cannot conceal our fear that not a few mistake the natural sympathetic influence of one mind upon another for the direct influence of God's Spirit. We are greatly grieved at the self-deceit to which emotional people, such as these, are subject, but in the present state of human nature we can expect no revival which does not stand exposed for this danger. However this may be, we thank the Lord we have good reason to affirm that since the revival began many have been added to the Lord's flock some of them who had been living in open sin, others again, perhaps the majority, were men of unimpeachable character in the eyes of their fellow men, but in the light shed upon them and their actions by God's Spirit they discovered the depth of their inward depravity and the sad estrangement of their souls from God. In some cases the feeling of misery was for a time overwhelming, and this realisation of their uncleanness and of the transcending holiness of God, was not as a rule, the direct result of the preaching of God's Word."

In 1862 Mrs. Murray's father died, Mr. Murray writes thus to his mother-in-law : " What made us specially grateful was that there was light enough poured down from the open gate of Heaven not only for him to go through, and in, but also to enable you and all who remained behind to follow in thought his spirit to worship and praise with him ; light enough to make all the dark days of your mourning bright with the peace and joy of Heaven. I have prayed specially that you may receive the chiefest grace, a quiet and expectant mind, simply waiting for God to do His work, and that knows He will comfort and sanctify and teach and guide most faithfully. Oh if we did not so often hinder Him with our much serving, and much trying to serve, how surely and mightily would He accomplish His own work of renewing souls into the likeness of Christ Jesus. What secrets He would whisper in the silence of a waiting heart, even the hidden mystery of how the Eternal God hath in Jesus Christ, a Father and a Brother-heart, and no human sympathy can be so near, so real, as that which the Eternal Love bestows upon us through the Holy Spirit." Of the Revival he writes : " To my mind the most striking proof that we truly had the Holy Spirit among us in the late movement, is to be seen in what He is now doing in stirring up in the hearts of believers a desire after more entire surrender to Himself and His Service."

Although the Dutch Church numbered only fifty-three ministers they had, as recorded in an earlier chapter, decided to start mission work among the natives of the Transvaal, and now in company with the additional ministers who arrived from Europe two came as missionaries : a devoted French-Swiss gentleman and his wife, Rev. and Mrs. Gorim, who rendered many years of consecrated service in connection with their adopted Church. Mr. McKidd, a Scotch minister, was also of the number, whose outlook is best expressed by the first words he learnt to speak in the Dutch language, " Beetje bidden," " pray a little." He did not live long, but left a rich legacy of prayer into which his successor entered with visible tokens of great blessing.

When Mr. Murray and Mr. McKidd used to pray together they would sometimes be hindered by visitors or other causes. Mr. McKidd would say : " Satan is trying to keep us from praying," but the reply would be, " No, these interruptions come from God to fulfil some design of His."

It was decided that when Mr. and Mrs. Gonin were ready to go North Mr. Murray should accompany them and make arrangements for the starting of the work. Concerning this he writes : " Even the prospect of a three months' separation can hardly be said to be a shadow amid all the brightness, for we feel it a high privilege to part in connection with such a work, especially with its important bearing on our Church. These are our first Foreign Missionaries going beyond the boundary of the Colony, the fruit of many prayers, and we trust the beginning of better days. How father would have rejoiced could he have heard of one farmer who is to accompany us, who is selling his farm for £1,500 that he may devote himself to mission work as a layman. The first African Boer that has done such a thing. A proof I trust that the Revival has been of God."

Mrs. Andrew Murray gives the story of Mr. Murray's journey to the Transvaal from her side, in this letter to her mother :—

" My Dearest Mama,

" Andrew left at 8 o'clock yesterday morning and Frederic at 2 p.m., he had come up from town with Andrew the Monday previous. I hope his short visit refreshed and did him good. A. has a comfortable little spring wagon, not such a one as he usually travels in, the seats are fine, all have stuffed backs, and can be let down so as to convert the wagon into one bed, quite a full size for two people ; but as usual he has too many people with him, there are eight, but two go only to Beaufort, these are Mr. Meiring, a minister ; and Leslie, a missionary of our Church. With Andrew are three of our farmers, two deacons, and a third very good man, full of faith, one of the Naude's, on whose farm the revival began, these three volunteered to go for the good of the cause, our idea is of forming a mission settlement, or colony farm, with drafts out of this congregation, one, a young man of the name of Stofberg, has sold his farm here with the desire to devote himself to work for God in the interior. He has a fine little boy of five years old, his eldest, whom he dedicated to the service of God two years since, and he has now with the others left his wife and young family behind. It is a great comfort to me that these three are with Andrew, because I think them three of the most earnest, devoted Christians and prayerful men in the congregation, and they are sincerely attached to Andrew and will do all in their power to aid, strengthen and comfort him on a very difficult and serious mission. Poor fellow, when I last stroked his thin, worn face, and felt his bony hands, my heart sank within me to think how that poor worn mind and body was to stand all the anxieties and fatigue of such an undertaking, and I almost but yet not quite, repented that I had myself urged him to it, but I felt no one was so fit for it in our Church and that it was of great importance in the history of our Church. David Naude with a strong mind has all a woman's tenderness, he is an excellent husband, all the Naudes are, nursing their babies and saving their wives fatigue in a way not common. I expect him to be very thoughtful and fatherly towards Andrew, and he is the eldest of the party. I think although in some points it is a serious loss to a congregation having no settled minister for three months, that yet to those who are converted here it may prove a blessing, the fact of such an embassy having gone out of our midst will stir up many to prayer and increased missionary zeal ; yesterday I believe the young girls meeting was a very serious one and in the working party to-day they were not forgotten in prayer, indeed I believe daily prayer is offered in many a household for success in their work and for the welfare of those gone ; to the unconverted even, in our midst a three months cessation from such earnest appeals may give them more force when Andrew returns, if it please God, *for I have noticed that many after feeling at first, are apt to get hardened when regularly listening to Andrew's sermons,* and I expect and believe a blessing will attend his meetings in the various places he passes through because it has always pleased God to bless in a particular manner those sermons in other congregations. It was of importance that Andrew should go because the Boers in the Transvaal Republic are, as a people, opposed to mission work, so that it requires a man of wisdom and sound judgment, and good temper, to bear the burden of our brothers' prejudices, as well as to love the mission work. Andrew has the affection and confidence of those Boers above any other minister, because when they were without

a minister he laboured incessantly for them, so that he
has a better chance of overcoming difficulties, and coming
to a good understanding with them and with the Native
tribes than any other minister; he also knows the country
best and, therefore, how to choose a good spot for a Station.
The missionaries are two young men, he must pioneer
the way and give them advice. I do not regret the
sacrifice although yesterday I felt it to be a heavy burden,
left alone with my five infants without a counsellor, but
the people are very kind. . . . "

From Bloemfontein he writes to his wife : " Difficulties
are becoming more thick. I feel a quiet but strong
confidence that the work is the Lord's and that if I may say
it, the responsibility of it is His. I only pray we may have
grace to keep our hearts more habitually and undividedly
open to wait for and to receive the influence of His indwelling
grace, He will make us meet to be the Executors of His
will and partners of the business through whom He will
accomplish the great purpose of redeeming Love."

Again from Rustenburg he writes to his wife : " We
were all full of the confident hope that we should witness
the triumph of our King (it was Ascension Day) in the
opening of the door here. When the large gathering of
some forty petty chiefs was asked whether they would
have a teacher, they all answered ' No.' It was no slight
disappointment to us, but it drove us out to celebrate our
festival in faith, and the day with its service in the open
veldt will not be soon forgotten. We are now all uncertainty
waiting for God's leading. We are thus kept waiting on
the Lord—an exercise not easy but I trust profitable."
With regard to Mr. Kruger (afterwards President) he tells
his children, " Mr. Kruger says that when God gave him
a new heart, it was as if he wanted to tell everyone about
Jesus' love, and as if he wanted the birds, the trees and
everything to help him praise his Saviour ; and so he could
not bear that there should be any poor black people not

knowing and loving the Saviour." He closes this letter with the following message to the children : " Papa is longing for his little darlings but cannot say for certain when he will be able to come—perhaps the middle of July. He hopes you will be very good indeed to Mama and very loving to each other, and that when he comes each one of you will be able to say a little hymn and a little text."

To his wife he writes : " The two days of waiting before Whitsunday at Paul Kruger's were not lost. It was during these days that I felt that which I wish I could retain and impart to you. The thought of the blessing of the indwelling Spirit appeared so clear, the prospect of being filled with Him at moments so near, that I could almost feel sure we would yet attain this happiness. The wretchedness of the uncertain life we mostly lead, the certainty that it cannot be the Lord's pleasure to withhold from His bride the full communion of His love, the glorious prospect of what we could be and do if truly filled with the Spirit of God—all this constrains one to be bold with God and to say, " I will not let Thee go except Thou bless me."

" I yesterday preached from the words ' Be filled with the Spirit ' and am only strengthened in the conviction that it is our calling just to take God's Word setting forth what we are to be, as it stands, and seek and expect it, even though we cannot exactly comprehend what it means. In all experience of the blessings of the Gospel, the intellect must follow the heart and life."

The door of work for the missionaries did not open immediately so Mr. Murray left them at Rustenburg to study the Dutch and native languages but before two years had passed each had founded a work that became permanent.

In 1850 Mr. Murray had refused a call to the Transvaal but had promised to train any sons they might give him as ministers. His first protegé was a boy who came with him from Bloemfontein in 1860, remaining till Mr. Murray went to England, when he was sent to a Boarding School from which he went back to his mother. The second, now Rev. Dr. Bosman of Pretoria, was one he brought with him on his return from the mission journey, who for nine years found a second father and mother in Mr. and Mrs. Murray, and has become one of the leading ministers in the Transvaal. From this onward, for the next 60 years one or more young people, chiefly boys, lived in the parsonage, being educated in the hope of supplying the need for Christian workers. It was wonderful to see how Mrs. Murray opened her heart to these children. In her home letters one can hardly distinguish between the interest in the formation of the character of her own and her adopted children. It was no easy task that fell to her share. All the duties of a minister's wife, an open house for any of God's servants, a growing family of her own to be cared for, on a salary of £300. Mr. Murray was always very fond of children and they loved him in return. His children's sermons were always popular. When away from home, preaching in the early years he would gather the children round him when disengaged and would tell a story and hear them recite their texts, and hymns, and give some to be learned for next time. He retained his interest in and hold on them till the very last. It was a touching sight to see how attentively a congregation of some 300 young people listened to him, an old man of eighty-six, as he explained the way of salvation and at the close of three days services over a hundred professed to find Christ.

To the elder children of the family the memories of Worcester are very precious. He was freer then than later, and loved to romp with them on winter evenings, or read Dr. Moffat's book *Rivers of water in a dry Place,* making it more vivid by imitating a lion's roar. In summer the whole family would go out for tea and he would play with them. What a pleasure it was to drop their weekly sugar money into the mission box on Sunday. On the wall hung a map of the religions of the world and he pointed out to them where the Americans were fighting to set the slaves free. To these memories are linked the kindly face of Dr. Duff who during his visit to the parents, at night told the children stories of India and asked them if they too would not become soldiers of Christ.

At Worcester Mr. Murray began the custom of monthly Baptismal Services when he would preach directly to the parents on the subject. The result was that in 1864 we find him writing a book in Dutch entitled : *What Manner of Child Shall This Be ?* The basis of his book : *The Children for Christ.* His thought on the subject is revealed in the following letter to his wife written in 1860.

" Did you ever observe the promise applicable to parents when God grants them children, Whosoever receiveth a little child in my name receiveth *Me.* If we only knew how to receive our children in His name, as given by Him, to be educated for Him, and, above all, as bringing a blessing to the home where they are rightly welcomed, how rich the reward would be ! There would not only be the thousand lessons they teach, and the joys they bring, but the reward of receiving Christ. I think constantly of our little darlings. What a comfort it would bring, amid all regrets of lost opportunities, and defects apparently incurable if one could leave children behind who have really profited by our experiences, *not* ' like their fathers a stiff rebellious race.' Surely this is obtainable, and instead of parental piety being diluted in children—this is so often spoken of as what we must expect—each succeeding generation of a God-fearing family ought to rise higher and higher. This principle of progression is acknowledged in all worldly matters and also in religion, so far as concerns its general effects on a nation or a large portion of society ; and surely a true faith in God as the God of our seed also, should not be afraid to expect this for the individual families. This subject of parental and

domestic religion may be more closely connected with
ministerial success then we think.   Paul, at least, thought
so when he spoke of the necessity of a Bishop's knowing
how to rule his own house well ; and so did our Saviour,
since in answer to the disciples' question : ' Who is the
greatest in the Kingdom of Heaven,' He replied : ' He that
is like a little child,' and then ' He that receiveth the little
ones in my name.'   The faith and the simplicity required
for training children would perhaps be better training for
the ministry than much that we consider great."

The consciousness he had of the need for help of the
many young converts of the Revival and of God's chidren
generally led to the publishing of the book which afterwards appeared under the title *Abide in Christ*. It at
once became a much beloved companion of many a heavenward pilgrim. At the same time he simultaneously
published another for those whose feeble faith needed
strengthening and this too was afterwards published in
English under the title, *Why do You not Believe ?* These
books were dictated, as already his hand was unable to
write long.

The Synod of 1862 elected Rev. Andrew Murray as
Moderator though still young, being only thirty-four years
old. This was a peculiar mark of the confidence felt in
him by the ministers and elders, for the difficulties of the
Synod that year were great and the decisions made history.

Rev. Andrew Murray, senior, Minister of Graaff Reinet,
was present at the Synod, as a member, when his son was
elected as Moderator, and when later on he, the father,
rose to address the Synod, and did so by courteously
addressing the Moderator first, as is the custom ; the
young Moderator at once sprang to his feet and remained
standing till his venerable father had taken his seat again,
and he did this right through the sessions of the Synod
when his father spoke. What a comment on the home
training and its effects ! It reflected credit on both father
and son.

The stirring story of the trials through which the Dutch Reformed Church was at this time called on to pass are well told in Professor du Plessis' Life of Andrew Murray. It is contrary to the aim of this unpretending book to do more than refer to the facts as they were woven into the life of Andrew Murray junior.

In 1864 a call came to Mr. Murray from the church in Cape Town and as it seemed to him to be the call of duty he accepted it and with his family took up their residence in the city.

Mrs. Murray tells her mother how she felt about it and also gives a glimpse into the loving relationship which existed between them and the people of Worcester. She says :—" On Saturday and Sunday the church was over-crowded, a hundred carts, many horse-wagons, whole families, came to the farewell meetings. On the day we left many carts and wagons accompanied us out of the village. After half an hour's drive we all knelt in a circle, Andrew praying, after singing a Dutch Hymn. Old men were weeping like children, and the leave takings were heartbreaking. I felt quite ill when I got to the farm near Wellington where we stayed. How I shall miss the dear Worcester people, they have been so kind and loving, and after all the wonderful times we have passed through together, I don't know how I shall get on in Cape Town, t will all be so stiff, not like our own dear homely people."

Chapter VIII

CAPE TOWN
1864—1871

THE call to Cape Town came to him in 1864 when he was in the midst of the great conflict which arose between the Modernists and the Orthodox sections of the Synod. As Moderator of the Synod, a leading part in this conflict fell to him, and nobly did he discharge his duty. It was the first time in the two hundred years of the Church's existence that the Government had allowed a congregation to call a minister by the vote of the elders and deacons. This of course made the call more important. To his father he writes : " I am sure I will have your sympathy during my present time of trial. As far as my own impressions go, and the advice of friends outside of Worcester, everything appears to point to Cape Town, but it is difficult to bring my mind really to say ' Yes.' So much is implied in that little answer, by which I venture to undertake such a great work. I shall be glad of your special prayers that I may be kept from going, unless it be with very special preparation from on high." After accepting the call to Cape Town he says : " If God wills to bless, no instrument is too weak, and blessed it is to be the instrument which He condescends to use."

The work in Cape Town was very heavy for one so deeply interested in the salvation of individual souls, and who had such a sense of the importance of pastoral visitation. There were three ministers in charge and they preached in turn in the two large churches caring for 3,000 communicants and about 5,000 adherents. With Dr. Faure, the senior minister, a man of wide evangelical sympathies, Mr. Murray formed a close personal friendship but soon Dr. Faure retired from the active work of the ministry and not long afterwards died. The other colleague

was one of those ministers who conscientiously fulfil their
official duties but do not attempt much more. He was
also Professor of Dutch literature and language and tutor
of Hebrew in the South African College. Mr. Murray
found it exceedingly unsatisfactory when after a week's
hard work of pastoral visitation he would on Sunday
have an entirely different set of people in his audience,
people with whose spiritual needs he was not at the time
conversant. He wished to preach to those he had visited
during the week whose spiritual requirements he definitely
understood. During the first eighteen months much of
Mr. Murray's time was taken up by the Law Courts and
owing to the death of his lawyer, he was obliged to plead
the cause of the Church himself. In the address to the
Courts among other things he says : " Under such circumstances I desire to appeal to the kindly forbearance of the
Court, should my language or arguments not always be
in accordance with the practice of a Civil Tribunal ; while
on the other hand I trust nothing will escape my lips that
is derogatory to the respect due to this Court, or that can
dishonour the cause which has been entrusted to my
poor defence." In delivering the verdict Judge Bell,
spoke in these terms : " There can be but one opinion as
to the ability and conscientiousness with which you have
pleaded your cause. Few advocates could have done it
equally well." The Attorney-General, no mean orator,
remarked : " he had listened with interest and admiration
to the earnest and eloquent speech."

In 1866 Mr. Murray went to England to carry the Church
case before the Privy Council. Here the case dragged on
for ten months. The whole family went with him and
Mrs. Murray much enjoyed visiting her mother and other
relations. To Mr. Murray it was a time of much helpful
spiritual intercourse, for he loved the society of his fellow
Christians. When at a Bath Conference the powerful
addresses he delivered there were published in *Evangelical
Christendom.* He also took great interest in religious and

philanthropic work such as the Field Lane Ragged Schools where he addressed the gathering.

An interesting experience was addressing 200 thieves on Christmas day before they had their Christmas dinner. When he began to preach they began to cough him down; taking out his watch he said, " One at a time gentlemen, one at a time, as the sailor said to the minister while the donkey brayed, either you or the donkey. So I will give you five minutes to cough and you will give me five minutes to preach." At the end of the five minutes they were so interested that they forgot to cough any more till the service was ended. Mr. Murray's presence even then exerted a powerful influence on those who met him. A niece who was then a passionate child of nine after his death thus writes of him, " I still remember the impression he made on me as a child—a rather frantic child. If he came into the room when I was in a passion, Peace— palpable, like a cool breath of sweet scented spring air came in with him, and I felt I could not be naughty or wild so long as he was there."

During his absence in England his revered father died. He had retired from the active work of the ministry in his 70th year and was succeeded in the pastorate by his fourth son Charles, who remained in it and in the old Graaff Reinet home till his death. His widowed mother lived with him the rest of her life, most tenderly cared for. Andrew writes thus to his mother : " The news of our dear father's departure has just reached us. You will not think it strange if I say that I could not weep. I felt that there was too much cause for thanksgiving. How indeed can we thank God aright for such a father, who has left us such a precious legacy in a holy life so full of love to us and labour in his Master's work. May his example be doubly influential now that we have him glorified with His Saviour. For he is still ours. I cannot express what I felt in church yesterday, we received the tidings on Saturday evening, at the thought of what his meeting

with His Master must have been, and what his joy in the
perfect rest of His presence. It must be a joy passing
knowledge to find and see One of whom the soul has been
thinking for fifty years, for whom it has longed and thirsted,
grieved and prayed, spoken and laboured—all at once to
find Him and to find everything it has said or felt or tasted
in its most blessed moments, but a shadow compared with
the inexpressible reality. What a joy, what a worship,
what a love that must be when with the veil of the flesh
torn away, the ransomed spirit recovers itself from the
death struggle at the feet of Jesus.

> " Jesus, the very thought of Thee
>   With sweetness fills the breast;
> But sweeter far Thy face to see
>   And in Thy presence rest."

I feel as if the thought of his being with the Lord, and
having entered into his reward, should work with power to
make us look with clearness and assurance to the time
when we too shall receive our eternal inheritance. The
Saviour who has done it for him will do it for us. He is
ours as well as his. It is this He loves to accomplish in us—
to prepare us for. Surely we should give ourselves up
afresh to him, to live in the light of that blessed prospect.
May God give all our dear father's loved ones grace to do
so !

" And I feel confident that my dearest mother has
tasted in abundant measure the comfort and support which
the Saviour gives. Not but what there must be some
dark and lonely hours ; but they will make the Saviour's
presence more precious, and help the more to lift the heart
heavenward in the prospect of an eternal reunion. We
cannot but be grateful for the kind providence which has
arranged for Charles taking Papa's place and keeping unchanged and sacred so many memories which would
otherwise have been lost. May the God of our home
still dwell there and abundantly bless. And I need hardly

add that you must please accept of all the tokens of love and service which Charles gives as coming from us all. I could envy him the privilege of being the deputy of the rest to cherish and cheer her whom our dear father has left behind to us."

" From Charles' letter you will hear what our movements have been and what our prospects are. I feel almost doubly ashamed at having been in the midst of enjoyment, while others were not only working hard but sorrowing too ; but I can only hope, as I do expect, that it will be sealed of God as the means of greater bodily and spiritual strength."

Mr. Murray visited Holland and much enjoyed renewing the old friendships of student days. In England and Scotland old friendships were revived and he had many opportunities of preaching in various churches. After his return to the Cape he had a call to Marylebone Presbyterian Church in London and, there is reason to believe he was approached with regard to a call from Regent Square Presbyterian Church as well, though a call was never received. In 1868 his mother-in-law writes, " I am pretty much persuaded I shall see you all again, several have an eye on Andrew, they are greatly at a loss for some one to take Mr. Hamilton's place."

That a man of Mr. Murray's judgment knew what he was doing when he refused the call to London is self-evident. When his wife asked him whether he would accept the call he replied, " No, my church needs me, my people need me, my country needs me, I must sacrifice myself for them." It appears that he never spoke of it again as a sacrifice, but threw himself heartily into every sphere of work that opened for his people and country. One of the lawyers he met in connection with the Privy Council said, " It is a pity you are a minister and not a lawyer, you would be an ornament to the profession."

Mr. Murray returned to Cape Town early in 1867. During his absence, a Dutch minister licensed in Holland, had established a Unitarian congregation in the city called the Free Protestant Church. Religious controversy ran very high at this time, the Dutch newspapers were full of it. Finally this minister, the Rev. D. Faure, published his views, in book form, under the title, " Modern Theology." In reply to this Mr. Murray delivered thirteen lectures in Dutch and published them under the title of " Modern Unbelief," these lectures led Mr. Faure to confess that both as regards matter and manner it represented the only serious attempt to meet argument with argument. For the benefit of the English-speaking people Mr. Murray lectured on the same subject on a week evening and one of the English papers published his address in book form. The lectures were described as keen in thought, scientific in treatment, and as profoundly philosophical in essence as they were eloquent in expression." At the Synod of 1870 Mr. Murray was Actuarius and Ex-Moderator.

The following sketch of Mr. Murray by an opponent will be of interest : " First let me sketch the men of the ultra-orthodox party, who pose as watchmen on the walls of Zion. Under this category I begin with Rev. A. Murray— a worthy leader. Eloquent, quick and talented, he has an acute mind and clear judgment. He instantly divines the weak points in his opponent's arguments and knows how to assail them. He carries the meeting with him : he is too clever for most of them. He understands the art of making his ideas so attractive to the elders and small minds among the ministers (who all look up with reverence to the Actuarius) that they very seldom venture to contradict Demosthenes, or, as another called him, Apollos. It would be sacrilege to raise a voice against the Right Reverend the Actuarius, Andrew Murray. There is no member of the assembly who possesses more influence than Andrew Murray and certainly there is no one among the conservatives who better deserves his influence. He is consistent and consistency always demands respect."

The poor and ignorant were always very much on his heart. Busy man as he was there were a number of poor fisher folk and others whose needs led Mr. Murray to have two week night sevices for them. Their appreciation of the services was shown by their placing gifts of fish, eggs and other things in the pulpit before the service. For the sake of helping his fellow Christians he had an English service after the Dutch which often entailed his preaching thrice on Sunday. Many leading citizens attended these services.

Shortly after his arrival in Capetown he wrote an appeal in the official organ of the Church containing this paragraph: " Merely to build schools and churches for the poor is to offer them stones for bread. There must be living, loving Christian workers, who like Elisha of old, will take the dead into their arms and prayerfully hold them close, until they come to life again. Is there not a wide field for such labourers in Cape Town, and are there not men and women who will declare themselves ready to undertake it ? God grant it."

Mr. Murray set the example for he was most faithful in visiting the poor, even fearlessly going to see the sick during a severe small-pox epidemic which claimed many victims in the Cape Town area.

When Mr. Murray came to the city he found there The Mutual Improvement Society, which he joined, but he soon felt dis-satisfied with it. He wanted something broader and more spiritual, so in conjunction with friends who were like-minded he got established a branch of the Young Men's Christian Association, and threw himself heartily into the work of making it a success by organizing a course of winter lectures.

His influence over young is illustrated by the following letter from one who as a young man stayed some months in the house in Cape Town. The parsonage was a large house, with a garden in a beautiful part of the town near to great pine forests. He writes : " From the time, now more than forty years ago, when you opened to me your own beautiful home life, with your personal kindliness and Mrs. Murray's sweet and gracious motherliness, you planted in me a reverence, affection and gratitude which have never withered. Life has put barriers between us, but to me it is always a privilege and an honour to come and see you, and a keen pleasure." In another place the same writer says that in spite of the heavy strain under which Mr. Murray was living he was never irritable or " nervy." " Why how is it you never get angry ? " he was once asked, " It takes too much trouble to recover your good temper," was the reply.

Often in those days at Cape Town the beautiful hymn by by Bonar was sung in the home :

> " Calm me my God and keep me calm,
>   Soft resting on Thy breast,
> Soothe me with holy hymn and psalm
>   And bid my spirit rest "—

or else :

> " As helpless as a child who clings
>   Fast to his father's arm,
> And casts his weakness on the strength
>   That keeps him safe from harm."

> " As restful as a child who sits
>   Close to his mother's knee,
> And feels no want while he can have
>   That sweet society."

> " So I to Thee my Saviour look,
>   And in that face Divine,
> Can read the love that will sustain
>   As weak a faith as mine."

How he was interested in young people, seeking in every way to help them the following extracts will show. The first was in reference to a poor widow who came for help. Dear Brother, give advice. About three years ago a worker came to live here, Mrs. or Miss R. (there is something mysterious in her history) with her son. She is half Moravian and connected with a Moravian missionary. Her son was first in a grocer's shop, and later with a photographer. He conducts himself well and appears pious but is now without work and desires to devote himself to school or mission work. I should like you to see him and talk to him, and give me your opinion as physiognomist and secretary of the Mission Committee. May I send him to you for a day, say Saturday, to remain over Sunday, or would you prefer Thursday? It is possible that he might become a good worker. His mother has little to live on." He did not prove suitable for mission work but became a well-to-do business man.

Writing to a mother about a son concerning whom she was anxious he says : " Let H. come and stay three or six months. He can learn much through new companions and I think a strange atmosphere will help him to self confidence and a manly carriage." Another student was sent instead of H. and a new outlook given to him which influenced his whole after-life and ministry.

His catholicity of spirit and consideration for the opinion of others appears in the following letter written to his brother, Professor John Murray of Hellenbosch : " I think of taking a service for the Moravians. The friends want me to dispense the Sacrament and I have practically promised to do so. Let me know if you three see any objection. You know in the law there is absolutely nothing in regard to dispensing the Sacrament in other denominations." The three here referred to were Rev. Mr. Neethling, Mr. Murray's brother-in-law ; Professor Murray his brother, and Professor Hofmeyr, both of the Theological Seminary and sometimes referred to as the Stellenbosch Triumvirate.

In 1870 the Synods of the Anglican Church and that of the Dutch Church were both held in Cape Town, both had just passed through troublous times, this gave rise to an interchange of messages on the subject of Christian Unity. The Anglican Church wrote, " The Synod of the Province of South Africa, deeply deploring the manifold evils resulting from the divisions among Christians, is desirous of discussing the principles upon which a reunion in one visible body might be effected." The Dutch Reformed Synod replied : " That the Synod especially rejoices in any sign of such nearer approximation in the case of the English Church when it remembers the ecclesiastical intercommunion which existed in the period following the Reformation between the English Church and the Protestant Churches of the Continent—an inter-communion of which the National Synod of Dort in 1618-1619 saw a clear proof in the presence of the deputies of the English Church who took a part in the proceedings of the Synod." A Committee was appointed to discuss the matter but is was not long before it became clear that *absorption* into the English Church, and not affiliation was the object in view. This of course was not possible and the effort proved abortive. Even the suggestion of an interchange of pulpits was rejected.

In addition to all his other work Mr. Murray did a good deal of literary work. He edited the official paper of the Church. He wrote in Dutch thirty-one meditations on the fifty-first Psalm, which were afterwards published in English under the title, *Have Mercy upon Me*, and dedicated it to the Cape Town congregation. He printed a small tract, *Do you Believe This ?* and did some writing for a Dutch newspaper of a higher tone, in the hope of cultivating a sane and ideal political outlook among the leaders. News of the day and instructive articles were given in it, but all bitterness was excluded. Later on it was amalgamated with another paper and still upholds high ideals.

Mr. Murray found the Cape Town pastorate very heavy and trying. Miss Murray writing of it says : " Often my dear Mother would come to me and say, ' I am sure your dear father will kill himself, see how exhausted he is.' She would try to persuade him in January or some other hot month to go to a lonely seaside place for rest. When he received the call to Wellington, many people came up to our home, Craig Cottage, to beg of him not to leave. There was a good man, a Deacon of the Church, who lived at the bottom of the street, who used to stop the people and tell them, " You need not bother, Andrew Murray will not leave us, he will soon be first Minister of Cape Town and that is a fine position and he knows better than to leave." It came as a surprise to many that he took as *they* thought a backward step on the road to fame. He chose the small congregation of Wellington with its limitations, leaving the glitter of the City and its opportunities of advancement and took a lowlier place. But God's ways are not our ways, nor his thoughts our thoughts. The quiet, contemplative life led to a deeper, truer knowledge of God and ultimately as a writer of religious books he was made a blessing to God's people in all lands.

Chapter IX

ANDREW MURRAY AS PASTOR

Wellington

1871—1906

WELLINGTON, to which Mr. Murray received a call in 1871, was then a village of about 4,000 inhabitants all told, white and coloured, but it was the centre of a large and prosperous farming community. The reasons for accepting the call are clearly stated in a letter to his eldest brother : " Thanks for your kind notes. It shows how each one must at last decide for himself. Just the things which you think insufficient for a decision weigh with me. The first attraction is the state of the Wellington congregation. The second, a sphere of labour where I can have the people, old and young, under my continuous personal influence. Perhaps it is my idiosyncrasy, but the feeling of distraction and jointlessness in preaching and in other labour grows upon me as I flounder about without a church to preach in, or a congregation to labour among systematically, or the opportunity for regular aggressive work among those who stay away from Sunday services, simply because they have never been taught better. As to your arguments I cannot see that either Cape Town or Wellington throw much into the scale of a possibly more prolonged life . . . I do think that I have honestly and in child-like simplicity said to the Father that if He would have me stay here I am ready and willing . . . Pray that He may not leave me to my own devices. I dare not think He will."

He accepted the call and the induction sermon was truly prophetic, *Acts* xiv. 1 " And it came to pass as they so spake a great multitude believed."

So came Mr. Murray to the place where he was to spend the remaining forty-five years of his life, and where now lies resting all that is mortal of him, in the midst of the people whom he loved so well, and who loved him so warmly in return. Wellington has been described by a visitor as "beauty in the lap of grandeur. On the south and east is a range of mountains whose rugged peaks present a panorama of ever varying delight to the eye, till the setting sun bathes them in exquisite rose and purple tints. Down the valleys, like broad green rivers lie the vineyards and on the hill slopes climb the orchards with their luxuriant foliage, blossoms and fruit."

The past years of strenuous toil and strife had told upon his health which was so precarious that one old farmer when he heard of the call said, "Why call him, in two years time we will have the expenses of another funeral." But the country life and above all the satisfaction of preaching to his own special charge proved most beneficial in spite of the hard work.

The congregation was largely composed of descendants of the Huguenots who had fled from persecution in France and had found a refuge in South Africa. The French names, Malan, Rosseau, Le Roux, were common. They were a deeply religious people who faithfully attended the ordinances of religion. The revival of 1860 had also visited them and some souls had come into very clear light. Mr. Murray was not unkown to them, as ever since the pass over the mountains between Worcester and Wellington had been opened communication was easy and the distance not great. From the beginning of Mr. Murray's residence there, the roomy parsonage was always open to any of God's children passing through the town, and as it lay on the main road which connected Cape Town with all the northern settlements and towns, the stream of visitors was very considerable, but the reputation for hospitality which centred round the old home in Graaff Reinet centred round the Wellington home as well, right up to the end of Mr. Murray's life. The ground in the neighbourhood was very fertile, and as a consequence the farmers devoted their attention chiefly to the cultivation of the vine, and the farms were comparatively small. The people were frugal and had the name of being inclined to hold what they had, but when the time came that the hoarded treasure should be used for the Lord's service it was not withheld. Under skilful spiritual training they learned to give more and more, the ideals set before them never allowing them to rest satisfied with what had been done, until they became almost a model congregation in giving to the support of missions and benevolent purposes.

His relations with his people were ruled by love, the poorest and most ignorant had the same courteous interest shown them that the rich and wise received. They were simple folk, not learned in the lore of books, but rich in practical knowledge of their work and blessed with shrewd mother wit. He learned well how to draw on this knowledge and to apply it spiritually in his teachings and writings.

As to the love of his people for him, the following account of a welcome they gave him after a four-months' absence on a tour bears witness. " Our respected minister returned home on Friday last, after an absence of four months. Shortly after midday vehicles numbering more than one hundred, gathered from all quarters and made their way towards Bain's Kloof, and at half-past one a large crowd had assembled in the pass. At two o'clock the reverend gentleman made his appearance, accompanied by some of the Elders who had gone on still further to meet him. As soon as Mr. Murray stepped down from the cart the Dutch metrical version of *Psalm* cxxxiv. 3 was sung, after which the Rev. S. J. du Toit, the assistant minister, presented him with an address of welcome and handed him a purse of £50 from the women of the congregation. In replying to this address, Mr. Murray appeared to be much affected, and asked the friends to kneel while Mr. du Toit offered prayer, after which he spoke in a touching manner, thanking God for the protection, assistance and blessing which he had experienced on his journey. . . . Mr. Murray's parsonage was decorated about the doors with garlands of flowers, and with the motto 'Welcome Home' worked in orange blossoms which can only be described as exquisite. The cart and horses with which Mr. Murray performed his journey were subsequently sold for £90, and this amount was handed over to him as a mark of gratitude and esteem.''

Sometimes his temperance principles clashed with the interests of the wine farmers, but he was wise in dealing with them. Preaching to his congregation who were unacquainted with temperance principles he said : '' When a farmer trains a young horse it will often shy at a stone or something else. The wise farmer will quietly lead the horse to the unfamiliar object and let him look at it and smell it till all fear passes, and it will not shy any more. So I will not force temperance upon you, but we will speak and preach about it till you are familiar with it and approve of it.'' So successful was he in the matter that for many years there have been only four saloons in Wellington in contrast to the neighbouring village, where, at the same period, there were forty.

Soon after he arrived he started a movement to secure the closing of some of the many public houses in the town. '' Mr. Murray, the congregation will be torn asunder by your temperance sentiments,'' said an irate wine farmer. '' Never,'' he replied, '' we will, if necessary, take the scissors of love and cut it in two, having one section for temperance and the other not, but we will live together in love.'' Some earnest Temperance reformers of later times have little knowledge of what Mr. Murray did in the cause of Temperance in days when such activity was almost unknown. One of his daughters relates her recollections of those days as follows : '' When father came to Wellington there were seven Canteens in Church Street alone, but he soon got four of them closed, and also in other streets he got the Canteens closed. These people were very angry with him, and sought to burn down down the parsonage. We had to be on the watch constantly, for rags soaked in paraffin were thrown in at the windows near the lace curtains, so as to cause them to burn. God, in His mercy, graciously protected us, but we exercised great care and watchfulness at this time."

In 1890 the jubilee of the village was to be celebrated, and the question arose how that should be done. Mr. Murray, with the more earnest Christians desired to help some missionary object, but the more worldly party wanted a church tower. Everyone was greatly surprised when a list was handed round for the church tower to find it headed by a handsome donation from the minister. When one of his earnest Christian friends remonstrated, he said, " Let us draw them into the Church by love," which proved to be the case. The erection was spoken of as " the tower of love," and many of his opponents became his warm friends. Even when men opposed him he had sympathy with them. Of an opponent he said : " He is a born leader, if he cannot lead the one party, he must lead the other, so do not blame him." " I have no patience with a lazy man," said a fellow-worker. " Have you ever thanked God you were not born lazy ? " was the response.

Mr. Murray was always in great request as an Evangelist, and he trained his people to help in the work by prayer. Here are a few sentences from letters written in 1874 from a congregation where he was having special services. " Here the Lord has been blessing us. Last night more than 20 stayed (to be spoken to). Although I should be glad of a little rest I do beseech the Lord that the spirit of prayer may be given abundantly to His people for a new and mightier work of the Holy Spirit." " I feel anxious to get God's people together to point out the need of intercession and entire consecration." " Ask for prayer for us here." " I have a strong feeling that God will give our people the spirit of prayer to ask and expect new and more mighty blessing when I return." " Give yourself entirely to Him to have your whole life, every moment of it, filled with His Presence and with

His love." " Especially I long to know that there is a spirit of prayer for a new and more powerful work. Stir the people up to pray for us." When a number of retired farmers came to live in the village, he suggested that God had brought them there to be intercessors, and he trained them for the work. Here is his prayer for himself : " May not a single moment of my life be spent outside the light, love, joy of God's presence. And not a moment without the entire surrender of myself as a vessel for Him to fill full of His Spirit and His love."

He was too practical not to require them to work as well as to pray. Writing about this time to one of his daughters, who was at school in Holland, he says : " I have been very much occupied with what we call our Home Mission work—in Germany they call it ' die innere Mission.' We have been interesting ourselves in our coloured people, arranging for Sunday Schools and Evening Schools on the farms around us, under a strong conviction that a missionary can never reach our farm people properly, unless the masters be his helpers in his efforts to instruct the servants. We have received great encouragement by the willingness with which the people have taken up the work and the readiness with which the coloured people attend the classes. I have great hope that God may make it a means of bringing down blessing upon our congregation. Working for Him cannot be unblessed."

His preaching to his congregation on sin was deep and searching. During Lent when the sufferings of Christ were specially remembered, his hearers were made to realise something of the price that was paid for their redemption. Its effect on the people was thus described by an old member of the congregation speaking to one of Mr. Murray's family : " When your father arrived we felt ourselves worthy of the front seats in church, but soon we realised that for such sinners, a back seat was more becoming for us. He did not leave us there, we next felt unfit for any place but the doorkeeper's, but now he has

cast us right out into the street and rolled us in the mire."
There was a very deep work of grace in many hearts, so
that a large proportion of the congregation was truly
seeking to live for God and enjoyed assurance of acceptance
in Christ. As Mr. Murray expressed it, God had been
very gracious to his congregation.

Speaking at the unveiling of the Stone that was erected
to his memory, one who had known him during the later
years of his life said : " His object in life was nothing
less than ' to present every man perfect in Christ Jesus '.
To that end he laboured all through his ministry, making
the best use of the powers and talents which God had
entrusted to him, and with singular devotion he applied
himself to the task."

The members of this congregation in particular know
how he exerted himself for their spiritual upbuilding, how
continually in his preaching he laid stress on the necessity
of growing in grace and in the knowledge of our Lord
Jesus Christ. Incessantly he sought to lead believers
into a life of closer union with Christ by faith, into a deeper
spiritual experience to a more fruitful, more holy and
more consecrated life. For all this the congregation owes
a deep debt of gratitude to God."

Miss Murray gives an inspiring account of one of the
many remarkable Communion Services held in the
Wellington Church in those days :

" Can one ever forget the Communion seasons at this
time ? There, gathered round the Lord's Table, 500 or
600 Communicants, and a Holy influence permeated the
Church. Can we forget the Holy Awe, the deep reverence,
the joy and often the rapture written on father's face ?
The holy joy that filled heart and soul at these never-to-
be-forgotten seasons of communion, when ' Heaven
came down our souls to meet ! ' One communion season
I remember well. Father seemed to have really been
taken up to the third heaven and a holy awe and deep
solemnity rested on us all before he spoke again, and his

words were, ' I live, yet not I but Christ liveth in me, and that life which I now live in the flesh, I live in *faith*, the faith which is in the Son of God who loved me and gave Himself for me.' More especially he emphasised those words ' *who loved me.*' Oh ! the wonder of it ! the pity of it that we so little understand, and so fail to bask in the sunshine of this great love ! Let us love Him and trust Him more and more !

" We left the table feeling that we had indeed been fed on heavenly Manna, and we rose with a deeper love, and fuller determination to do and dare all for our adorable Lord and Master. We were strengthened and refreshed as with new wine, and in the afternoon, the Thanksgiving Service was a time of wondrous praise, not from the lips alone, but from the heart. ' What shall I render unto the Lord.' After one of these refreshing times I remember a farmer coming to father, with £50 for the Mission cause or for the cause of education."

It is characteristic of this devoted and successful Servant of the Lord Jesus Christ that he had always a low estimate of his work or attainments. In notes of reminescences supplied by Miss Murray, she says :—" How often have I heard him say ' I wish I had more of a Shepherd's heart, to seek after and find the lost.' He was not able to walk much but his desire for this heart was very intense, and he would blame himself because he had not more of it. But no one could welcome more graciously some quarrelsome person who called to ask him to settle personal quarrels or disputes which had arisen among neighbours or friends. He had a very gracious way of getting rid of cranks without hurting them. He had always many things awaiting his attention and would excuse himself with great courtesy. But he would leave the most important things, however pressing, for some poor brokenhearted person who sought his help. He had more of the Shepherd Heart than he knew."

Truly he walked humbly with his God.

CHAPTER X

THE
CHRISTIAN EDUCATIONALIST AND EVANGELIST
Wellington
1871—1906

WHEN in the order of Providence, Mr. Murray was called to pass through some special experience he always was attentive to the call which such an experience was intended to be. It was generally a call to some special work. The death of his darling little daughter became to him a call to the putting forth of fresh efforts on behalf of the children of his people, and this was deepened by reading of the wonderful work Mary Lyons had accomplished in America. There was a certain similarity of conditions in both America and South Africa which entirely differentiated both countries from Europe. Each of these two countries had been a refuge for those who fled from religious persecution. Both were young countries with a sparse population which made it difficult to obtain educational advantages. The great hope of both lands lay in its farming population, and the farmers often had manifold difficulties to contend with. Mary Lyons had adopted for her motto that which had become the motto of Mr. Murray : " The Children for Christ." Early in her teaching career she embraced an ideal which she set herself to realise, it was then winning every child that came under her care for Christ, and the training of them as Christian workers. Her missionary zeal expressed itself in the words, " If we would have the whole Christ in our hearts we must embrace the whole world in our love." For these things she lived and laboured and prayed.

Her ideals crystallized in the founding of Mount Holyoke

Seminary for the daughters of those who had but moderate means. For the sake of economy and also to train the girls as the heads of the future home-makers of the land, most of the domestic work was done by the girls themselves. The institution was under a Board of Trustees, to whom the interests of the Church of Christ were of the highest importance. In a series of articles written to prepare the way for the introduction of the same kind of education into South Africa, Mr. Murray thus describes her work : " She was marvellously successful in rousing her pupils to aim enthusiastically at uniting the highest intellectual development with the most decided piety. First the Kingdom of God, but after that most certainly all science and knowledge."

The Colony (as it was then called) at that time had only about 350,000 European inhabitants scattered over its immense area, and to supply the needs of its members the Dutch Church had started a Boarding School a short time previously in Capetown, but this was for well-to-do parents. Mr. Murray was ever seeking to help those in more straitened circumstances. He had noticed in his travels the difficulties mistresses had to get servants, and he felt that if the young women had a practical training in housework, many homes would be the brighter. In after years one of the school inspectors bore witness to the practical value of such training by stating that he usually recognised the presence of a " Huguenot " girl by the refinement that was evident in the home-life on the farm.

But Mr. Murray not only awakened interest among his people, but he also wrote to Mount Holyoke in America, asking that a teacher should be sent, and he, himself, personally guaranteed her salary, at the same time stating that he expected Government would assist in the matter later on. Much earnest prayer was offered by Mr. Murray and the congregation after the letter was sent. Eagerly an answer was awaited ! Meanwhile tracts were circulated and the congregation educated by a series of sermons on the privilege of consecrating and educating their children *for the Lord's work*. He emphasised the spiritual possibilities of a teacher's influence. He awakened them to an intelligent, prayerful and practical interest in the new venture, so that when at length a circular was issued calling a meeting to consider the whole question of raising funds, £1,500 was raised in Wellington alone. It was decided that the Institute should be named in commemoration of the French refugees, The Huguenot Seminary.

When a letter came from America saying that they felt it would be better to send two ladies, the faith of those interested was ready to accept this increased responsibility, and it expressed itself in action by purchasing a property as site for the Institution.

On November 16th, Miss Ferguson and Miss Bliss arrived to devote their lives to God's service in South Africa. These noble women are among His choicest gifts to South Africa, one of His best and greatest gifts to the womanhood of this country. Only in the days to come will it be fully revealed what they have meant to the cause of education, missions and Christian life in its many aspects. In spiritual aspirations and missionary enthusiasm, the Murrays found in these ladies kindred spirits. Their selfless devotion to their life work has seldom been equalled. Miss Ferguson's constant reply to the various questions that arose was " What is best ? " Never did they turn aside in their pursuit of what seemed to be the highest good of the work. Miss Ferguson was a woman of vision, and bravely did she and Miss Bliss steadily materialise each successively revealed possibility. In Mr. Murray they had an unwearying helper, and adviser, and true friend.

The school was opened in the beginning of 1874, under the now widely known name of The Huguenot Seminary, with 40 boarders, who soon proved to be just the stamp of girls required and were very responsive to all the influences brought to bear upon them. By the end of the first year many of them had been definitely won for Christ. The increasing numbers who applied for admission soon made another building necessary, so Mr. Murray, besides stirring up his own congregation to greater generosity, undertook a four months' tour to raise the necessary money. Before starting, he had, in quiet faith, claimed from God £100 for every Sunday's services and for the week-day services £50. It was remarkable how wonderfully the Lord arranged that His servant's request should be fulfilled in spite of many difficulties and even dangers from flooded rivers. In almost every place he received the required sum ; some congregations even giving more than the sum asked for. What his thoughts were busy with during the tour is shown in the following extract from a letter to his brother-in-law : " You will have heard from Wellington this and that about the journey. The collections were fair, the interest in giving children to the service of the Lord fair, the meetings not without fruit, the preaching not unblessed. I long much to hear of you and your's. I feel so cut off from intercourse with you and know not what has happened in your home. Here is something of interest for you. I have found here and in the Free State more than one young man who would like to become a minister, but distance hinders more than money. Write me how far you are on with the Boarding-house and what the charges are. There are young persons here in the Free State and in the Colony who desire to become teachers but are too advanced for our school. Let me know, if they have nothing, and you can only count upon a £15 from the Church and £12 from Dr. Dale, if you see a chance of finding them support and education. If we can set the current flowing, then you will have a considerable number from down country.

The spirit of the world is already very powerful and it is of inexpressible value that the young should be brought under the sway of a powerful, decidedly religious influence.

In visiting down-country congregations it is clear to me how much ground we have already lost with the young people by the influence of a worldly teacher, and we have not an hour to lose if we want by means of pious teachers to win the younger generations for the Lord."

After his return the second building was opened in 1875, with room for fifty students, and was filled almost immediately. The previous six months Mrs. Murray had had sixteen girls and a teacher boarding in their home. Speaking of the speedy success of this second building, Mr. Murray said : " On my return from the opening of the new building my mind was full of one thought, ' He purposed doing it, He has done it ! ' "

When the new school was opened and still more room was needed, Mr. Murray, in 1876, made another tour extending over seven or eight weeks. Some extracts of letters written to his wife on this tour will show how God was leading him : —

" I did thank my God with my whole heart that you had been kept in peace and I pray very earnestly that He may increase it to you yet more abundantly. The more I travel the more I see that the great need of our Church is Evangelists. And though I cannot in the least see it would be possible to give up Wellington, or to arrange for long absences, it does almost appear wrong not to undertake the work when one knows that there are hundreds ready to be brought in. It appears terrible to let them go on in darkness and indecision when they are willing to be helped. I have been much struck in reading the notes on *Exodus* by the words of God to Pharoah : ' Let My people go that they may serve Me.' He does hear the cry and sighing of the thousands of seeking ones and wants His servants to lead them out of bondage. And how can I help saying that if He will use me I shall only consider the honour too high. It is sad to preach one or two earnest Evangelistic sermons to see the impression made and to go away feeling sure that if one could devote a little more time and individual attention to the work, souls would come to light and joy.

" The thought suggests itself whether with such precious opportunities, so short and rare, it is right to preach a sermon for a collection. May the Lord direct and guide. We have said and do say that *entire* consecration to His work and will is our choice and our life. And we know that for all difficulties and questions that come we have an infallible solution in the assurance—Christ Who lives our life in us, is sufficient for all that comes and will guide and keep us in perfect peace."

This journey was attended with some dangers. " On Saturday morning we came on here and found the first crossing of the river quite easy. Some people were doubtful about our getting through the Poort (gorge) with its 30 drifts (fords)—but the hotel-keeper assured us it was quite passable. So we went on—got through the first drift quite nicely—but at the second the water had come down afresh and we were hardly in before the cart upset—we think owing to a hole washed in the road by the flood. We were all out in the water—and through God's goodness all safe. A boy we had with us fell under the cart and was some time under water, but God spared us what would have been a terrible blow, and he came out. Fortunately the horses turned round towards the river bank so that after we had with difficulty lifted the cart on its wheels we got out on the same side as we had gone in . . .

" In the solitude of last night and this morning I thought a great deal of ' the backside of the desert.' The ' Let My people go ' is continually before me. In travelling these last three or four days I have met ever so many people who appear so willing to accept Christ but have not the needful knowledge or help. I have felt so deeply that if one had a Divine enthusiasm, the warmth of faith and love to compel them to come in, one might be a blessing from home to home. I have this day sought to lay myself afresh on the altar, and to look to the Great High Priest presenting me to the Father, an acceptable and accepted sacrifice, and engaging by His Holy Spirit to appropriate and use the Sacrifice. How, I know not fully, the want, the universal want, of a dealing with souls in the fervency and joy of a living faith, rests heavy upon me. But whether there is any prospect of my doing the work I cannot say. Or whether by training workers, teachers and missionaries, the Lord may permit me to do more, I know not. But it is sad to see souls in multitudes seeking and not finding, sighing and not helped apparently because there is none to show them the way of the Lord. Oh ! why should not our hearts be filled full with the love which wrestles for souls unto death."

The next letter shows how he regarded his disappointments. " You think because I have not been so successful that this is a sign that the journey is not the Lord's will. I think we must be careful in judging thus. In the notes on *Exodus* there was a very striking remark : ' Apparently Providential openings are sometimes our most dangerous temptations,' sent by God on purpose to test our principle. And so with failure—we cannot judge of our path by this, for God may send it to try us. The great thing is to have our minds always in a childlike state when we are considering or fixing our plans—and thus we shall know that God is guiding our path, even if it were a mistaken one, to very blessed issues. Failure, though perhaps I ought not to call it failure, even though I have not got quite as much as last time—but even comparative failure, has not for one moment made me think I was not in the right path. But one thing has been very heavy on me all through . . . the idea of being on a mission for *money*, and having no time or opportunity to work for *souls* . . . It is really a terrible thought, thousands of souls, willing and apparently ready to be led to Christ, and even earnest ministers without the power to take them by the hand and to take the decided step. It appears to me so mysterious, so terrible that they should be ready to be saved and have no one to press them simply and earnestly to accept of Jesus. May God send help. It only makes me feel more than ever the need of our Institution for training Christian young men for teachers who can act as missionaries too. And oh ! how deeply I have felt the sight of children entrusted to unconverted teachers ; Christ's lambs given to the charge of the world."

On one of his collecting tours, as he was getting into his cart on a farm near Fraserburg, the old farmer advised him not to go too fast. He urged the need of care for the horses. " Uncle Piet," said Mr. Murray, " what would you do if a jackal had got into your sheep kraal (sheep fold) ? " " I would run to kill him or drive him out as quickly as I could." " Well, Uncle Piet, there are two jackals among my sheep," and with that he touched the horses with his whip and was off.

When he returned home his first care was the establishment of a boys' boarding home where missionaries and teachers might be trained. Again he looked to America for one who could do the work, but above all, it was prayer and quiet waiting upon God that gave him the confidence to step out in faith on this new venture.

The following letter to his sister shows how well he was learning the lesson of trust :—

" MY DEAREST SISTER—Many thanks for your letter and its contributions to our Seminary and Training-school. I accept them as a pledge ot your prayer and love. As to our Training-school, we start the work with 10 boarders —5 preparing for teachers and perhaps for mission work too—nice hopeful boys—and we have been led most kindly in regard to our teacher, Mr. Weich, an assistant whom God has just provided too, and the domestic arrangements. God appears to be doing everything for us so that though there is at present no prospect of Mr. Ferguson's coming I am full of confidence that God is in His own way and time, step by step, going to unfold to us the blessings He has in store, and the kindness He is going to show us in the establishment of this Institution. So you can think with such a prospect I feel as if I have but one lesson to learn better and I am learning it, just to sit and adore and say to Divine Grace, that there is nothing I cannot expect His wondrous kindness to do."

At the end of 1877 he returned from a trip to Europe and America, accompanied by Mr. Ferguson, a brother of Miss Ferguson. He was another of God's gifts to South Africa ; a holy man who carried the sense of the presence of God with him wherever he went ; a man of prayer who exercised a powerful influence over those with whom he came into contact. Previous to entering on his ministerial career he had been an engineer, a training which gave him some practical ability. The material which he had to work upon was not always responsive at first. There was the tall, blue-eyed shepherd David, who had learnt the whole English dictionary by heart, but whose courage failed when he had to speak in English, so he grew homesick and returned to his sheep. There was Ben, who arrived with all his worldly possessions tied up in a red handkerchief in one hand, and the spear that killed Bethuen—whose murder had occasioned a small Kaffir war just ended—in the other. There were others, more fitted for training but most of them not very far advanced. But many of them became inspired to devote themselves to a life-long service of the Master's. Such was the beginning of an Institute which has provided 145 ordained missionaries out of the 178 who are now working in connection with the Dutch Reformed Church, beside those who have passed beyond the veil after a longer or shorter service, as well as many Christian teachers.

The following extract from Mr. Ferguson's Biography reveals the man and describes his manner of work : " He had to begin at the very commencement, teaching them the rudiments of reading and writing. It was the day of small things, yet he never complained. Patiently, he toiled with them, giving them of his best. Often it seemed as if he had left the great calling of the ministry to do a lesser work, yet he never complained or doubted that he was in the place God had appointed."

Once when asked why he studied so carefully when he was taking class after class over much the same ground, he said he must bring to his class a living truth. If it did not become a living truth to his own heart it would be a dead thing to his class. "He not only studied his message but he studied his students and learned to help each individually."

In 1905, this Institute passed into the hands of the Synod of the Dutch Reformed Church, which passed the following resolution :—" The Synod expresses its cordial appreciation of the work performed for the Church during upwards of a quarter of a century, by the revered first minister of Wellington and his collaborators in the training of missionaries. It accepts the gift (of the Training Institute) which has cost more than £5,000, and is offered to the Synod unencumbered by debt, with sincere thanks to the Lord and to the donors."

The following extracts from an appeal to the children of Christian parents, entitled " Labourers for the Harvest " (*Matt.* ix. 36-38) show how Mr. Murray's heart was yearning after them for Christ's Service :—

" When Jesus saw the multitude, scattered as sheep without a shepherd He was moved with compassion. What did He do ? He turned to His disciples for aid. He said they must pray for labourers ; God's provision for the need of the world would be accomplished by the co-operation of His people first in prayer and then in work."

" The need of labourers is the subject of the Lord's address. The Lord Jesus has committed the interests of His Kingdom to His people on earth. He has exempted no one. He expects every one of His subjects will be willing to live and die for Him. He expects that every one who belongs to Him will be interested in the concerns of His work and Kingdom and live entirely to establish His glorious empire on earth.

" I wish specially to speak of the need of Christian workers, other than ministers, such as teachers, missionaries and individual Church members for such work as they can do, all—all are needed.

(1) *Teachers.* Throughout the whole country there is a call for teachers. Believing teachers are indispensable for the wellbeing of the Church. If the lambs are entrusted to careless shepherds how shall the flock increase ? There are in our country thousands of children who receive either no education at all or a bad one, or else good secular, but irreligious education. Of these thousands of children Jesus says ' the fields are white to harvest.'

" Lord Jesus pour Thine own love to children into the hearts of Thy people. May it become impossible to bear the burden of the children's need any longer. Teach Thou them what they must do that no single child of the Church who bears the mark of the covenant on the forehead may grow up without Thy grace and Thy word.

(2) *Missionaries.* The Mission committee has long spoken of extending the Foreign Mission work, but talking does not help ; there are no labourers, and the work has been carried on for years with only three workers. Young men are not coming to be trained for the work. And thus it goes on year after year, and the heathen among whom we ought to labour are left in their darkness. The harvest is great and the labourers are few. The harvest is lost in the fields—Satan has no lack of men for saloon keepers —but the Lord Jesus seems to call in vain for missionaries.

(3) *Other workers.* What has been said does not include all. Every Christian is called to be a worker for God. The secret of a truly religious education is to train our sons with this as the great thought of their lives—that

they not only belong to the Lord but each one must work for Him. Work for Him must be the main object, not a side issue in whatever position or business they are, they must know that they live only to serve the Lord, and to say of all their money, their influence, their talents, I hold it every hour at His command.

"Is it an impossibility to make the idea of entire consecration the foundation of education? Would it not be highly desirable? Are there not many parents who would count it a joy to seek such an education for their children? Without definitely saying the child must become a teacher or missionary gladly would they have been prepared to enter life with the Word of God engraven on his heart. None of us liveth to himself. This will cause our children to answer the purpose of God."

It will have been noticed how in the midst of all his efforts to raise money for the great educational work he had in hand, Mr. Murray was ever true to the Evangelistic call he had received from God, and it will appear later on how wonderfully God used His servant as an Evangelist at an age when most men feel the work of their lives is finished. He tells how he was led to break through the conventions of a lifetime and to get into personal touch with seeking souls. Very wonderful was the harvest God enabled His faithful old servant to gather.

This lesson he learned theoretically while on a journey and had an opportunity to carry it into practice immediately after his return home. He says:—" A week before I started I received from Edinburgh, an account of the work Mr. Moody was carrying on, with reports of his addresses and statements as to his methods. As I travelled from one parsonage to another, these things were the subjects of earnest conversation, and we often asked whether we ought not to venture on after-meetings. More than once we were just ready to begin when prudence held us back. In a wonderful way God loosed my bonds. In our Dutch Church it is customary to have daily prayer

meetings during the ten days between Ascension and
Whit Sunday. In my absence they had been held as
usual at Wellington. At the first prayer meeting after
Whit Sunday, the question was asked, " We have prayed,
why have we not received ? " The answer was given :
" If we persevere we shall receive." They resolved to
begin again. The next week I arrived at home and joined
them. We continued prayer for a week and then felt,
it is now time to work for the unsaved. This was done
and the after-meetings during the next five weeks proved
such a blessing that the fruit remains till this day."

Undoubtedly this experience powerfully influenced all
Mr. Murray's later Evangelistic work. His eldest daughter
gives an interesting account of that remarkable work of
God, which supplements what Mr. Murray himself has
written. She says :—

" The first Whitsuntide after Father's return from
England God granted him a wonderful ingathering of
souls at Wellington. The elders requested him to preach
on ' Hell ' and he did so. Many a man and woman trembled
under that sermon, but it was under the tender wooing
of God's great love to us in the gift of Christ that they
found peace. For three weeks he preached to a crowded
church, which had sitting accommodation for over 1,000
people, night after night, on one text only : *John* iii, 16 ;
" God so loved the world that He gave His only Son."
I can never forget his tender earnestness, as with simple
but telling illustrations he brought the truth home to us
personally. God loved the *WORLD*, loved *YOU*. He
GAVE His SON . . . WHOSOEVER believeth . . .
HATH EVERLASTING LIFE. How anyone could
withstand his pleadings, and refuse to surrender to God
used to puzzle me. Often Mrs. Murray and other workers
were in the church till late at night, dealing with anxious
enquirers. Mr. Peter Stuart, whom Father called a
' Buttonhole Christian,' assisted him greatly. He had
the faculty of getting hold of people in the street, or

elsewhere and holding on to them while he presented the claims of Christ. Many were thus reached who would not have been led to Christ by the ordinary methods."

The wonderful pile of buildings which goes under the name of The Huguenot Seminary, and those also connected with the College for Women are a material monument to his memory, but far more precious is the fact that such numbers of souls there and throughout South Africa have been led to a knowledge of Salvation through faith in Jesus Christ.

In front of his old church his friends have erected a beautiful marble statue of him with the face towards the street, and so great was the reverence felt for him, that drunken coloured people who would be staggering to their wretched hovels, feared to pass that way home, for, said they, " Ou Minheer sal ons sie." " The old minister will see us." They did not wish him to see them in their cups, even when intoxicated and incapable, they had a consciousness of fear to pass by even his likeness in stone.

Chapter XI

EUROPE AND AMERICA VISITED

In 1877 Mr. Murray was elected by the Synod of the Dutch Reformed Church to be Moderator for the second time, and it appointed him and Rev. Mr. Fraser to represent the Church at the Pan-Presbyterian Council meeting in Edinburgh. His brother Charles, who succeeded their father as minister of the church in Graaff Reinet accompanied them.

Mr. Murray wrote several articles for the *Kerkbode*, the official paper of the Church, in which he gave from time to time accounts of what he saw and heard, which he thought would be of interest to his congregation and large circle of friends.

He states in these articles that after his duties in connection with the Pan-Presbyterian Council have been discharged he had three objects in view as he travelled about from place to place :—

1. To study the condition of the Church,

2. To enquire into problems concerning Education, and

3. To consider the Spiritual Life of the Countries visited.

As regards Education he was able to state some things with confidence. He says :—" The educational work of our churches (in South Africa) is only in its first beginnings. Hitherto we have been so occupied in seeking the teachers so badly needed that the great educational questions, which are being discussed in Europe, have not yet been considered. I hope that whenever opportunity offers, I shall use my eyes, on my own and the churches' behalf, noting what is being done to train teachers for a profession on which both church and country depend so much.

He looked forward with the greatest pleasure to meeting those men whom God had raised up as " witnesses of what He can do for His children."

He reported some of the things which were said in the Council which deeply impressed him, and undoubtedly what was said about the missionary work of the Church left an indelible impression on his mind which had already been prepared by the Holy Spirit for just such seed, so that he became one of the greatest missionary enthusiasts of the universal Church and his influence was felt throughout the world. It was in the old Graaff Reinet home that his young heart and mind had been prepared for a willing responce to the call of the Spirit later on.

He reports a statement made by Dr. A. Hodges at the Council which impressed him :—" The same force in the Reformed Churches, which in former ages had opposed tyranny in the Church and State, must now do battle against the modern enemy—the lawlessness which defied all authority and exalted man and nature above God."

But perhaps what that prince of modern missionaries, Rev. Dr. Duff said on missions impressed him most of all : " I wish to take the highest possible Scriptural ground with reference to the sole and supreme duty of the Church of Christ to devote all the strength it has to the cause of missions. With the exception of the brief apostolic age there has been no period in the history of the Church when this actually has been done—to the great shame of the Church. Holding this conviction, a conviction which has been gathering strength these forty years—you will not take it amiss in me, standing as I do upon the verge of the eternal world, when I give expression to my immovable assurance that unless, and until, this supreme duty is more deeply felt, more powerfully realised, and more implicitly obeyed, not only by individual believers, but by the Church at large, we are only playing at missions, deceiving our own selves, slighting the command of our blessed King, and expending in all manner of fruitless struggles the powers, the means, and the abilities, which should be devoted with undivided enthusiasm to the spiritual subjugation of the nations."

Andrew Murray made his own important contribution to the deliberations of this Council, on the Church's duty towards its Young People. The Reporter says: " Rev. Andrew Murray, Cape Town, addressed the Council on the training of the Young, giving it as his opinion that the Lord had Himself given to the children a place in the Church which it scarcely realised. The best pastors of the Church should give themselves to the work of the Christian training of the young, and there should, more-over, be a link connecting together the home, the school, the Church ; such a cord could not be broken."

On another subject dear to his heart—" Christian Fellow-ship," he said : " I believe in the Communion of Saints, and am firmly convinced that such an exercise of Christian fellowship carries a rich blessing with it. The power and courage of the individual soldier depends largely, not merely on the confidence he places in his general, but upon the power and faithfulness of the *army* to which he belongs. Everything that strengthens this conviction in him increases the qualities which are indispensible in any army that is to conquer, namely, enthusiasm and courage. In the Church of Christ we have not merely " one Spirit " but " one body," and everything that tends to emphasize the unity of the body brings a blessing with it."

On one occasion when sitting on his stoep (verandah) in Wellington, a minister was conversing with him about some of his difficulties.˙ Mr. Murray listened very patiently and with deep sympathy, for he knew the speaker was a devoted servant of the Lord Jesus Christ, but he also knew that some of the minister's difficulties were due to the general state of the Church, and when he had finished Mr. Murray said : " My brother, you forget that you are a member of a body that is sick, very sick. If your own body is ill, every joint feels it, and cannot escape the inconvenience and pain till the body itself regains health." He often urged this as a reason why Christians should unceasingly pray for the Church *as a whole*. In its health they, as individual members, would also flourish. He felt that this fact of the unity of the body was too often lost sight of and altogether too little regarded. He was never weary of repeating " Believers ARE ONE. They have not made nor can they unmake the unity. It is ours to RECOGNISE it and act upon it as one of God's facts. Recognise the unity." He wonderfully exemplified his teaching in his practice. Few men have ever manifested a wider catholicity than Andrew Murray. In the hospitable home at Wellington, ministers and members of any or all of the Churches acknowledging our Lord as Head and Saviour were cordially welcomed as brethren beloved, and made immediately to feel themselves at home. He did not merely talk about Fellowship, he taught it truly, but first he practised it himself, and he did it as an expert, as hundreds testify.

After the Council had finished its work, a Conference was held at Inverness, in which Mr. Murray took part. He writes :

" In the house in which I was staying and in intercourse with laymen, I could notice very distinctly the influence of Mr. Moody's work. There is much more readiness to talk out on spiritual things and much more warmth. I had noticed in Edinburgh, too, that the whole religious tone of Scotland has been lifted up, and brightened most remarkably. I do praise God for it. Then, too, there is much earnest work being done, though I get the impression in many places that the activity and joy of work is regarded too much as the essence of religion. . . . "

" For myself I have learnt this lesson, that it does not do to emphasise too much the one side of holiness— communion with Jesus apart from the other side of work. There is no joy like that over repentant sinners, no communion closer than ' Go ye into all the world and teach—and lo ! I am with you alway.' And yet the joy of work and revival *is not enough. God's children must be led into the secret of the possibility of unbroken communion with Jesus personally.*"

Here is another extract : " In the evenings we had evangelistic services and I gave addresses on two evenings. By the third evening the impressions were deepening, and we all felt the need of continuing them. I think some were blessed that night."

Then follows an account of a journey by steamer and coach on his way to Bonskeid where the deeply spiritual Mrs. Barbour, mother-in-law of Dr. Whyte, lived, and here he had much delightful fellowship. Then he went on to a Conference at Perth. He says : " On Sunday I preached twice and felt the need of after meetings. I feel myself bound hand and foot to Wellington and to my home— otherwise it would be a glorious thing to be an Evangelist. One feels as if there were an immense harvest waiting everything and as if there is indeed nothing like ' the joy of harvest.' But the Blessed Father knows exactly what the work is He wants each one to do. . . . Good- bye, my love to all friends. I really cannot write, this is my first quiet day since being in Scotland."

After visiting his many friends in Holland he went on to Germany and Switzerland to visit Barman and Elberfeld, being present at a Missionary Feast and was interested in the missionary training centre there.

From Europe he, in company with his brother Charles, went to America in search of more teachers to supply the increasing needs of South Africa. There he much enjoyed what he saw of Christian work, especially Mr. Wanamaker's Sunday Schools.

Writing to his sister from New Haven, Rev. Charles Murray gives an interesting account of their tour, and incidentally shows how great and widespread was the influence of his elder brother. The relationship between

the brothers was peculiarly affectionate. He says:
" The state of utter mental and spiritual and physical
degradation into which my cross Atlantic voyage threw
me made me despair of ever being able, in America, to
muster courage to begin a letter to you. I now have
courage enough in a sense, though I feel vexed at being
unable to give you an idea of the rate at which we are
going on. Last night we had been four days in the country
and I caught myself wondering how it was we had seen no
Sunday Schools yet nor heard any celebrated minister.
If ever you want change, then, of all places in the world,
come to the United States. If you had been with me
your brain would have reeled or you might have gone wild.
If I try to pray after such a day of excitement my efforts
at prayer resolve themselves into efforts to bring my
thoughts to a standstill. You think you are praying, but
before your closed eyes there passes a clear panorama of
streets, ships, hotels, human beings and what not, as if
you had in the orthodox fashion paid 2/6 to see it.

" I trust the children told you something about our
treat at Brooklyn, and that Amelia told you about the
first days after our arrival. You will have noticed that
Graaff Reinet work and variety of months is crowded
into a day here. We have stayed a day with Mrs. Allen,
not unknown to you by name. And such a woman as
Mrs. Allen is ! I do not say lady. Woman is far higher.
You have no idea of the value I attach to such a peep
into American home life. What a contrast to the hateful
hotel life preferred by some. Should you ever come over
here, Miss Ferguson's name is an ' open sesame ' to hundreds
of hearts. Last night (we had spent the day with Miss
Bliss's mother and brother) a large company of gentlemen
—professors, ministers, etc., with their ladies, were invited
to meet Andrew. He is Mr. Murray. I introduced
myself as the other Mr. Murray. As two or three little
coteries were in danger of monopolizing him, old Dr.
Bacon took a chair right opposite him and began catechising

him for the benefit of the whole company, on the political, social and religious condition of South Africa, and, of course, on the state and prospects of the Huguenot Seminary. I couldn't realise I was in North America when I felt how much at home we were.

" There was really nothing of the distinctive American, such as we always expect it coming from such a distance. What was especially pleasant was the absence of all formality and stiffness, and the ease with which we passed through the whole evening. Andrew is in the circle in which we move quite a lion. Such regrets that he cannot stay on to spend the Sabbath and preach. He is a precious brother and very convenient to travel with. On his back, not literally, but metaphorically, I get in anywhere. You can't think how precious his conversation and society were on board, only he is awfully troubled on the point of first-style dress, manners, e.g., he had no peace till I had purchased a hateful high hat. Once he was horrified at seeing me eating an apple in the train, and made me swallow a mouthful unchewed when he noticed a known gentleman coming in.

" Boston. Dear me how much we have gone through and heard Moody-Sankey, Dr. Cooke, Dr. Cullis, Mrs. Cullis, Mr. Brooks and whom not ? To-day, coming out of Dr. Cullis Convention meeting, met Mrs. Farley, go to spend to-morrow afternoon there, spent last night with the Peabodys at Salem : attended a first Revival meeting, and this morning went right through a large Normal Training School there. The day after to-morrow we go to the Gilsons, Friday to Wellesley, Saturday to Mount Holyoke, and Sunday at Amhust, or perhaps with Mrs. Ayres. Next week Andrew and I may part. He to visit other teachers, friends, and I to go to Chicago. We do not find half an hour unoccupied, and every day have new cause for regret that our time is so limited.

" I shall say nothing about Moody, etc., to you. If I find time, which does not look likely, I shall write to the

Kerkbode (the official paper of the D. R. Church). I do wish American ingenuity had discovered some way of putting down your thoughts in a tenth of the time now required. I feel we have set too little value upon them (Miss Ferguson and Miss Bliss) when I see what they have left to come."

This last sentence has reference to the change of surroundings which Miss Ferguson and Miss Bliss experienced when they exchanged the United States for South Africa. Certainly they left behind them there many of the conveniences of life which were not then common in South Africa, but they found their life work in Wellington, and lived to see it become the centre from which blessing flowed to all parts of South Africa—and they were so happy in their work they never returned to America save for an occasional visit to their friends and relatives, and what was mortal of them awaits the trumpet of the Resurrection Morning in the Wellington cemetery.

Nothing can more clearly show how entirely her heart was in her work in South Africa then the following letter written by Miss Ferguson, Dr. Ferguson (as she then was), to a dear American friend of hers as she left New York, after a visit, to return to Wellington. She writes:

" I have a cabin to myself, and it has seemed a very sacred place since this first consecration of it. Ellie, darling, I am very very glad to go back to South Africa, very glad that the Lord is letting me take up the work there again, and O darling, pray, pray much for me that it may be in a new spirit of love with a new power, a new consecration for service, taking hold by faith of the resources that there are in God for me as I have never done before. My whole soul is stirred within me with the desire to be all that God would make me in this service He is giving me. I want all my girls Christians, all who ever shall come to the Huguenot Seminary . . . I want them built up in Christ, strong for His Service, wise in His wisdom, taught of Him to help other souls. I am reminded frequently of nearly eight years ago when Miss Bliss and I were on our way to Africa, of the cry of my heart then for a blessing on the work that was waiting for us, and I feel now that I want the Lord to do exceeding abundantly for me and for the work, above all that He has done, above all that we have asked or thought as yet, and my heart's longings include all the other schools that have been established in His name, that each may become what the Lord wants to make it. I think, darling, that our danger is in letting other things absorb us rather than the great thing. We want ourselves to become just as near perfect as possible for the sake of Him whose we are. I do not think in a certain way we can be too ambitious for them. We are working for the King and we want to do the very best work, but we must remember that the work is His. He is the head. He has His plans about everything, and if our eagerness and enthusiasm run away with us, we shall make a sorry tangle, marring His work. I think we need to hold ourselves loose so that we may wait on Him to know His plans, His way, and O, darling, do let us pray continually and let us with all our hearts determine that God and the things of God shall ever only always be first."

This letter lets us catch a glimpse of the inner life of that remarkable woman whom God sent to Wellington to the help of His servant Andrew Murray. A close and abiding friendship and fellowship in the great cause of Christian Education enabled them to accomplish the great work to which so much of their energies had been devoted. Who can measure the greatness of the blessing to South Africa that resulted from the sending out of hundreds of well educated girls to become the mothers in new homes, and to pass on to their children the ideal of full devotion to the Lord Jesus Christ as the thing of most importance.

One of these teachers writes : " In 1877 Revd. A. Murray with his brother Charles, visited the United States with the special object of arousing interest in the educational work in South Africa. They addressed the professors and students of various colleges in every case receiving a hearty welcome. So many were the invitations that poured in upon them to visit these institutions that the brothers had to separate. Once, Mr. C. Murray introduced himself thus : " You must please understand that I am not *the* Mr. Murray. I am the other Mr. Murray."

During their stay they were successful in obtaining ten lady teachers for girls' schools in Wellington, Stellenbosch, Worcester, Swellendam, Beaufort West, Graaff Reinet and Pretoria. The Revd. George Ferguson was also secured in order to take charge of the Mission Institute to be commenced at Wellington. The whole party, who sailed together from England, included another minister and his wife and some other teachers. . . .

Soon after the voyage began, Mr. Murray proposed a daily class for the study of Dutch with himself and Mr. Stucki as teachers on alternate days. So excellent was the instruction, and so great the enthusiasm aroused, that after the voyage was over two at least of the learners were able to undertake correspondence in Dutch.

Mr. Murray used to spend most of his time on the voyage in a quiet corner of the deck, absorbed in a book ; but we soon discovered that he was quite ready at any time to put down his book for a helpful chat with anyone who desired it. Some of those talks will never be forgotten. Mr. Murray continued to manifest his interest in the teachers he brought out even after they had all been dispersed to their different spheres of work. It was very pleasant to observe the affection that existed between the brothers and their evident enjoyment in recalling the experiences of their boyhood and in discussing, as they walked up and down the deck, their plans for future work.

He had also engaged in Scotland a well-qualified Christian Principal for the new Normal School which his church was starting in Cape Town, who gave over forty years of faithful and successful work to the country of his adoption. In his first sermon after his return he dwelt upon relationship between the minister and his congregation, and exhorted all to praise God for past blessings, to make intercession for the future.

He found much work awaiting him, especially that of caring for the new ventures, the Mission Institute and the Boarding Home for those boys who had been sent to him, most of whom could afford to pay little or nothing. The Boys' Public School had not yet secured a suitable teacher and it was not till 1880 that the right man was obtained in answer to much prayer. Mr. McCrone knew how to inspire his pupils with high ideals and to make even the laziest work, and exercised a powerful Christian influence over them. In 1880 Rev. Mr. Paauw was appointed as Minister of the Coloured Church and Teacher of Dutch in the Missionary Institute. He was well qualified for his work and had the power of awakening enthusiasm for their calling in the hearts of the students. His practical knowledge of local conditions was of great value. This twofold appointment of Mr. Paauw marked the accomplishment of two things for which Mr. Murray had long worked and prayed. He had long desired to see some definite work undertaken for the coloured people in Wellington, and in Mr. Paauw he found one who earnestly and with great wisdom and devotion threw himself into the work and succeeded in establishing a thriving church.

Mr. Paauw was also peculiarly fitted for teaching and helping the young men who were coming to the Institute to be trained as missionaries, to be employed chiefly among the coloured people, in the congregations which were being formed in many places throughout the country. It is the least romantic and in many respects the most difficult kind of mission work, and it is very remarkable what the Dutch Reformed Church has done in this way during the last 30 years, and she has been able to do this work largely because one of her sons, Andrew Murray, had a vision of the needs and possibilities of that work if only men were found to do it. The Missionary Institute in Wellington supplied the want and prepared men for work among these hitherto largely neglected people, men who had not the means nor opportunity to take the more extended and more expensive training necessary for entrance into the Ministry of the European Dutch Reformed Church.

Chapter XII

SUNSHINE AND SHADOWS

Jubilee—Retirement

1898—1905

Up till 1892 Mr. Murray had been sole minister at Wellington, In that year Rev. J. Albertyn was called as second minister. He was an earnest, spiritually minded, gifted preacher, between whom and Mr. Murray there arose a very tender affection. When he was called to become Mr. Murray's assistant he hesitated fearing he and Mr. Murray might not be able to get on together, so he wrote asking " what would happen if I cannot agree with you ? " " Come along my Brother," replied Dr. Murray, " I will agree with you, only be sure you are always in the right." That attitude of mutual give and take was the characteristic of all their after intercourse. He came with the understanding that Mr. Murray should be free to have Evangelistic services when he wished. Mr. Albertyn also exercised his gifts in that direction, and in the later years of his ministry he also travelled a good deal, strengthening and confirming the brethren. Mr. Murray vacated the Parsonage and built for himself a house on a most beautiful site. He became much attached to this home, and " Clairvaux " as he called it, was noted for its boundless hospitality, ministered under the loving care of a host and hostess who overflowed with courteous kindness, and under that hospitable roof great numbers of God's children found refreshment for body and soul.

Mr. Walton thus describes the Wellington home, " This is a Bethany indeed, just fragrant with the Master's presence. Mr. Murray seems to live in heaven, and certainly heaven is in him, and with it all there is such perfect simplicity and humility, and a joyful willingness to be the servant of all. It has been a privilege to work with him, and our talks have been most searching to my own heart. He has led me to see and realize more of the blessed life. We talked much about Christ in us, and he thinks there is much more to be realised than many at present teach. This visit has been a season of untold blessing to my soul."

How crowded their days were with work a letter of Mrs. Murray's shows, " It was one of those rare days to look back upon in after years, *when I had my husband all to myself for a few hours,* but in the evening the public claimed him." In these busy times he said, " Meals are a providential institution at which the family gathers and the members give themselves up to one another's interests and learn to know one another. It ought to be a time of real social intercourse." During their visit to England one wrote : " Meals with the Murrays are like Holy Communion."

In 1898 he celebrated his 70th birthday, and it was also his ministerial jubilee for he had been ordained on his 20th birthday. For almost a week there were celebrations of one kind or another in Wellington Church, Schools, Congregation, all joined to do him honour. His old University conferred on him the honorary degree of D.D. The Huguenot Seminary held its semi-jubilee at the same time. It was a great cause of gratitude to him that nearly 1,000 teachers had gone out since the school had been established. When asked by his colleague what he would wish as a jubilee gift he replied £1,000 to pay off the debt of the newly opened Women's College, an out-growth of the Seminary. Gladly and speedily the gifts came in.

With a gift of furniture for his study the Dutch Reformed Church presented this address :

" Right reverend and highly honoured brother. This day, which for you is so rich in memories of God's love and faithfulness constrains us to assure you, in the name of your fellow-ministers in the whole of our Church in South Africa, of our sympathetic association with you in your joy and gratitude. While you look back upon a life of rich and blessed experiences, you readily appropriate the words of the Psalmist, ' I will sing of the mercies of the Lord for ever.' We too, desire gratefully to acknowledge God's mercies towards you. We may not, on this festive occasion, forget what the Lord has bestowed upon His Church through you during the half century that has elapsed since your ordination . . . for the Church in general as well as within this Colony.

"The visits which during the first years of your Gospel ministrations you paid to our co-religionists who had emigrated northward, your special Gospel services of later years in almost all the congregations of our Church, in the Colony and beyond, your labours even in foreign lands, especially England, Scotland, Holland and America, in the way of sermons and convention addresses—all bear witness to the extent of your toil in the great vineyard of the Lord. Then, we have not even mentioned the still wider circle, in which you have promoted the interest of the Divine Kingdom and served your great Master by means of your writings.

" We call to mind, likewise, the services rendered to our Church in days of struggle and difficulty, when you pleaded her interests with the utmost ability, not merely in the ecclesiastical assemblies, but before the tribunals of the lands, and even before Her Majesty's Privy Council in England. We remember also your able guidance as Moderator of the highest Assembly of our Church, at six of her Synods ; your zealous labours as chairman or member of many different committees in connection with our Church institutions ; and all that you have been enabled by the Divine blessing to do by way of establishing in-stitutions, where our young men can be trained as mission-aries and our young maidens as teachers, as well as what you have done for the cause of education generally.

" With you and for you we bless the Lord who has bestowed on you wisdom and strength for all these undertakings, and who has crowned your many-sided labours with such abundant blessing. To Him be ascribed all honour."

For nearly a quarter of a century—and but for Mr. Murray's high sense of duty it would have been longer—he held the highest office of his Church, that of Moderator, a position for which he was peculiarly gifted. He knew the strength and weakness of his Church and had initiative and persistent energy enough to carry through his purposes. His business acumen, insight into the true bearings of any matter, knowledge of Church law, gave him an almost unerring judgment. His knowledge of human nature was remarkable, and he knew how to intervene in a debate at the psychological moment, while his ready wit and humour often cleared a highly charged atmosphere of dangerous elements. He was firm, tolerant, impartial, courteous, tactful in public, and readily accessible in private.

From the Ministers' Association, Cape Town, came this telegram : " The Ministers' Association send hearty greetings. We thank God for your work, friendship and help, and pray you may long be spared. *Heb.* vi. 10." Well might they mention his friendship, for his love to all ministers of all denominations was very tender. When well over seventy he used to catch the 6.15 morning train to Cape Town, reaching there at nine so as to be able to attend the monthly breakfast and conference of the Ministers' Association, and he much enjoyed the fraternal intercourse.

An outline of the speech made by his brother-in-law, and of that made by Mr. Murray himself are thus given in a newspaper report, printed at that time :

The Rev. J. H. Neethling, of Stellenbosch, Mr. Murray's eldest brother-in-law said, " Mr. Murray valued far more than a present the love of his fellow-ministers. And that he had. He knew now what to say. There was the experience of a lifetime to speak about. He had known his brother-in-law since boyhood. One day, he (Mr. Neethling) squeezed a little boy's nose, and then placing his thumb between his two fingers, told the lad that was his nose. Mr. Murray gave him a smart box on the ear, and though he was by far the stronger of the two, he had no chance to fight, for Mr. Murray, when challenged, coolly remarked, " we'll discuss the matter later on." His brother-in-law's influence on him when they studied in Holland was always for good. In the early days of the Transvaal they travelled together for months, sleeping by night in the same wagon, and preaching by day when they came to a village or a number of farmers. Jonathan and David were not truer friends than he and Mr. Murray in those days and he still loved him as much as a man could love a brother. They thanked God for the wonderful constitution He had given their brother, and if it were not that he had had an accident some time back, his step would be as elastic as ever. Humanly speaking, there was no reason why he should not live and work another twenty years. It was said that " life was a harp with a thousand strings," and he thanked God that the harp of their brother's life had for so many years been kept in tune. Not only had Mr. Murray done much for the Church and for the education of the people, but by his life, his position, and his outspoken evidence, as a man of high character he had done much for society.

" The Stellenbosch Theological Professors had asked him (Mr. Neethling) to tender their most sincere congratulations. When the Rev. Professor de Vos thanked God in the church on Sunday for having spared Mr. Murray for so many years, he felt that the entire Church would say ' Amen ' to it."

Telegrams from the Governor, the Prime Minister and others conveyed expressions of warm appreciation.

Dr. Murray's address was marked by the simplicity and humility which increasingly characterised him.

After a feeling acknowledgement of the many good wishes,

Mr. Murray said that "the lesson of half a century of ministerial work to him was that God had for every man a sphere of work and a plan of work. The more unreservedly a man submitted to God's will the more completely God's work was wrought. He emphasised this by reference to various periods in his own career at Bloemfontein, Worcester, Cape Town and Wellington in the ministry, in connection with education and in writing for the religious press. He said that throughout his life, any success was secured only by following God's guidance. Incidentally he mentioned that he had just declined an invitation to take a four months' tour in India and China visiting the various Mission Stations.

The following day was " Schools' Day " and it was a great cause of joy to Mr. Murray to see the church crowded with 1,100 scholars and students from every part of South Africa. At the Teachers' Dinner, the day previous, many bore testimony to the fact that they owed much to his influence, especially the realisation of the nobility of the office of teacher. The one thought in his mind was " Soli Deo Gloria."

Later in the year he made a tour in the Free State to attend the jubilee celebrations of the four congregations which were formed at his induction to them. Here he threw himself so energetically into the work that Mrs. Murray wrote : " I fear sometimes he will be laid to rest in this country of his first love." On another occasion she says, " Andrew has had two of the hardest working weeks possible. The first with our mission feast and we had twenty-six ministers to tea that evening and then days of Committee meetings and the last with the Synodical Commission and choosing a fourth professor for the Theological Seminary. Both weeks he has returned from Town at midnight on Friday and preached twice on Sunday. I have ceased to be anxious about him but just trust. It is God who gives him strength and will give it as long as he sees best, but some one remarked that when he is gone six ministers will not do his work. He is reading Eugene Stock's "Hundred Years of the Church Missionary Society" and is just head over ears in Missions and what can be done to rouse the Church to its calling to live for the Kingdom."

The next year dawned brightly, but towards its close clouds gathered quickly and the Anglo-Boer war broke out in October. It was a sad and awful experience for Mr. Murray, and men like him whose loving hearts bound them to dear friends and relations on both sides. Now that the bitterness of that strife has abated it is possible to judge more justly than many were able to do at the time, the part Mr. Murray took in sympathy with his people. Those who knew him best, and were most closely associated with him never heard a word nor saw the manifestation of a spirit that was unbecoming to his profession, but he felt deeply the fact that many of his old friends turned away from him, on the side of the English-speaking people because he was too pro-Boer, and on the side of the Boers because he was too pro-British. Oh! it was a sad, sad time, but it came on both sides because of the failure of the church leaders both Boer and Briton to come together in humiliation and prayer before the storm broke. Each side was ready to pray for its own success—" but," said a Quaker Editor of one of the Midland papers, " I feel I can never forgive the ministers and Churches that not one voice gave a call *for both sides to come together to pray.*" Andrew Murray did sound this call, but it was unheeded. The one power which rejoiced in that strife was Rome, for her it was a matter of congratulation that misled by Jesuit intrigue two Protestant peoples were at war with one another and it mattered not on which side men fell—there were so many Protestants less in the world.

Not long after the commencement of the war, Boer prisoners of war began to be gathered into camps. With true spiritual statesmanship Mr. Murray applied himself unwearingly to supply their souls' needs. It was no easy task to find deeply concentrated spiritually-minded men who would be acceptable to both Boer and Briton. When the right man was found it required endless correspondence to remove the many obstacles that beset his way to the camps. When no one could be found for Sea Point Camp Mr. Murray twice took charge for some weeks, and held three services daily during the whole period.

But the strain of the war told terribly on him. He felt for both sides, his own children and relatives suffered by it, and finally his health gave way. Then the Lord in mercy made it possible for him to go with his wife and two daughters to Switzerland, through the kindness of two Christian ladies in Cape Town. Here he could give himself to prayer but his tender heart was spared the harrowing tales of suffering which he could not relieve. An answer to these prayers was given in connection with the camps of the prisoners of war. Close intercourse with spiritually minded ministers who acted as Chaplains among them, exercised a powerful influence on the prisoners. In all the camps there were members of Christian Endeavour Societies and when the war was over many of these members brought with them to their homes new spiritual life. Two hundred names were given in of those who were willing to enter into training to become missionaries, and *over one hundred and fifty of them actually entered Training institutions*. Some, on their return home, were hindered from studying, but the results called forth profound gratitude to God, and greatly rejoiced Mr. Murray's heart.

After peace was declared Mr. Murray returned home. He visited Mr. Head as he passed through London and Mr. Head writes, " I remember one morning Dr. F. B. Meyer came to breakfast with us. It was interesting watching these two writers questioning one another as to what they would write next, until Miss Murray raised a laugh by exclaiming, ' Oh Father has eight books on his brain ! ' "

In 1905 Mr. Murray attended the Synod for the last time as a member. Mrs. Murray writes, " He is interested in what is going on but too deaf to always listen quietly, while he is invaluable in giving advice. He attends Committee meetings for schools and missions and often makes his influence felt. When he does speak in Synod his words carry weight and he feels that being here he can often over-rule things for good as he generally has his way." The Synod was held just after the war and feeling ran high and the loving sympathetic influence exercised by Mr. Murray was much needed and was of much value.

This same year brought a heavy blow to Mr. Murray in the sudden death of his wife from apoplexy. She was a singularly devoted wife and their's was an ideally happy union of hearts. His daughter says, " It was wonderful to hear his prayer of thanksgiving, immediately after her passing away, because of what she had been to him and her children. It took us into the very vestibule of heaven." The following Sunday he preached from the text : " With Christ which is far better." The great thought was : Let us seek to draw nearer to Christ so shall we come nearer to our beloved. God's sustaining grace was great, though the sorrow seemed more than flesh could bear. He threw himself into work with the result that he himself had a slight stroke which confined him to his bed for some weeks. When he recovered he said to his daughter : " I now begin to see the glory of God's Will." He then decided to retire from the responsibility of being in charge of a congregation, and so after an active ministry of 57 years he became Emeritus, continuing to live at " Clairvaux," and was appointed by God to a still wider ministry which was to continue for nearly twelve years longer, twelve years of experience of the grace and power and love of God and to be a witness of these things to thousands of hearers. Well might Dr. Whyte speak of him as " happy man ! "

CHAPTER XIII

CONVENTION SPEAKER AND LEADER

LIKE St. Paul Andrew Murray was always forgetting the things which were behind and pressing on to that which was before and it is very interesting and instructive to notice how, long before the Keswick Convention was even thought of, God had been teaching Andrew Murray the secret of victory over the inner, or heart sin of a child of God. He had been leading him into an experience of the cleansing efficacy of the Blood of our Lord Jesus Christ, through the power of the Holy Spirit dwelling within the believer's heart. He did not at this time give expression definitely to his own experience, but his daughter says that Mrs. Murray's spiritual life mirrored that of her husband, and bearing this fact in mind much light is shed on the character of Mr. Murray's teaching as far back as the Worcester Pastorate by some extracts from her letters written at that time.

In 1864 she tells a friend : " Andrew says there is a step higher than looking forward to Heaven and being weaned from the world we may have our life so in Christ, that even here below we may enjoy peace and happiness in Him, which no earthly events can shake or destroy ; not by despising or trampling upon earthly things, but living above them ; willing, and loving to live for His glory, and the good of others, and counting it all joy even in tribulation, for His sake. It is the one lesson He is trying to teach me lately, perfect peace and quiet of mind under all circumstances, which of itself imparts strength, nothing interferes more with work, or renders it more difficult, than fretting or worrying. In such a state of mind we can do nothing well, yet it is not stoical indifference one must cultivate, but the childlike acknowledgement of God's will in everything, with His peace in our hearts, and a truly humble walk with God, a bowing to His will."

Mrs. Murray also writes, " We need not wait to enter heaven to have a noble, holy, great mind. It is attainable even here . . . it may be ours through the indwelling of the Holy Spirit of God, through receiving Christ as our Sanctification, as well as our Justification ; through an entire, unconditional surrender of ourselves to Him, and an entire cessation from our own efforts and works, while waiting for the suggestions and influences of the Holy Spirit, through believing in His indwelling, and expecting His guidance, even in the minutest concerns of our daily life. It is a solemn truth, but still a truth, " Ye are the temple of God and the Spirit of God dwelleth in you." *I Cor.* iii. 16. Christ is in us. His word is " Abide in Me," *John* xv. 4. It is not NEAR, nor WITH but just as close as the branches are to the vine.

Of themselves apart from the vine stock they can do nothing, joined to it they have only to let the sap flow through them. Let us see that we put no hindrance in the way of Christ's work and especially when we fall into sin let us not despair but just say " Lord Jesus I can't make myself holy, Thou must do it." *I am convinced holiness in a very high degree is attainable.* It is not the power, but the faith and will which are wanting. We have received it as ' a *must be* ' in our creed that we must sin so long as we are in this world, and so there is no effort, or only a partial, half hearted effort to make it otherwise."

" I think in the present day there is not enough retirement to seek teaching from above, there is too much human teaching. Tersteegen says : ' Within, within the heart to be with God alone, and if you need a friend or a book He sends it,' but we are so prone to seek teaching from man and to be content with streams instead of going to the fountain head. Therefore there is so much work, with so little result. If we waited more upon God, and followed more simply the teaching of His Holy Spirit, greater blessing would result, even if we were to do less ; but this is the hardest lesson of all, the surrender of self,

and it is just self which is ' the dead fly ' in the ointment."
How little, as Mrs. Fletcher says, are we content to be
fools in the sight of others, or have that deep self abasement
of soul that can really esteem others better than themselves ; it is the Holy Spirit alone who can teach such
lessons. It must be a daily surrender of self and self-
will and a pure desire that the will of God shall be done
in all things in and by you." Here we have true Convention
teaching in pre-convention times.

Then again, his eldest sister, who was of a peculiarly
kindred disposition writes, in 1867, an account of how
she claimed the fulness of the Spirit, " After reading the
Acts and other passages on the Holy Spirit, I tried to be
earnest and feel much desire—but the prevailing feeling
was one of God's great goodness—He giveth to all men
liberally and upbraideth not. In the evening I felt very
unhappy, my language was, ' Lord, I have believed in
Thee—and yet streams of living water have not flowed
from me.' I have drunk of the water of life Thou gavest
me and yet I thirst—then I was unhappy at the thought
of reproaching my Saviour, for I saw my unbelief was the
cause. . . . " I remembered how near believing in this
way on the Lord I had been when Mr. Taylor (later Bishop
Taylor of America) was here. I tried to follow his advice—
I could only feel the Lord's great love in offering to be to
me a present Saviour from sin—and that He was made
to me of God wisdom, and righteousness, and sanctification,
and redemption ; and I do believe I was enabled to accept
Him anew as my complete Saviour." Later she writes :
" Let me tell you with what joy and gratitude we heard of
what the Lord has done for you. Oh, we could thank
Him for giving you such sweet rest just when the work
presses. She then goes on to mention others who found
the same blessing.

Providentially the father of educational missions, Dr.
Duff, from India, during his visit in 1864, which kindled
much mission interest, proved to have been guided to the

Colony at that time to show by his life the reality of Christ's indwelling power. Mrs. Murray writes : " What a noble old Scot he is, as grand in his humility and simplicity, but in very delicate health, quite unequal to any excitement. I greatly enjoyed his conversation. He is the exemplification of the doctrines of quietism in action, if you understand what I mean. All those expressions of being ' dead to self ' and ' lost in God ' which one finds in Madame Guyon seem to be exemplified in His experience and life."

One source of great spiritual blessing was the annual Whitsuntide ten days of prayer commencing on Ascension Day. Ever since the Revival of 1860–61 these ten days have been set apart for prayer throughout the D. R. Church of South Africa, to seek for the outpouring of the Holy Spirit on the Church. The responsibility of providing the meditations for these meetings fell on Mr. Murray and he either wrote them himself or requested others to do the work. Some of the subjects were " The Holy Spirit in Believers," " The Holy Spirit and the Unconverted," " The Holy Spirit and Missions," " Types of the Holy Spirit," " The Full Blessing of Pentecost." Here again Convention truths are emphasised. The reports that came in from all over the country showed the quickening of believers and the ingathering of souls as the result.

While all this was going on in South Africa and already centering round Andrew Murray ; both in England and in the United States the Holiness Movement had begun. Dr. Boardman was at work in America and Mr. and Mrs. Pearsall Smith had come over to England where they powerfully stirred up Christians in connection with the Oxford and Brighton Conventions, in which they were aided by the saintly William Pennifather, Rev. Evan Hopkins and others. A profound though quietly wrought change was taking place in Mr. Murray. A born ruler of men, he sought and obtained from God a remarkable measure of the meekness and gentleness of Christ. It was wonderful how these qualities, united with a humility and

patience marked the following years, without any loss of
strength.

In private prayer notes which he kept for himself, under
the date 1874, he prays " to be made a fountain of love
to all around." From that time he grew ever more loving
as the years went on. If any one of the family would
turn to him for confirmation of some sharp criticism of
others he would say : " My child try not to say what is
unloving."

In 1879 he writes : " More correct spiritual knowledge
is what we need (*Eph.* i. 17). And then if the need be
felt, spiritual teaching will show us the living Jesus,
personally communicating, personally maintaining, each
moment His life within us. It is no new Christ or
Christology, but Christ in a new and nearer aspect. The
Lord teach us this blessed secret, an open secret to those
whom He teaches."

Thus the Lord was graciously leading His beloved child
into a deeper knowledge and experience of the truths he
was to pass on to others. It was the steady silent dawning
of light growing more and more into the perfect day.

It was during these years also, he read the reports of
George Muller's work, and preached about it, to stir
Christians to a stronger faith and closer walk with God.
The writings of Dr. Boardman, Dr. Cullis, and Hudson
Taylor left their own mark upon him. He read regularly
both " The Life of Faith " and " The Christian," and thus
kept in close touch with the Spiritual movements of the
world.

In the Bible he used at this time he had written the
following sentences on the front page, revealing his attitude
of mind when reading or studying it. " The central
thought of this book is *God !* Its one object is to reveal
God, His Glory, His Will, His Love. In reading it our
chief desire ought to be to know God. God cannot be
known except as He pleases to make Himself known. He
does this to the heart that bows in deep dependence, that

worships, and loves Him. Prayer is the great power that moves the Blessed God in Heaven to reveal Himself on earth. God is to be found and known in prayer. Let our heart and life be as full of God as the book is. This the God of the book must Himself work. Our great danger is to think that the words through the thoughts and words they suggest will do us good. No, the words as they came from God must lead us to God, they can only point to Him. *He Himself must work in us what they tell.* Scripture can only direct us to God, who does what it cannot do, and tells us of something it cannot give."

Elsewhere he writes :—" It is wonderful that after all God has bestowed that He should condescend to bind Himself to us by His Word. How little we realise this and how little do we make use of it. How little do we have a clear conception of what we may expect Him to do. How little in reading His blessed word do we seek first the Spirit to guide us into all truth. We expect to understand it intellectually, not distinguishing between spiritual and carnal understanding. Did Christians pray more the prayer of *Eph.* i. 17–23, how much fuller and richer would their lives be."

Among the lessons God had been teaching him was the importance of true Christian love in our relation with others. Two extracts from his private notes and correspondence illustrate this fact. The first is taken from his personal note book. He says : " This great and wonderful God of ours wants to live out His own life in us. He can only do it as we live in love. We can only live in love as Christ lives out His life in us when we are fully yielded to Him. Let us then surrender ourselves to Him that more of God's great and wonderful life may be lived in us."

Then in a letter written to his wife in 1881, he writes in regard to a trying relative : " Love hopeth all things— perhaps if we shut our eyes to failings, and love and labour and pray in hopefulness the good may be strengthened. It has struck me much in reading Genesis how with Isaac and Jacob God overlooks and tolerates a vast amount of evil, and works out His purposes with very deficient instruments. Though in the New Testament we are on higher ground, the same principle holds true. If we could be thoroughly imbued with the thought of God's forbearance, and cultivate the power of love to lay hold of what is good and encourage and strengthen it, all God's children would get nearer each other and be more helpful in building up those who are weak. It is a wonderful thing to think of Love, love, love, being the one lesson Christ came to bring from heaven to earth—gentle, patient, self-sacrificing love being the one thing God had to teach from heaven to men on earth.''

During his two years of silence his thoughts were occupied with the work of the Holy Spirit as well as with the Bible Union just started. Asking his eldest daughter to join it he writes : '' Try and give time to let God's Word get deep down into the heart. We all acknowledge that the Holy Spirit is given us, but we hardly know how to make use of the knowledge, and how to get the blessing He is ready to work out for us. I have said, if God allows me to preach again, I do hope to realize more, and to teach the congregation to realize more, the presence of the Holy Ghost in all our religion. And it is in secret that we must begin to give ourselves to the power and working of the Holy Ghost. What we need are two things. The one, *faith that He is in us*, and will do a Divine work in teaching and sanctifying us. The other, is *quiet waiting to realize His presence*, to hush our own thoughts, and to crush all our *natural* activity, so as to give Him time and opportunity to take possession, and become the new principle in our lives. Let us pray God earnestly for each other that we may know how to behave towards the Holy Spirit and how to place ourselves before Him that He may complete in us all that perfect and glorious work which He is given by the Father to do in us.'' Again : '' I think continually on what the presence and the power of the Holy Spirit should be in the Church, in the preaching and in the lives of God's people. I see more and more that the one thing needed is to die to our own will and to enter into and live in God's will. That is the new and living way into the Holiest of All."

In 1895 Mr. Murray went to England at the invitation of the Keswick Convention Council, to take part in their meetings for he was now recognised as one of the leading Holiness teachers of the world. While in England Mr. and Mrs. Murray made their home with Mr. and Mrs. Head at Wimbledon. Such was the love and care they bestowed on them that Mr. Murray called them his father and mother. Of course this made the son their brother. The relationship was claimed on both sides and a close affection sprang up between them.

The following extracts from Mrs. Head's letters show with what affection they were regarded. " It is indeed a privilege and joy to have dear Mr. and Mrs. Murray in the house. He is so intensely loving and humble and full of Christ that one feels the presence of Christ whenever with him. He arrived on Monday, and on Tuesday we went together to Mildmay for the Annual China Inland Mission Meetings. In the evening Mr. Murray gave a wonderful address so full of power and fire ! We were quite amazed at the dear old man. He is so thin and worn-looking, and certainly such addresses must use up his bodily as well as spiritual strength. We feel indeed, that he has come to this land as God's messenger, and he is so simple, depending utterly on the Lord to use him as His channel of blessing to His people. This morning we all went up to Exeter Hall for our Reception Breakfast. This was a most unique gathering of about 120 leading Christians of all denominations, including Revd. C. A. Fox, F. B. Meyer, Lord Kinnaird, Lady Hope, Mr. Denny, Amanda Smith and others. We had some pretty menu-cards printed on which were the verses of the hymn : " Lord Jesus we are one with Thee," to be sung before breakfast.

Mr. F. Paynter said grace, and at the close we sang " Perfect love," and Mr. Fox spoke most beautifully.

" Mr. Head spoke a few words of welcome, followed by Mr. Meyer representing the Convention, Lord Kinnaird spoke for Scotland, Mr. Inwood for Ireland, and Mr. Eugene Stock for Missions. None exceeded five minutes, and all went straight to the point. Then dear Mr. Murray spoke for half an hour most beautifully and with such a message to the Church of Christ as will leave a deep impression in all hearts, and intensify the expectation of what God is going to do through His servant. Later, Mr. Murray gave us a beautiful address on ' the Heavenly Treasure in earthen vessels.' He illustrated it by mentioning that on Sunday on our dinner table there was a silver jug of milk, but there was also a little brown earthen pot—not worth a penny—full of rich cream. We all preferred the cream, notwithstanding the common pot, rather than the milk though it was in a beautiful silver jug.

" The following incident made a deep impression. One evening when the whole party returned together from a great meeting where a rapt and crowded audience had been addressed by Mr. Murray, he found awaiting him a letter from a well-known man, filled with severe censures upon him for teaching error. The way the criticism was expressed stirred indignation in all, *except Mr. Murray*. He only said in his gentle way that if he had been teaching anything wrong, all that he asked was that the Lord would show this to him, that he might make it right. Quite simply they knelt down, and put up that petition ; then rising they went in peace to rest. Next day being Sunday, Mr. Murray stayed in bed to rest. For his own guidance he wrote these lines :—

In time of trouble say :—

First, He brought me here, it is by His Will I am in this strait place : in that fact I will rest.

Next, He will keep me here in His love, and give me grace to behave as His child.

Then, He will make the trial a blessing, teaching me the lessons He intends me to learn, and working in me the grace He means to bestow.

Last, In His good time He can bring me out again—how and when He knows.

Let me say I am here,

(1) By God's appointment.   (2) In His keeping,

(3) Under His training   (4) For His time.

Next day Mr. Murray went straight to the writer of the letter and by his loving intercourse made him his faithful friend."

Of the Keswick Convention Mrs. Head writes : " I cannot describe to you the deep heartsearching teaching of Mr. Murray's evening addresses nor the power and authority with which they were delivered. Every word seemed to come straight from God with living power, and went right to the hearts of the people."

Writing in the *Life of Faith*, Rev. Evan Hopkins says : " The main feature of this convention has been the presence of our beloved brother, the Rev. Andrew Murray from South Africa, whose addresses have come home with peculiar power. As message after message was enforced by one who has evidently been the marked minister of God this time, it seemed as if none could choose but let Christ Himself, in the power of His living Spirit, be the One to live, although the cost was our taking the place of death."

From England the Murrays went to America to the Northfield Convention, at the urgent invitation of Mr. D. L. Moody. In addition to the general public not less than four hundred ministers attended these meetings, and large numbers of them including Mr. Moody himself testified to having received great blessing. Here again it was the life that gave power to the word. Every day he had the second address at the morning meeting after " a closely reasoned and spiritually powerful one preceding it." Many left after the first address but " those who remained were led by the frail-looking speaker to the place where he already seemed to have placed his foot, within the veil, in the very presence chamber of God." Mr. Moody would not allow anyone to go in or out during these addresses.

Dr. A. T. Pierson testified to having received much blessing at Northfield as the two speakers, Rev. Webb-Peploe and Mr. Murray, dwelt on " Faith." He wrote : " Never did I see so clearly my privilege of resting moment by moment on the Word of God. I entered that day into the consciousness of the rest of faith, and Thursday night sealed my new consecration in the farewell meeting. Henceforth my motto is ' That God may be all.' " He joined Mr. Murray in other Conventions, speaking at Toronto, Boston, Chicago and elsewhere. His deepened spiritual life led him to lay somewhat less emphasis on the *work* of foreign missions and more on the *Spirit* of Christ in all life and service.

During these Conventions Mr. Murray was never weary of calling for the hymn beginning :

> " Dying with Jesus by death reckoned mine,
> Living with Jesus a new life divine,
> Looking to Jesus till glory doth shine,
> Moment by moment, O Lord, I am Thine "—

with the refrain :

> " Moment by moment I'm kept in His love,
> Moment by moment I've life from above.
> Looking to Jesus till glory doth shine,
> Moment by moment, O Lord, I am Thine."

From Northfield he went to Chicago, New York, and other places and the meetings were crowded in spite of the hot summer weather. Canada was also visited, and there he met members of the other branch of the Murray family, of whom mention has been made in Chapter I.

After his return to England he crossed to Holland where a remarkable succession of meetings took place. He was pressed to visit the missions of the Dutch Churches in India and the East but could not go. He paid also brief visits to Ireland and Scotland. Then came the final meetings for Christian workers in the East End Tabernacle attended by probably 3,000 people. One writes concerning these meetings : " His one aim and object was ' to bring us to God ' and it was indeed with overflowing hearts full of praise to God that the vast multitude sang, ' Praise God from whom all blessings flow ' at the close." This series of meetings closed with a day of prayer at Exeter Hall, which was thus described : " In each address God spoke with mighty power ; from the beginning *God Himself* was the One to whom all hearts were drawn and His Presence was revealed."

At Keswick he was asked to give his experience and his address is thus recorded in *The Christian* of August 15th, 1895. It is the only record of the kind Mr. Murray has left behind him. He was ever fearing to draw the attention of his hearers from Christ to any experience.

He said : " When I was asked to give my testimony I doubted whether it would be desirable, and for this reason : we all know what helpfulness there is in a clear cut testimony of a man who can say : ' There I was, I knelt down, and God helped me, and I entered into the better Life,' I cannot give such a testimony, but I know what blessing it has often brought to me to read of such testimonies for the strengthening of my own faith. And yet I got this answer from those who wished me to speak : ' Perhaps there are many at Keswick to whom a testimony concerning a life of more struggle and difficulty will be helpful.' If it must be so I replied let me tell for the glory of God how He has led me. Some of you have heard how I have pressed upon you the two stages of the Christian life, and the step from the one to the other. The first ten years of my spiritual life were manifestly spent on the lower stage. I was a minister, I may say, as zealous and as earnest and as happy in my work as anyone, as far as love of the work was concerned. Yet, all the time, there was burning my heart a dissatisfaction and restlessness inexpressible. What was the reason ? I had never learnt with all my theology that obedience was possible. My justification was clear as the noonday, I knew the hour in which I received from God the joy of pardon, I remember in my little room in Bloemfontein how I used to sit and think, ' What is the matter ? ' Here I am knowing that God has justified me in the blood of Christ, but I have no power for service. My thoughts, my words, my actions, my unfaithfulness—everything troubled me. Though all around thought me one of the most earnest of men, my life was one of deep dissatisfaction. I struggled and prayed as best I could.

" One day I was talking with a missionary. I do not think that he knew much of the power of sanctification himself—he would have admitted it. When we were talking and he saw my earnestness he said : ' Brother, remember when God puts a desire in your heart He will fulfil it.' That helped me. I thought of it a hundred times. I want to say the same to you who are plunging about and struggling in the quagmire of hopelessness and doubt. The desire God puts into your heart He will fulfil.

" I was greatly helped about this time by a book called ' Parables from Nature.' One of these parables represents that after the creation of the earth, on a certain day, a number of crickets met. One of them began, saying : ' Oh, I feel so happy, for a time I was creeping about looking for a place where to stay, but I could not find the place that suited me. At last I got in behind the bark of an old tree, it seemed as though the place was just fitted for me, I felt so comfortable there.' Another said, ' I was there for a time, but it would not fit me '—that was the grass cricket. ' But at last I got on to a high stalk of grass, and as I clung there and swung there in the wind and the air, I felt that that was the place made for me.'

" Then a third cricket said : ' Well, I have tried the bark of the old tree, and I have tried the grass, but God has made no place for me, and I feel unhappy.' Then the old mother cricket said : ' My child, do not speak that way. Your Creator never made anyone without preparing a place for him. Wait, and you will find it in due time.' Some time after these same crickets met together again and got to talking. The old mother cricket said : ' Now my child what say you ? ' The cricket replied : ' Yes, what you said is true. You know those strange people who have come here ? They built a house and in their house they had a fire, and, you know, when I got into the corner of the hearth near the fire I felt so warm that I know that was the place God made for me.'

" That little parable helped me wonderfully and I pass it on to you. If any of you are tempted to think that God has not a place for you, just trust God and wait, and He will help you, and show you what is your place. You know God led Israel forty years in the Wilderness ; and that was my wilderness time. I was serving Him very heartily, yet it was dark very often and the great burden on my heart was, I am sinning against the God who loves me. So the Lord led me till in His great mercy I had been eleven or twelve years in Bloemfontein. Then He brought me to another congregation in Worcester, about the time when God's Holy Spirit was being poured out in America, Scotland and Ireland. In 1860 when I had been six months in the congregation, God poured out His Spirit there in connection with my preaching, especially as I was moving about in the country, and a very unspeakable blessing came to me. The first Dutch edition of my book *Abide in Christ* was written at that time. I would like you to understand that a minister or Christian author may often be led to say more than he has experienced. I had not then experienced all that I wrote of : I cannot say that I experience it all perfectly even now. But if we are honest in seeking to trust God in all circumstances and always to receive the truth, He will make it live in our hearts. But let me warn you Convention Christians, *not to seek too much satisfaction in your own thoughts, nor in the thoughts of others. The deepest and most beautiful thoughts cannot feed the soul ; unless you go to God and let Him give you reality and faith, you cannot know satisfaction.*

" Well, God helped me, and for seven or eight years I went on, always enquiring and seeking and always getting. Then came, about 1870, the great Holiness Movement. The letters that appeared in *The Revival* (now *The Christian*) touched my heart ; and I was in close fellowship with what took place at Oxford and Brighton and it all helped me. Perhaps if I were to talk of consecration I might tell you of an evening there in my own study in Cape Town. Yet I cannot say that that was my deliverance, for I was still struggling. I would say that what we need is complete obedience. Let us not be like Saul who after he was anointed failed in the case of Agag to accept God's judgment against sin to the very uttermost. Later on my mind was much exercised about the baptism of the Holy Spirit and I gave myself to God as perfectly as I could, to receive this baptism of the Spirit. Yet there was failure : God forgive it. It was somehow as if I could not get what I wanted. Through all these stumblings God led me, without any very special experience that I can point to, but as I look back I do believe now that He was giving me more and more of His blessed Spirit *had I but known it better.*

" I can help you more, perhaps, by speaking, not of any marked experience, but by telling very simply what I think God has given me now, in contrast to the first ten years of my Christian life. First of all, I have learnt to place myself before God every day as a vessel to be filled with His Holy Spirit. He has filled me with the blessed assurance that *He, as the everlasting God, has guaranteed His own work in me.* If there is one lesson that I am learning day by day, it is this : that it is God who worketh all in all. Oh, that I could help any brother or sister to realise this !

"I will tell you where you fail. You have never yet heartily believed that *He was working out your salvation.* You believe that if a painter undertakes a picture he must look to every shade of colour and every touch upon the canvas. You believe that if a workman makes a table or a bench he knows how to do his work. But you do not believe that the everlasting God is working out the image of His Son in you. As any sister here is doing a piece of ornamental or fancy work, following out the pattern in every detail let her just think : ' Can God not work out in me the purpose of His love ? ' If that piece of work is to be perfect, every stitch must be in its place. And remember that not one minute of your life should be without God. We want God to come in at times—say in the morning ; then we are to live two or three hours, and He can come in again. No, God must be every moment the Worker in your soul.

"I was once preaching, and a lady came to talk with me. She was a very pious woman, and I asked her, ' How are you going on ? ' Her answer was, ' O just the way it always is, sometimes light and sometimes dark.' ' My dear sister,' I said, ' where is that in the Bible ? ' She said, ' We have day and night in nature, and just so it is with our souls.' No, no ; in the Bible we read ' Your sun shall no more go down.' Let me believe that I am God's child, and that the Father in Christ, through the Holy Ghost, has set his love upon me and that I may abide in His presence, not frequently but unceasingly. The veil has been rent ; the holiest of all opened. By the grace of my God I have to take up my abode there, and there my God is going to teach me what I never could learn while

I dwelt outside. My home is always in the abiding love of the Father in Heaven. You will ask, are you satisfied? Have you got all you want? God forbid. With the deepest feeling of my soul I can say that I am satisfied with Jesus now: but there is also a consciousness of how much fuller the revelation can be of the exceeding abundance of His grace. Let us never hesitate to say, that this is only the beginning. When we are brought into the holiest of all, we are *beginning* to take our right position with the Father.

" May He teach us our own nothingness and transform us into the image of his Son and help us to go out to be a blessing to our fellow men. Let us trust Him and praise Him in the midst of a consciousness of failure and of a remaining tendency to sin. Notwithstanding this let us believe that our God loves to dwell in us; and let us hope without ceasing in His still more abundant grace."

From 1889 till his death, that is for 28 years, he was the Father of the Keswick Movement in South Africa. A short history of that movement will help to a fuller understanding of its aims and teaching. Eternity alone will reveal the wonder of its results.

After a series of remarkable Evangelistic Services conducted by Mr. Spencer Walton in different parts of the country, the Cape General Mission was established with Mr. Walton as Director. The first party of Mission workers arrived in Cape Town in August, 1889. From the beginning Mr. Murray manifested the deepest interest in the movement.

The one burden ever weighing heavily upon his heart was " The state of the Church," and this subject was introduced into one of the first conversations he had with a leader of the " Cape General Mission," which later on became known as the South Africa General Mission. It was then that the proposal was made that an annual gathering should be held in South Africa, along the lines of the English " Keswick " Convention. This Convention stands for whole-hearted consecration to God and proclaims the possibility of a child of God being so filled with and led by the Holy Spirit that a life well pleasing to God may be lived here on earth. All the Mission Workers were clear exponents of " Keswick " teaching of Entire Surrender to the Lord Jesus Christ ; Complete Cleansing from sin through the precious Blood ; and the Fulness and Anointing of the Holy Spirit for life and service. It was Mr. Murray's special wish that the workers of the Mission should undertake to organize the Convention, of which he became President and Chairman, and he continued to occupy that position until his Home-call. These annual gatherings were first held in what is known as the " Goodnow Hall," in Wellington ; in the grounds of the Huguenot Seminary, an educational institution for girls which was started by Mr. Murray, who was then in charge of the Dutch Reformed Church in Wellington. Those who were privileged to be present at the early Conventions will never forget the powerful messages given by our beloved President, and the sacred sense of the nearness of God throughout the week spent together in His presence. Most of those who attended these meetings were led to a new place of surrender to Christ and of fellowship with God.

The far-reaching results of the Convention held in Goodnow Hall upon the Church of Christ in South Africa will never be fully known ; but let it be said that many of the outstanding workers of to-day in the different churches and missions ; ministers and laymen who have been used mightily of God, received their inspiration and equipment in these gatherings ; later known as the " South African Keswick."

One of the outstanding features of these Conventions was the number who entered into a very definite experience of the Fulness of Blessing, and reached a place of real victory and power over sin which was seen and felt by their friends on their return to their homes in different parts of the country, and this was the means of causing the blessing to spread. This was partly due to the expressed desire of Mr. Murray that the speakers should be very definite in their teaching, and also to the fact that he was unwilling to ask anyone to speak who could not strike the definite Convention note. Powerful messages have been given from that platform by many well-known Keswick speakers from England, but while in his humility he was among them, like his Master " as one that serveth " Mr. Murray was ever the man with the most outstanding and powerful message.

South Africa being such a large territory, it was found quite impossible for many who longed to attend the Wellington Convention to do so, owing to the great distances to be travelled, and the high cost of travelling. This led to arrangements being made for the holding of similar Conventions in various towns through the Country, including Johannesburg, Cape Town, Port Elizabeth, Durban, Pietermaritzburg and Kroonstad. Some of these have continued year after year, and others have only been held periodically at longer intervals.

In every Convention held by Mr. Murray his first object was to get into touch with the ministers of the various Churches. He had a heart large enough to take them all in, and generally they responded to the transparent brotherliness and sincerity of his call, though they were not by any means so ready, all of them, to accept his teaching on the surrendered and consecrated life.

One who was present at a Convention Mr. Murray held in Durban writes :—" The effect of the Convention on the lives of many a Christian was permanent, but perhaps the outstanding feature of this Convention was the number of ministers and missionaries who attended, and who from that time became themselves flames of fire. Several meetings were held for ministers only, and coming out of one of them, a little group gathered round one of the most argumentative and perhaps least sympathetic of the local ministers of that day, and as they gave expression to the various feelings with which they had listened to God's old servant, this man said : ' Well I do not accept his teaching, but one is left in no doubt as to *what* he teaches, it is clear as daylight.' Alas ! it became evident in later days, that there was a reason why he could not accept of the teaching."

Towards the close of that week of remarkable meetings it was announced that there would be a half night of prayer and many ministers attended it, but when it became known that Andrew Murray was not to be there and that he had handed over the conduct of the meeting to a member of the S.A.G.M. some were grievously disappointed. One of them telling the next day what God had done for him, said, that so great was his disappointment when he found Mr. Murray was not there he was rising to go home but did not actually go. When later on the leader asked those who were willing to surrender all to Christ, to come forward and kneel down at the front, this missionary said to himself, " If Andrew Murray had been there and had asked me to do this I would have done it." Suddenly he saw that Mr. Murray, in his own name, would have had no right to ask him to do such a thing, and then, as suddenly, he thought that perhaps God was calling him by the leader's voice, and the question was would he obey ? He had grace to do so, to his own great joy and blessing in the following years.

One of the remarkable addresses Mr. Murray gave at that Convention was on " Be FILLED with the SPIRIT." His divisions were striking in their simplicity and depth of insight combined.

I *MUST* be FILLED. It is absolutely *Necessary.*

I *MAY* be filled. God has made it blessedly *Possible.*

I *WOULD* be filled. It is eminently *Desirable.*

I *WILL* be filled. It is so blessedly *Certain.*

Mr. Murray has often been spoken of as a Mystic. Perhaps in one sense he was, but he was a Mystic full of common sense, and with a mind that grasped truth clearly, and he had the power of expressing it simply, but beyond all doubt it was the constant presence and inspiration of the Holy Spirit, who dwelt so fully in him, who clothed his word with such power, and made the results so permanent.

It was at Mr. Murray's instigation that the Convention Hymn Book, " Hymns for Life and Service," was compiled. At one of the Council meetings he mentioned the need for a special Hymn Book, and, with the alertness which he always showed, turned quickly round to the brother who led the singing and said, " I think we must ask you to undertake the work for us." When he mentioned the great amount of labour and difficulty involved in such an undertaking, he placed his hand upon his shoulder and, with a twinkle in his eye, said, " Never mind my dear brother, you do the work and we will promise to pray for you." God's blessing has been graciously on the undertaking, and although the sale of the publication had to be restricted to South Africa in order to overcome the difficulty of many copyright pieces, over 50,000 copies of the edition of words only have been sold.

Soon after the Wellington Convention was started, in the course of conversation with Mr. Murray the subject of the spiritual needs of the country came up for consideration, and Mr. Murray said, " How I wish the teaching we have here could be given in the small towns and villages throughout the land ; could not the Mission arrange for the villages to be visited ? " He then said in that beautiful humble spirit which was always his, " You will not find it easy work, but the need is very great, go ahead with it and I will pray to God to bless your efforts." This led to the starting of " Village Work " in connection with the S. A. General Mission. No branch of the Mission's activities has been more wonderfully owned and used by God than this ; thousands have been reached by the Gospel in this way, and numbers led into a life of full deliverance and victory.

As age came on, Dr. Murray invited certain ministers who had long been associated with him in Convention work to become a Council, to work with him and after his death to carry on the work of the Convention.

During the last years of his life, when his hearing was very bad, it was pathetic to see him, still in his old place in the chair at the Convention, quite unable to hear what was going on, but kept in touch by one or another giving him running notes of the addresses. All felt the spiritual atmosphere was being purified by his prayer. What a man of prayer he was ! His whole life was lived in the spirit of prayer, and he appeared to be always in open communication with Heaven. Was not this the secret of his wonderful life, and the wonderful power he had in influencing others ?

In the following letter written to his sister there is much food for serious thought. Not a few of those who are seeking after " The Full Blessing of Pentecost " are suffering from the same kind of difficulty as that mentioned in the letter, and the reply is of the greatest importance.

There is some obscurity in the part where Mr. Murray reports what Mr. Palmer said. The words " It may be a temptation of Satan... If this brother has truly surrendered everything, etc," evidently refer to Mr. Murray himself. To those who learned to look up to him, as such members did in after years, it seems strange that he should ever have been an enquirer himself. Yet it is only in those who knew him from afar that such a feeling could exist, for he was humble enough to learn gladly from the most unlikely teachers, and was ever seeking to know more and more of that love that passeth understanding.

The personal references are left as written for they give a glimpse of the tenderness and true humanity which so characterised him. Dear, strong, tender, gentle, brave, humble man that he was ! To God be the Glory.

" On board *City of Richmond,*
" *27th June,* 1877.

" My Dearest Sister,

" Charles has read me your letter. Let me try and give you an answer to what you say to him about your intense wish to unburden your soul to R. P. S. and Mr. Boardman and ask them for the secret of their success. I almost think I could give you the answer they would give. I spoke to Mr. Boardman on the point. Many feel as if the full baptism of the Spirit was wanting. His answers all ran in one direction. You must trust Jesus in the assurance that He will make everything right in due time. You really rest on Him for it. In your desires for more blessing you must see that your joyful rest in Him as an all sufficient portion be not disturbed. The joyful praising acknowledgment that you have everything in Him, that unutterable fulness dwells and that you are complete in Him must not be dimmed by the desire after what you do not yet see or feel. I spoke with Mrs. C. about it. She said we must remember the diversity of gifts and operations in different people and at different times. Mrs. H. W. S. was still seeking for a baptism of the Spirit while everybody thought she had it remarkably—it might be we mistake in the idea we form of it. Experience, feeling, success were not given to all in the same degree. At Mr. Moody's enquiry meeting in B. after I have been helping, speaking to the anxious, God sent an old man to deal with us. He said : ' Brothers, may I ask whether you enjoy the full rest.' I gave an honest answer. In the course of conversation he said such wishes may be a thought of the old nature leading you off from what you are in Christ—say at once you are dead to every such thought of discontent and dissatisfaction. The Holy Spirit who has been given you in His fulness is equal to every need and emergency. I spoke about it with Mr. and Mrs. Palmer who have for forty years been holding Holiness meetings in their drawing-room in New York. Mr. P. said ' It may be a temptation

of Satan. If this brother has truly surrendered everything he must beware of being led off from his faith in
Jesus by what he seeks in his experience. And we had a
very precious prayer meeting together. And after a
prayer meeting at Mrs. Keene's in Philadelphia we had
another talk. I spoke of the feeling I had that in the
fellowship with other believers the blessing came more
easily. She said she had more than once attended Holiness
meetings and seen people attain experiences of which she
could not speak. Sometimes people who were but little
prepared and whose surrender was not so deep or full as
that of others who apparently got less of blessing. Her
chief thought, too, was maintain the assurance of your
surrender and your trust, and then ask and expect with
patience His guidance. See, then, my dearest Ellen,
what I have been taught in America if not in the words
of the speakers yet in substance. And I have taken the
lesson and am rejoicing and will rejoice whatever comes,
because Jesus Christ the living Saviour is all I need.
And you will take this lesson and no more speak of the
feebleness of your consecration. Our mistake is, I think,
forming an ideal of an abiding exhibition of power and
success which is not according to the mind of God. We
cannot live so that every word we speak shall be blessed
to the conversion of a soul, but we can live so that every
word shall be to the glory of God—spoken in quiet obedience
and trust and then committed to Him who giveth the
increase. Now good-bye. Charles has written you what a
time of enjoyment our month in America has been. The
spiritual life of the pulpit has not struck us so much as
that of the home and the individual. As in England, the
pulpit aims too much after literary culture and cannot
get this without paying for it—a heavy price—the ' wisdom
of words making the Cross of none effect.' Holyoak is
very much what I expected—its religious influence more
valuable than ever. Could we fill our land with teachers
of such a spirit. Once again, good-bye. God bless you.

My kindest love to Maria. Emmie sent me her message about resting and taking care. We have not rested but have enjoyed so much that I am sure we are both physically and spiritually the better. Charles thinks he is getting fat, and the lines in his face faint, and I look quite young. Dear Maria kiss her for me.   How many said as we showed the family group and told of the nine sons in the ministry— how happy she must be.

" Your most loving brother,
" ANDREW MURRAY."

Two short letters written to a Christian Sister who had appealed to him for help and teaching will form a suitable conclusion to this chapter.

" MY DEAR SISTER,

" I am in receipt of your note of 25th.   Do not apologise for writing—We live to help each other, for we are so wonderfully the members of one Body.

" Your great difficulty is SELF-OCCUPATION.   Your only cure will be SELF-OBLIVION, forgetting yourself. You say, ' Ah, that is just it.   How can I attain that ? ' The way is this :

" First, let it be a settled thing that you are not going to trouble about what you find or do not find in yourself ; what you feel or do not feel in yourself.   Be occupied with Jesus and the souls He came to save.   Don't pray too much for yourself.   Pray greatly and patiently for others. Do leave you yourself in God's hands quietly.   He will work in you without worrying.   Secondly, Believe that the Holy Spirit of God is deep hidden in you and enabling you to believe and love.   Do not look for Him in sudden thoughts and impulses and suggestions.   He lives deeper down where you cannot at first find Him.   Honour Him then in the dark and believe that He is working in you. Trust, in the confidence that He is working.   Wait quietly on God.   Be assured you have the power to do this because

God's Spirit is in you. Thirdly, Praise God the Three in One for His wonderful Salvation and rejoice in what Christ is. Don't be such an anxious worrying child with such a kind Father, and such a Saviour. Just fold your hands when you sit still and say : ' What a God. What a love. What a Saviour.' You do God's work OUTSIDE. LET GOD ALONE DO HIS WORK INSIDE YOU.

" With much love and true prayer for God's blessing,
" Ever yours."

" MY DEAR SISTER,

" I am in receipt of your note. I can only say ' Thank God,' for it is an unspeakable blessing that the Lord who is going to perfect His salvation in you, is beginning to discover to you what it is you need to be saved from. Be very sure that the light which is now revealing the darkness will expel it. Remember that however much you abhor what is revealed of self within, and however much you long to be delivered from it, no effort of your own, no self-abhorrence, or self-crucifixion will bring you the slightest relief. IT IS GOD WHO MUST DO THAT. Trust His Beloved Son Whom the Father has given to be and to do in you what He asks you to be and do : to enable you to behave in your present circumstances, whether in the trials from without or from within, just as you ought. If He does not do that at once, He will do at once what is far better, He will put you right with it by putting you right with Himself.

" So you see I have only one word of advice : Rest in the Lord and wait patiently for Him. Put yourself very quietly—without needless self-reproach or struggling before Him in perfect impotence. Just rest in entire dependence upon Him, in His time and way, by His power to give deliverance. Neither man, nor self, nor devil can harass you if you give up all to Him.

" My greeting to Miss D. The Lord bless you.
" Yours in Him."

Chapter XIV

DIVINE HEALING

Experience and Teaching

OWING to the strain of the constant preaching, not only in his own church but on lengthy tours for Special Services, Mr. Murray's throat became relaxed towards the end of 1879 while he was on one of his tours. The doctor whom he consulted warned him to be careful, and advised him to stop preaching at once, as the condition of his throat was serious, but Mr. Murray felt he could not take the needed rest till he had fulfilled his engagements. The result was that for the next two years he was able to preach but little.

In 1880 he went to Murraysburg to be under the care of an able doctor there, and also to enjoy the benefits of the dry Karroo air. A few extracts from his letters to Mrs. Murray will reveal what he felt and thought. The letters were written between January and April of that year.

" On my arrival here I saw the doctor at once. He says he can say nothing positive. He must try for a fortnight. . . . and then will be able to give an opinion as to what he thinks of a cure. I have to see him once a day . . . and to speak as little as possible. . . . Mima (his sister) is very much concerned about my being so solitary in my room, but I enjoy the quiet, and have not yet found time hanging heavy upon me. . . . You know what I have said about the two views of affliction ; the one always seeing it as chastisement for sin, and the other regarding it in the light of kindness and love. And you know what very great kindness I have felt it, to have such a time for the renewal of bodily strength, and for mental refreshment and quiet, for the work before me. The thought has come whether I might not be in danger of overlooking the former aspect. . . . I have been asking the Lord to show

me what specially He wants changed.   The general answer
is a very easy one, and yet it is difficult to realise at once
distinctly, where and how the change is to come.   What is
needed is a more spiritual life, more of the power of the
Spirit in the life first, and then in the preaching. . . . If
the Holy Spirit were to come in great power and search
out and expose either individual failing or the general
low state of devotion in the soul, this would be the first
step towards forsaking what is behind. Let us pray
earnestly that our gracious God would search and try us
and see if there be any evil in us."

In March he writes : " When I saw the doctor to-day
I was a little bit surprised to hear him say that by the
end of next week the treatment would be at an end. . . .
There is nothing needed but care and gradual and gentle
use of the voice."

In April he is able to report : " I preached again
yesterday. The doctor says it has done me no harm.
Let us bless the Lord for again permitting me to preach
Christ and pray that it may henceforth be in the power
of the Holy Spirit."

During this time of silence and quiet he wrote in Dutch
his book on " Like Christ," as well as notes on Bible
readings for the use of members of a Bible Union he had
started, which now numbers 15,000.   It is also noteworthy
that his mention of the two aspects or views of affliction
shows that his mind was dwelling on things he had heard
and seen during his student days concerning the problems
of sickness and the relationship of the child of God to it
and the possibility of Divine Healing. It was during
this time of trial he learned the value of silence, as practised
by The Friends (Quakers) which counteracts one of the
central weaknesses of Protestantism.

He returned to Wellington in time for the Pentecostal
prayer meetings of that year, and his congregation was
delighted to have their beloved minister once more leading
the meetings, and they expressed their gratitude to God

in their prayers. With that instinct for seizing opportunities which characterised him, Mr. Murray asked them to prove their gratitude by deeds and to build the Missionary Training Institute for which there was so much need. For seven years he had prayed and waited and now God was sending the answer in an unexpected way. Only a couple of years before Mr. Murray had written : " The Institute is not yet built, but we know in God's good time it will be, so now we work on and trust and praise for what He has done and will do. I try to grasp the promise and trust God's leading."

His people responded now to his call, and as a token of their love and sympathy they subscribed the needed £2,000 for the erection of the building.

In Wellington he resumed his preaching, but with great care, and his voice seemed to be getting stronger, but in a letter to his brother John at this time he says : " My throat was improving, but got set back partly by a cold . . . and partly by the strain of the New Year and Prayer Week services." This relapse, however, was serious enough to lead his people in Wellington to arrange for him, along with Mrs. Murray, to take a trip to England so that he might consult a specialist and in the hope also that the voyage and rest might do him good. The foundation stone of the Missionary Institute was laid on the eve of his departure on this voyage. How ill he really was appears from the fact that one of his nephews wrote to his parents : " Uncle Andrew is very ill, you had better come and say good-bye to him before he goes to England." Not a few of his friends went as far as to condole with Mrs. Murray on the prospect of her being left so soon a widow—but Mr. Murray assured them that he did not expect to die in England, but to come back quite well.

When in England, he was led to consider afresh the whole question of Divine Healing, a subject on which he had often thought since his student days. After much prayer and consideration, and after consultation with the widely-known Pastor Stockmayer, Mr. Murray decided to enter Beth-shan, a home opened in London by Dr. Boardman for such suffering believers as wished to be instructed in Biblical teaching on disease and healing, in answer to the prayer of faith, as understood by these devoted servants of Christ. Here he remained for some weeks, and in the mercy of God left it, completely healed, so that never again was he troubled by any weakness of throat or voice. His throat, in dependence constantly upon the Lord for its use, in spite of the heavy strain imposed upon it for the rest of his life retained its strength till the end, and his voice retained its clear, musical, penetrating quality.

After leaving Beth-shan, Mr. and Mrs. Murray spent some weeks in Switzerland. Here they met Miss de Watteville, a devoted follower of the Lord, and with her they took a tour amidst Alpine scenery and formed with her what proved to be a life-long friendship.

On his return home to Wellington, he had an immediate opportunity to exercise his faith in the Divine power and willingness to heal. An old and tried friend of the family, Miss McGill, was lying seemingly at death's door. She said to Mrs. Murray : " I am waiting only to hand over my charge to you before I die." " Oh, no," said Mr. Murray, " God needs you still in South Africa. He will restore you in answer to prayer." At first she was doubtful, but later on was led to claim by faith her healing, and God graciously heard and answered the prayer, and she was spared to work for years in the Y.W.C.A. in Capetown.

Many questions have been asked and not a few misstatements made on the attitude of Dr. Murray towards what is generally called Faith Healing. It is an unfortunate term, and has led to sad misconceptions. Those who first used it had no thought of any healing by faith apart from the Almighty God who was the object of faith. Divine Healing is a better name and sets forth more clearly what those men of God taught who influenced Mr. Murray's mind and action, and what Mr. Murray taught and believed till the end of his life, though with certain modifications perhaps. As the term is used to-day it covers such things as auto-suggestion and the miracles of the holy places of the Romish Church. As Mr. Murray understood it, it is not faith that heals, but faith is the hand that receives the gift from the Healer. Experience has taught the necessity of distinguishing things which differ in this, as in most other things.

The fairest way of treating this matter is to let Mr. Murray himself tell the story in his own words, as he does in letters written to his Congregation in September, 1882, and in other writings. He writes from Holland:

" Let me now relate to you a few of my experiences in Europe. Let me begin with the restoration of my health, since that was the chief object for which you sent me hither. I wish to tell you something about the way by which the Lord has led me in this matter.

" At the Cape I had already frequently given thought to *James* v. 14-16—' the prayer of faith shall heal the sick ' —and, in union with others, I had already made this matter of faith healing a subject of intercession. What I had read concerning the work of Dorothea Trudel and Dr. Cullis had removed from my mind all doubts but that the Lord, even yet, bestows healing *in answer* to the prayer of faith. And yet I felt that it would be a serious question for me whether I should place myself under the treatment of a physician, or should turn to those who appear to have received this gift of healing from the Lord. I thought that I would have time on board to think over this question and come to a decision.

" How it happened I do not know, but on the voyage my attention was not directed to the matter in any especial degree. I could only beseech the Lord to guide me. The man whom I desired particularly to see was Pastor Stockmayer, whom I had learnt to know in Switzerland five years earlier, as a truly spiritual man, of strong faith, and who now stood at the head of an institute for faith healing. But I did not expect to meet him before I got to Switzerland. And so it happened that, having received no clear guidance, I placed myself the day after my arrival in the hands of a famous London physician, Dr. Kidd. He prescribed a few medicines for me to use and sent me to a cold-water establishment in the vicinity of London, with directions that I should call on him from time to time. The following week was appointed for the Mildmay Conference, which was to last for three days, and I obtained permission to attend it.

"At this Conference, just a week after our arrival in London, I heard that Mr. Stockmayer was also present. I called on him and discussed my throat trouble with him. In the course of our discussion I said that I, too, had wanted to make use of *James* v. 14, but that it seemed to me that I could not reach that faith. Perhaps that was due to the secret doubt I cherished whether it was certainly God's will that I should be healed. Might it not conduce in greater measure to His glory if I remained silent and served God in some other capacity? Surely suffering and trial are means of grace which God employs to sanctify His people.

"Mr. Stockmayer replied: 'You are still fettered by the customary views of Christians about suffering. Observe how carefully James distinguishes in verses 13 and 14 between suffering and disease. Of suffering he says: ' Is any among you *afflicted ?* (or *suffering*), let him pray ' —for patience (*Jas.* i. 2–5, 12). But then again, ' Is any *sick* among you ? the prayer of faith shall save the sick.' There is no unconditioned promise that suffering, arising from the many temptations and trials of life will be taken away ; but there is such a promise in the case of sickness.'

"I was obliged to admit this, and subsequently I thought that I understood the matter still better. There is no promise of complete deliverance from that suffering that comes upon the Christian from the world without—it

must serve to bless and sanctify him. But it is different
with disease, which has its seat within the body, and not
outside of it. The body has been redeemed ; the body
is a temple of the Holy Spirit and for the believer who
can accept it, the Lord is ready to reveal even in the case
of the body His mighty power to deliver from the dominion
of sin.

"Mr. Stockmayer invited me to attend, in the course
of the following week, the meetings of Dr. Boardman,
writer of 'The Higher Christian Life,' on the subject of
faith healing. Shortly before my departure from the
Cape I had perused Dr. Boardman's other work, 'The
Lord thy Healer,' but it left no special impression upon
me, perhaps because in my opinion he built too exclusively
upon the Old Testament. I now learnt that only a few
months before an institute for faith healing had been
opened in London under his supervision. This institute
I visited in the following week, when everything became
clearer to me, and I decided to ask if I could not be received
as an inmate. The reply was that there would be a
vacancy in the course of a few days, when I would be
welcome.

"I entered the institute three weeks after our arrival
in London, and remained in it for another three weeks.
It would be difficult to describe how much instruction and
blessing I obtained during those weeks. The matron was
of the same name as ourselves—Miss Murray. Morning
by morning the sixteen or eighteen inmates were assembled
around the Word of God, and instructed as to what there
still remained in them to prevent them from appropriating
the promise, and what there was in Scripture to encourage
them to faith and to complete surrender. I cannot remember that I have ever listened to expositions of the Word
of God in which greater simplicity and a more glorious
spirit of faith, were revealed combined with heart-searching
application of God's demand to surrender everything to
Him,

" But why was it necessary to enter a Home, and to remain there for so long a time ? Is not the prayer of faith the matter of a moment, just like the imposition of hands, or the anointing with oil of which James speaks ? Quite true. Yet in most cases time is needful in order to learn what God's Word promises, and rightly to understand what the cause and purpose of the disease really are, and what are the conditions and what the meaning of healing. The stay in such a Home, with all its surroundings, helps to make this matter plain, and to strengthen faith.

" When Mr. Stockmayer prayed with me the first time, he made use of the expression which occurs in *I Corinthians*, xi. 31, 32, saying, ' Lord, teach him to judge himself, that he may no longer be judged or chastened.' In that whole passage we find the main thoughts concerning sickness and cure. Disease is a chastisement, because God judges us in love so that we may not be condemned with the world. If we judge ourselves in such manner as to discover the reason for which we are being chastised, then, so soon as the reason for chastisement is removed, the chastisement itself is no longer necessary. The disease was designed to bring us to complete severance from what God disapproved of in our life, and when the Lord has attained this purpose, the disease itself may be removed. It is not necessary for me to say that God judges us sometimes (though not always) for some definite sin. This may be lack of complete consecration, the assertion of one's own will, confidence in one's own strength in performing the Lord's work, a forsaking of the first love and tenderness in the walk with God, or the absence of that gentleness which desires to follow only the leading of the Spirit of God.

" It is difficult to express what a sight we sometimes obtain of the unutterable tenderness and sanctity of the surrender to which we are called, when we ask the Lord for healing by faith. It fills the soul with holy fear and reverence when we ask the Lord truly to impart to the body the eternal youth of His heavenly life, and when we express our readiness to receive the Holy Spirit in order to infuse health into the body which He inhabits, so that we may live, every day, in complete dependence upon the Lord for our bodily welfare. We begin to understand how complete the surrender of the body to the Lord must be, down to the very smallest particulars, and how the Lord, in thus giving and preserving health by faith, is really effecting the most intimate union with Himself.

"When faith healing is regarded from this point of view, one of the chief objections against it is removed. We are so apt to think that the disease and the chastisement bring us the blessing, that the thought hardly finds an entrance that the recovery from disease may bring even greater blessing. And if the recovery consists in nothing but the removal of the disease, our view of the matter would be justified. But if the disease is removable only after its cause has been discovered and removed, and after a closer contact with the living Lord, and a more complete union of the body with Him has been attained, then we can understand that such a recovery brings infinitely greater blessing to the soul than the disease could convey.

"I must bring this letter to a close. I write from the home of our brother Faure at Doesburg (Holland). We think of remaining here another fortnight, and still adhere to the intention of leaving for the Cape on the 19th of October next."

The following was Mr. Murray's second letter on the subject of faith healing :

"I was obliged to end my former letter on faith healing without having said everything I desired, and, therefore, I write further on the same matter.

"One of the first things that struck me as being in conflict with my expectations, was, that in most cases slow progress is made with the healing process. I thought, and others have expressed the same opinion, that if healing is an act of God's almighty power, there can be no reason why it should not be perfected at once. This point I discussed with Dr. Boardman and others, and the reply was somewhat as follows :

" ' First of all, experience has taught that, at the present time, most cases of healing are subject to this rule ; so that, even though we cannot understand why it should be so, we have merely to observe what God actually does. Then, too, we have to notice that this gradual recovery stands in close connexion with learning to trust in the Lord and to continue in constant dependence upon Him. It is as though the Lord, by this slow and gradual process, is educating His child to the increasing exercise of faith, and to a continuance in communion with Himself.'

" This leads me to tell of one of the most important lessons which I have learnt. When I arrived at the Home my mind was chiefly set on the *healing : faith* was a secondary consideration, which was to be employed simply as a means of healing. But I soon discovered that God's first purpose was to develop faith, and that healing was a secondary question. God's purpose with us, as with Abraham, is first of all to make us true believers. Disease and cure, to His mind, derive their importance from the fact that they can awaken in us a stronger faith. Faith again, is of value in His eyes, not merely as the means by which we obtain a blessing, but especially as the pathway to a fuller fellowship with Himself and a fuller dependence upon His power. And if there be simple souls, who with child-like faith cast themselves wholly upon the Lord, recovery sometimes comes to them at once. But if there be those whose minds must be brought to believe by the way of reason and conviction, the Spirit of God must, as it were, bear patiently with their needs, and take time to teach them fully the lesson of faith, so that they may obtain not only the blessing of healing by faith, but the much greater blessing of a closer union by faith with their Lord.

" I subsequently discussed this subject with Mr. Stock-mayer, who stands at the head of a faith healing establishment at Hauptwal in Switzerland. He told me how at one time he was wholly incapacitated from preaching by an affection of the head, and that even after he had accepted the truth of healing by the exercise of faith, the trouble in no wise disappeared immediately. For more than two years the head affection continued, and yet he was always able to perform his work in the power of fellowship with the Lord by faith. He was led at this time, as though in leading-strings (he also used the expression, like a dog at the end of a chain), and he assured me that he would not for all the world have lost what he learnt during those two years. An immediate cure would never have brought him the same blessing. He counted it a great privilege that God took him so completely in hand, in order to preserve him in continual fellowship with Himself by means of the body, and the daily bestowal upon it of supernatural power.

" At first I could not entirely assent to this view of the matter. I asked Dr. Boardman if it would not be a much more powerful proof, both for His children and for the world at large, that God hears and answers prayer, if the cure of disease were instantaneous and complete. I said that if I could write to my congregation that I had wholly recovered my voice as at the first, the thanksgiving would be more abundant to the glory of God. Would it not also be for the greater glory of God if I desired of Him this instantaneous restoration ? His answer was : ' The Lord knows better than you or your congregation what is for His greater glory. Leave it to Him to care for His own glory. Your duty is to hold fast to him as your Healer, in whom you already have the healing of your malady, and He will enable you, in such manner as He sees fit, to perform all your work.' In this point of view I was able, ultimately, wholly to acquiesce.

"So we see that in faith healing there is the same contrast as in the spiritual life between feeling and believing. The body must be brought under the same law of faith as the mind : it has been redeemed, and it is now possessed by the Holy Ghost, in quite the same way as our spiritual man. This idea is founded upon the expression which Matthew the evangelist quotes from *Isaiah*, ' He healed all that were sick, that it might be fulfilled which was spoken by Esaias the prophet, saying, Himself took our infirmities and bare our sickness.' (*Matt.* viii. 17). In the well-known fifty-third of *Isaiah* sins and sicknesses are placed alongside of each other in a very remarkable way, and are borne together by Him in the suffering of which the chapter speaks. By bearing both He overcame them both, and received power to deliver from their sway. We have severed the one from the other, and have accepted the redemption of the soul from sin as the fruit of Christ's sufferings, but without regarding the deliverence of the body from the disease as in like manner the fruit of His sufferings. The faith which says : ' He has borne my sins to free me from them,' must also learn to say : ' He has borne my sicknesses in order to deliver me from them also.' In the world there will be trial, and affliction, and temptation in abundance, from which the believer must expect no deliverance ; but from the disease of the body there can be deliverance through the Spirit who dwells in the body as His temple. . . .

"From these brief accounts you will perceive that faith healing has a much higher aim than the mere deliverance of the body from certain maladies : it points out the road of holiness and full consecration which God would have us follow. The question has arisen in my mind whether I may not perhaps possess the gift, and have the vocation, to devote myself, for a time at least, to this work. I notice in those who are engaged in this labour that they must give almost all their time and strength to it. In this manner only does faith acquire sufficient vitality and strength to enable them to wrestle courageously with all the doubts and difficulties of their patients. I spent last Sunday week at Mannedorf, where Dorothea Trudel laboured with so much blessing. Her successor is Samuel Zeller, and I found the opportunity of discussing this point with him. He acknowledged that it was not the vocation of every one who had been cured by faith to devote himself to the task of healing others. In this matter he said that one must wait for God's guidance, who would assign to each his work according to his ability. For some he acknowledged that the ordinary ministry of the Gospel might be a higher vocation. But he expressed the opinion that, if the Church were to flourish as in the earliest ages, and the leaders in the congregation were again to be characterised by true spirituality, the gift of healing would be found very much more frequently ; and that this would be the case especially in the ministers of the Gospel, who would thus find a powerful recommendation for their work in rescuing the lost and in securing the sanctification of the children of God. May the Lord in His own good time grant this ! Help me to pray that He would give me grace to preserve faithfully and use rightly the blessing which He has entrusted to me.

" I close with the prayer for God's richest blessings upon my congregation, and upon our approaching re-union as well as upon His whole Church in South Africa."

Mr. Murray wrote a small book in Dutch on the subject of Divine Healing which was translated into French and English. In the Introduction he gives the leading contents of the book thus :—

" FAITH HEALING—BY WAY OF INTRODUCTION.

" Are not these glad tidings that reach us from different quarters, that the Lord is again making Himself known to His people, as of old, by the name *The Lord thy Healer ?*

The number of witnesses daily increases, who can affirm from their own experience, that there is still truth in the promise, " The prayer of faith shall save the sick, and the Lord shall raise him up." Hearts are filled with the glad expectation that this is merely a sign that the Lord is in the midst of His people, in order to bless them with His presence and with the fulness of His Spirit.

" The Church has grown so unaccustomed to this action of the Spirit in curing the body, she has for so long ascribed the loss of this gift to the counsel of God rather than to her own unbelief; she has so persistently overlooked all the utterances of Scripture on the subject, or has explained them from the viewpoint of her own feeble life that the truth has remained hidden even from the eyes of many pious expositors and theologians. It is the purpose of this little book to enquire what Scripture has to say on this matter . . . and in this introduction are adduced from the Bible the chief reasons why we believe in Jesus as the Physician of the sick, and then the main conditions upon which a sick person may abtain health from the Lord.

" i. *The Grounds for Faith in Jesus as the Physician of the Sick.*

" 1. Because God's Word expressly promises the cure of the sick by faith : ' The prayer of faith shall save the sick.' (*Jas.* v. 15). ' They shall lay hands on the sick and they shall recover.' (*Mark* xvi. 18).

" 2. Because the Lord Jesus, our Surety, has borne our sicknesses as well as our sins in His body. ' Surely He hath borne our griefs ' (margin *sicknesses*) *Isa.* liii. 4). ' Himself bare our sicknesses ' (*Matt.* viii. 17).

" 3. Because Jesus has shown that it is His work no less than His desire to heal diseases as well as to forgive sins. ' And Jesus went about all Galilee, preaching the gospel . . . and healing all manner of sickness and all manner of disease ' (*Matt.* iv. 23). ' Jesus said unto the sick of the palsy, Son, be of good cheer, thy sins be forgiven thee . . . arise, take up thy bed and go into thine house ' (*Matt.* ix. 2, 6).

" 4. Because Jesus commanded and empowered His disciples both to preach the Gospel and to heal the sick. ' Then called He His twelve disciples together . . . and sent them to preach the Kingdom of God and to heal the sick ' (*Luke* ix. 2). See also *Luke* x. 9 and *Mark* xvi. 15, 18.

" 5. Because this is part of the work for which the Holy Spirit was given and has come down from heaven. ' There are diversities of gifts, but the same Spirit . . . to another the gifts of healing by the same Spirit ' (*I Cor.* xii. 4, 9). See also *Acts* iv. 30, 31 ; v. 15, xiv. 3 ; xix. 11, 12 ; xxviii. 8, 9.

" 6. Because the Apostles preached healing as a part of the salvation by faith in Jesus. ' By the name of Jesus Christ of Nazareth doth this man stand here before you whole . . . neither is there salvation in any other, for there is none other name under heaven given among men by which we must be saved.' (*Acts* iv. 10, 12. See also *Acts* iii. 16).

" 7. Because our body also is delivered from the power of Satan, and because the Holy Spirit reveals His power even in the body. ' Know ye not that your body is a temple of the Holy Spirit ? ' (*I Cor.* vi. 19).

" 8. Because the healing of the body and the hallowing of the soul are very closely connected, and because in union with each other they enable us fully to know and glorify Jesus. ' If thou wilt diligently hearken to the voice of the Lord thy God I will put none of these diseases upon thee, for I am the Lord that healeth thee ' (*Exod.* xv. 26). See also *Psalm* ciii. 3.

" 9. Because the Church must expect great outpourings of the Spirit in these days, and may reckon upon this gift likewise. ' I will pour water upon him that is thirsty and floods upon the dry ground : I will pour my Spirit upon thy seed and my blessing upon thine offspring ' (*Isa.* xliv. 3). Pentecost was but a commencement ; the promise is ' over all flesh.' Now that the Lord is beginning to bestow His Spirit, we may certainly expect a new manifestation of His wondrous power.

" What has here been touched upon may seem strange to many readers, but it is further explained in this little book. To each one, however, who is ready to accept these promises of God, we now give brief indications of the manner in which the believing sick may obtain healing from their Lord.

" ii. *The Rules for Faith Healing.*

" 1. *Let the Word of God be your guide in this matter.* Faith can build upon nothing other than the Word of the living God. The instruction and the encouragement which God's children give are of great value but if you found upon the word of men, men may also soon cause you to doubt. God's Word commands us to seek the imposition of hands or the intercessory prayer of His believing people : this is needful and brings a great blessing. But our confidence is not to be built upon them, but upon the Word of God. In that case, too, we will betake ourselves to the Lord straightway, if there should be no true believers at hand. Seek to know what God Himself speaks to you in His Word. You have here to do with God Himself, who says; ' I am the Lord thy Healer.'

" 2. *Understand that sickness is a chastisement on account of sin.* God makes use of the disease as a rod of correction, in order to discover to us our sin and to draw us to Himself (*I Cor.* xi. 30–32). In times of sickness we must suffer the Holy Spirit to search our hearts, and so we must discover, confess and renounce our sins. When sin has been confessed and forsaken, the Lord is able to remove the chastisement. He chastises only until His purpose has been attained. When sin has been confessed and renounced, forgiveness and the cure of the disease can follow at the same time.

" 3. *Be assured*, upon the strength of God's Word and God's promises that *it is the will of God to heal you*. Unless I am firmly persuaded that something is the Will of God, I cannot pray for it in full assurance of faith. I may indeed trust that God will do what is good and right, but I cannot pray the prayer of faith. We are so accustomed to think that we cannot know the will of God with reference to the removal of disease, that we do not believe His promise concerning it. Seek to obtain an insight into what the Word promises—what it says about the work and the person of Jesus as Physician, and about the new life of the Holy Spirit as affecting the body not less than the soul—and you will obtain the assurance that the healing power of Jesus will restore health to your body.

" 4. *Accept by an act of faith the Lord Jesus as your Physician*, submit your body to Him, and claim healing for yourself. Everything is as much a matter of faith as with the forgiveness of sins. The sinner accepts Jesus, surrenders his soul and all his sins to Him, and, upon the ground of God's Word, claims by faith the forgiveness of sins. Just so with faith healing. Though the sinner feels no change and finds no light in his heart, he says, Upon God's Word I know that forgiveness is mine. So, too, the sick one says, I have confessed and renounced my sin ; Jesus has pardoned me ; He who pardons is also He who heals ; believing in Him I say, I have the healing ; by faith I see that healing granted me in heaven in my Jesus, and commence to sing, ' Bless the Lord, O my soul, who healeth all my diseases.'

" 5. *Exercise your faith*. ' Stretch forth thine hand ' ; ' Rise, take up thy bed, and walk.' So Jesus commanded

the sick. He who believes that he is healed, even though
he may feel no better, must exercise his will and commence
to act as one who realizes that health is beginning to
return. Do this in confidence in Christ's word, with the
eye of faith upon Him, to His glory, and you will not be
disappointed.

" 6. *Do not be surprised if your faith is tested.* Health
by faith is an inseparable part of the life of faith, and
therefore here, too, faith must be strengthened by being
tested. Do not be astonished if the disease does not
immediately take a turn for the better. And if after
some improvement the disease grows worse, do not imagine
that it is all a mistake. If restoration to health is longer
in coming than you expect, do not be discouraged. These
trials are indications that Satan is unwilling to relinquish
his power over your body (see *Mark* ix. 26), but also a
proof that God is willing to strengthen you to be healed
wholly and solely by faith in Jesus.

" 7. *Dedicate yourself now, in the power of your Lord,
to a new life of faith.* This health, this new power, is
something exceedingly sacred. This new life is none
other than the Holy Spirit in the body. Your body is
not your own any longer. You have no rights over it.
Walk in tender obedience to the voice of the Spirit.
Healing and sanctification are closely united. Let your
motto for every day be, with quite new emphasis, ' The
Body for the Lord, and the Lord for the Body.'

" 8. *Be a witness for Him who heals you.* Do not
speak much to those who do not understand you. Do
not argue with those who have no longing for the Physician.
Rather offer yourself to the Lord to acquaint those whom
He may bring to you with His glory. Be not ashamed to
testify, as a witness to the faith who knows what he says.
Above all, work for Jesus with your renewed strength,
and bring poor sinners to the Saviour. Follow Jesus as
one who has been healed, and glorify God.

" These are the main outlines of the doctrine of faith healing, as we have attempted to explain them from Scripture. May it please the Lord to open the eyes of His believing people, by His Holy Spirit, that they may see His glory and by the Spirit's quiet power to reveal in their hearts His great name, ' *The Lord thy Healer.*' "

The following letter was written by him in 1899, to the wife of a minister who had experienced God's healing power, but was troubled by want of complete deliverance. This letter was written about 17 years after his own healing and so under his own hand, his mature views are here given :—

" MY DEAR SISTER—I read your letter with the deepest sympathy and we commended you to the Lord at once. With my whole heart I praised the Lord for the deliverance He has given, and it appears to me the symptoms that have troubled you have simply been allowed by God for the testing and increasing of faith. Faith that is not exercised and tried cannot possibly grow stronger or be given ever new experience of God's goodness and power. And so God allows symptoms to return, that we may learn not to regard the healing as a thing we have, but a continual living participation in the life of Jesus being made manifest in our mortal body. I have just been reading over again George Muller's life, and it is astonishing how God oftentimes allowed his faith to be tried for months, and even for years, by apparently withholding everything but just the scantiest supply of his need. And he always tells that he was sure it was only to teach him not to weary in patience and prayer that he might have the stronger proof after the trial that God does really hear and help. Be not afraid ; the God who healed you is caring for you. There may have crept in something of a confidence in things seen and felt in the healing you had, and our Father does so want us to live in perfect dependence on Himself alone, that He takes away the gift we were rejoicing in, that *He Himself* may become more our all in all. Shall we not patiently and courageously bear the trial and glorify Him by being strong in faith ? You may count on Him who has begun a good work to perfect it. I pray God very earnestly that He may Himself be your Teacher and the Finisher of your faith, as He is the Author, and your mouth may afresh be filled with His praise.

" Ever yours in the love of Christ,
" ANDREW MURRAY."

As the years passed, several severe tests were experienced by Mr. Murray, in the sickness and death of some for whom prayer had been offered and whose lives seemed of great value, but neither disappointment, nor failure to understand God's Providence, shook his confidence in the God of his life.

Although Mr. Murray never ceased to trust God for his bodily as well as for his spiritual health, yet for the sake of easing the minds of relatives and friends he did not refuse, as a rule, to see the doctor if they so desired. But this was not always so. As recently as 1907 he suffered from a severe attack of Influenza and it seemed as though he was likely to be carried off by it. Miss Murray says :— " Father was very ill and my Mother was quite broken-hearted and asked me ' What am I to do ? ' I went in to Father and said ' Father dear, which will you do ? will you have the doctor or will you have some one to anoint you and pray with you ? ' He said ' neither my child, I will have neither. You can hold as many prayer meetings as you like but I WILL TRUST IN GOD.' I went out and arranged for three different meetings for prayer to ask for his restoration to health. To the praise of God it is said he preached the next Sunday, a most remarkable sermon on the text, ' They limited the Holy One of Israel ' (*Ps.* lxxviii. 41). Once more he proved the faithfulness of God.

Miss Murray relates also the following interesting facts :—

" Soon after his return from England in 1896, he undertook a tour into Northern Transvaal where his testimony was mightily owned of God. It was an Evangelistic tour and he preached almost every night, even if it were only a farmhouse congregation. In the Standerton District he was thrown out of the cart which was conveying him to his next appointment, and by the fall his arm was broken. He bandaged it as well as he could, applying cold water compresses, and he preached that evening as usual. The broken arm was made a matter of prayer, and so complete was the healing that some months later he showed it to a friend of his, who was a doctor, and asked him if it had ever been broken. He assured him that it had been broken but had been most remarkably and perfectly set."

Miss Murray further relates :—

" Some years later he was thrown, along with Mrs. Murray, from a cart again, when he was on a similar tour in Natal. He was seriously hurt in the leg and back. This time the relatives insisted on calling in a doctor, and though he did not give up his tour he was never perfectly restored and had to give up travelling by cart again.

" Some time afterwards, one cool evening at Clairvaux, I was sitting on the stoep with him, and he said to me in his humble way : ' My child, I would so much like to hold Evangelistic meetings but God does not see fit to heal me.' He sighed as he said this and I felt it was a mystery that when God was using him so mightily as soul winner that this accident should have happened. But it was his Peniel. He became through this experience a Prince who prevailed with God in prayer. He was led through this seemingly strange Providence into a deeper Prayer Life, and was taught what the power of Intercession really was. The Church of God at large little knows what

it owes to those prayers. His remarkable books on
Prayer were written after that accident, and the influence
they have exercised cannot be measured nor told by man.
Thus God glorified Himself in His servant, and in spite of
his lameness which resulted from his accident, he lived to
a good old age, and at last sweetly fell asleep in Jesus—
'A shock of corn fully ripe.' "

CHAPTER XV

A GLIMPSE INTO THE HOME LIFE
Andrew Murray as revealed in his Correspondence.

MANY men who are great in the outside world fail lamentably in the home. An old saying represents them as as " hanging up the fiddle behind the door " when they enter their own home. They can be merry and agreeable enough with strangers, but now—home—ah, that is a different matter.

No sketch of Andrew Murray would be complete which did not give some insight, however slight, into the remarkable way in which his Lord had wrought out so much that was lovely and of good report in his servant. But those who have shared the pleasure of fellowship in his home, will feel that no description can give more than a poor idea of what it was in reality. There is material enough to draw on but space prevents the free use of it, and perhaps the best way will be to allow Dr. Murray to unconsciously reveal himself to those outside by letters written while he was separated from his loved ones.

Reference has already been made to the close and tender relationship which existed between Mrs. Murray and himself. How beautifully this is manifested in his letters to her.

On October 9th, 1883, he writes from the Synod in Capetown :—

" MY DEAREST LOVE—" To my utter amazement I am Moderator again. How or why I know not. May the Lord give me grace to act so that any influence I may exert may be for His glory and may testify for a religion that is higher than organisation and work . . . I think I could go on Friday evening to Mama, perhaps you can come and meet me there with F.G. and return with me on Saturday morning . . . Good-bye. The Lord keep us and unite us in His love. Love to the children.

"Yours most affectionately."

Writing from Laingsburg, where he had gone for special services, he says :—

" MY DEAR LOVE— . . . I have been praying that the Lord who is gracious and of tender mercy may be with you and help you to put full trust in Him. Do let us get hold of the thought that faith pleases Him and that He Himself delights to work in us what is pleasing in His sight. The one thing we need is to look up to that Love which wants to do all *for* us and *in* us. My love to all the children.

"Your most loving husband."

This was followed by another letter written soon afterwards :—

" MY DEAR LOVE—Your letter of Good Friday from Worcester, and Monday from Wellington just received.

" I do bless the Lord for what He is teaching and giving you. Do let us seek in great quietness and reverend worship to realise that God has invited us to WALK WITH HIM, to put ourselves under His charge and guidance. We shall ever have to confess that we have this treasure in earthen vessels. But it is blessed to learn that the excellency of the power is of God. And if we put everything in His hands, as He wants us, and has a right to expect us to do, if we walk with Him we shall find Him faithful in caring for our souls. What we want is to KNOW HIMSELF. Not to know about Him, nor to have beautiful thoughts, but to KNOW HIMSELF. This is Eternal Life. We cannot feed on thought. Thought is but the dish in which this food is served. We want the thing itself, the heavenly substance, the power. And this we have when we get beyond the thought to the

LIVING CHRIST HIMSELF. And to have Him, the soul must reach out beyond words and thoughts in living faith, in deep receptivity, and worship, that acknowledges His presence and rejoices in HIM. May the Lord teach it to you and me.

"I wrote you last from Riebeek. Our work was blessed to God's people I am sure, and some were helped to faith in Christ. Monday I rested . . . Tuesday, Kermalazze Station where we had services in the hotel dining-room with more than one brought into the light. The hotel-keeper's wife I baptized 38 years ago—when, as her father told her, I was ' a boy of 19 or 20 years old '—Converted under William Taylor and now full of zeal and fire, terribly burdened that her husband will not give up the bar and drinkselling.

"Came on here (Somerset East) yesterday morning, found all well. Annie had arranged to spend her holidays here when John, arriving at G.R. prevented it. I was expecting John this morning but he has not come. He may appear on Saturday morning.

"I enclose the second halves of the £15 sent from Grahamstown. Use what you need and deposit all you can spare in the bank. Let Emmie by all means have what you wish to give for her work.

"I thank God for hearing your prayer on Easter Sunday about the——. Let us walk with Him and all our needs will be His care.

"Your loving husband."

On New Year's morning, 1885, he writes from East London :—

"MY DEAREST LOVE—The Lord's richest blessing be upon you the New Year's morning. May His own peace fill your heart and keep it. Let us just believe in the infinite tenderness of His Fatherhood and be assured that He looks upon us as His very own. That He is delighted with every effort to please Him and serve Him ;

that the failures of the loving child do not make Him angry and that He has taken our whole training into His own hands. Oh, we may depend upon Him to make us what He wants us to be.

"The text I have sent to the Congregation for the year and that I want also to have printed for the Bible Union is this :—' The Lord will abundantly bless you, if ye will diligently hearken unto the voice of the Lord your God ? ' I am trying to take in that ' abundantly bless.' We want our hearts filled with the thought of as Mr. Lamb used so often to say in prayer, its being God's very nature and property to bless. He is just longing to reach us and pour down his blessings into us. Our imperfections, want of receptivity hinders Him. And now, ' hearkening to His voice ' does not mean a perfect obedience as the PRICE or CONDITION of the blessing, but just the childlike willingness to listen and be taught and led. Out of this the obedience will afterwards grow, but the hearkening, the silence, the patience, and waiting for God's teaching must first precede. But it will come if we just get our eyes fixed on this : ' The Lord will abundantly bless.' Faith in such a God of love and blessing will attract and make the hearkening diligently easy and natural. I cannot help trusting if I really see Him in His wonderful love and readiness to bless. May the Lord reveal HIMSELF so to us.

"Let us go into the New Year with this abundant blessing. God as our portion, and diligently hearkening as the one first desire and duty of our lives.

"As I sat yesterday and thought over the past year from our prayer about Evangelistic work at Simonstown, through the George Conference, and the blessing at Wellington, and then the blessing at other places, I felt that we surely ought to trust the Father for the year to come. I sent a telegram to the Congregation, wishing them a Happy New Year full of praise, faith, and obedience.

"We are going to spend New Year's Day as follows :—To write to you and the Congregation till 11.0 or so ; then lunch with Mr. —— formerly Magistrate at R., a Christian man who gave us yesterday in the street a very hearty invitation to their seaside cottage. Then in the afternoon Mr. S. drives us to the Horseshoe, a piece of beautiful scenery, three miles off. To-morrow—Friday—morning we start early for Maclear. Monday night we hope to spend with Mr. B. Tuesday and Wednesday nights at King Williamstown and then Friday afternoon begin at Adelaide.

"Now Good-bye. The Lord be with you. Love to the children. Remember me to the teachers.

"Your loving husband."

Two more short extracts from this striking correspondence are all that can be given :—

The first from Capetown where he had been taking some services, and the second from Johannesburg, where he had been conducting or taking part in special services.

"My Dear Love—I am glad you are better. I wonder whether you will be able to go to Worcester . . .

"Yesterday I had a quiet service in the morning for Mr. de Beer, and in the evening a good church full at the Gardens Presbyterian Church and a solemn, serious time. To-night I speak to the young men. May God help me to feel what I sometimes feel, what a thing it is to carry Christ and Eternal Life to men. I ask the Lord continually : ' Lord, what is to be done to teach Thy ministers and people the inconceivable glory of their calling ? ' Let us rest in faith that He hears and is working, slowly but surely. Faith says in face of every disappointment ' He is Love, He is working.' I shall be glad to be home on Wednesday evening.

"With much love and prayer,

"Your most affectionate husband."

" MY DEAR LOVE—Was very glad to get by Saturday's post your long letter . . . You say people ask for news. It is really difficult to say much special. The place would need much more systematic working up than has been given. A large number of backsliders have returned to the Lord. Some who were religious have been truly converted. We have had some cases every day to deal with. We cannot say there has been a striking work but the blessing is such as to give cause for praise. It is very much the same in connection with the Scotch Church : many cold ones quickened, and some careless ones reached— but not anything very striking."

After reading such intimate expression of thought and affection it might be truthfully said that Mrs. Murray was a happy woman to have a husband who could and did write such letters, but it is no less true that he was a happy man to have a wife who could draw forth such expressions from her husband. They were happy in one another because united in the love of God.

His relationship to his children was very close and tender.

When Andrew Murray returned to South Africa from college as a young minister he was overflowing with fulness of life and merriment, but under the strain of the great responsibility of the work in the Orange Free State and Transvaal he became greatly sobered and even severe. He dealt severely with himself and felt the need of strict discipline with his people.

Speaking of the earlier days of her father's ministry during the Worcester Pastorate, his eldest daughter writes, " that while all the children loved him and romped happily with him when he was free to play with them, they feared him also. It was after the time of ' Silence ' when God came so near to him and he saw more clearly the meaning of a life of full surrender and simple faith, that he began to show in all relationships that constant tenderness, and unruffled loving kindness, and unselfish thought for others, which increasingly characterised his after life, while at the same time he lost nothing of his strength or determination.'' Above everything else the wonderful, grave, and beautiful humility which can never be successfully affected but is the work of the indwelling Spirit alone was felt by all who came into contact with him. He was indeed a charming old gentleman, and till the end a model host. God wonderfully wrought out in him a likeness to his adorable Master and Lord.

Soon after he settled in Wellington problems in connection with the education of the elder children had to be faced. Both the Boys' and Girls' schools at Wellington at that time were in the hands of teachers whose influence was not what Mr. Murray wished for his children, and so it was finally decided to send the two elder girls to Europe, as Mrs. Murray had sisters who would care for them in England. They were sent to a Moravian school in Holland and travelled to England under the care of the celebrated pioneer missionary, Robert Moffat.

Mr. Murray's letters to them while away from home manifest his tender love and fatherly wisdom and show also how this man of affairs did not let his home duty be neglected, because he was busy with many things.

" How tenderly our hearts have been going out to you this morning, wondering where you are and what you have been feeling as you think of home. We have almost daily been following you on your travels, imagining where you would most likely be . . . And now comes your birthday to remind you of home and of how we will all be thinking of you. Dearest child, we have been asking the Lord this morning should you feel somewhat sad and desolate to let you feel that He is near, and to give you a place in His own tender heart, so full of gentleness and love. May the blessed Lord Jesus indeed do it, and help you to begin this year with Him. And do you, my dear child, try to get and keep hold of the precious truth that there is no friend like Jesus, and that even when we feel naughty and foolish and sinful, He still loves us and wants us to come to Him with all our troubles, that He may heal and comfort us.

"Yesterday was Papa's birthday. We thought of how you would be thinking of us and your usual morning work on my birthday, of arranging the flowers and presents . . . When I returned thanks for all God's mercies during the past year, I did not forget to mention His goodness in giving my children such a prosperous and happy arrival in England. May the prayers many people have offered for you be richly answered.

"But yesterday was more than Papa's birthday, it was Jesus' coronation day (Ascension Day). O! what joy for those who love Him to know that their Friend has been crowned with honour and glory, and clothed with all power in heaven and upon earth. I spoke much . . . of the blessedness of serving Jesus as the sure way to have His Presence with us. I trust, my dear child is trying to keep this one thought before her, that the value of education is to fit her for the service of the Lord Jesus wherever He may have need of her hereafter.

" . . . . I was delighted to hear you were getting on happily . . . Remember when difficulties won't accommodate themselves to your wishes, there is nothing like your accommodating yourself to them . . . Though spelling and grammar and the dull exercise of translation may not be very interesting, they are needful in more ways than one. For one thing, now at school, is the only time to learn such things. The careful and exact application required at school is what you will not cultivate when you afterwards become your own teachers, whereas the easier and pleasanter paths of general literature can quite well be explored by yourselves alone afterwards. And then another thing, the object of school life is not so much to impart a large amount of information, but to ' cultivate those powers by which you can afterwards gain information for yourself . . .'

" And if you are sometimes brought into difficulties by seeing true children of God indulging in conversation or engagements which appear to you wrong, ask Jesus to help you to act up to the light of *your* conscience. If their conscience is not fully enlightened on that point, that may be an excuse for them, but cannot be for you . . . Try and think, my dear little girls, that you are not too small to exercise influence. I think when your Uncle John and I went to Holland, though we were but very young, we did exercise some influence in this matter among our friends. Don't argue with others and don't condemn them, but simply try to show that there is a way of being engaged in religious exercises all day long without being sad or unhappy, and invite them to join in such things as reading or singing."

In 1872, the then youngest child of the family, a parcularly beautiful little girl of a very sweet disposition, of two and a half years, who had been consecrated to mission work and had wound herself very closely round her father's heart was removed to the Heavenly home. The father writes thus to his absent daughters : " My darling Children—Your hearts will be very sad to hear the news which this mail brings you. And yet, not only sad, I trust, for we have had so much comfort in seeing our precious little Fanny go from us, that we cannot but feel sure that He who has been with us will be with you too, and will let you see the bow He has set in the cloud— the bright light that our Precious Saviour has caused to shine even on the dark tomb . . .

" Since you left us she has been so very sweet, from early morning when she came tripping in to breakfast to say good-morning to Papa, and all through the day. How often she came to my room just for a little play. Darling lamb, we shall see her again, and, as Mama said, we cannot refuse her to Jesus. Do you try too, my darlings, to say this. Hear Him asking whether you are willing that He should have her. And when you look at

Him, and entrust her to His love, give yourselves too, my dearest ones. We want Him to take not only her, but all of us, so that whether on earth or in heaven we may be an unbroken family, praising and serving and loving Him, here in conflict, and there in victory and glory everlasting.

> " With tenderest affection,
> " Your most loving, FATHER."

Again he writes, " I am writing in the midst of Synod business. We are not without anxieties about your change from Holland to Scotland, but we desire to leave everything in God's hands. He has been so kind about other things that we do not doubt but He will care for this too.

" I feel very grateful to Mr. Cachet for his kindness in introducing you to friends in Edinburgh, and delighted to think you had the opportunity of seeing the General Assembly and so many of Scotland's best men. You should avail yourselves of every opportunity of seeing and hearing such men, in after life you will find the recollection of this more gratifying than all the sights or places you have visited. . . such a day's intercourse with the most earnest workers for the Kingdom as they devote themselves to speak and pray for the coming of the Kingdom may give you a stimulus for a lifetime."

" DEAREST CHILDREN ! How glad we shall be to welcome you back. We are sometimes anxious lest you should be led away from the simplicity that is in Christ Jesus amid the surroundings you are in. May the faithful Shepherd keep you.

" The gathering together of God's children for the more entire dedication to Him and to Holiness is one of the most delightful tokens of God's Presence in His Church. There is hardly a man in England I would like more to meet than Mr. Pearsall Smith. And if he should be in London holding meetings when you are there . . . you should spare no pains to be present at one or more. The blessing many have got there of knowing, not only that they are saved, but entirely consecrated to their God and His work, is of unspeakable value. May my dear children, when they come back bring a real blessing to their own dear home, in the devotion of their fresh young lives to the Kingdom of their Lord."

Writing about the holidays he says : " I can only do what our Father permits us to do and cast the care of the matter on Him too. I well remember one day in the Karroo, standing beside my cart when it was outspanned, it was the 12th of June, and committing the matter into the bosom of Him who cares for us."

After the children had returned home, when Mr. Murray went to Europe he writes thus to one of them :

" MY DEAREST CHILD, How often have I been thinking of you. I have felt it very strange to be so uncertain of all that might be going on at Wellington. . . . All I can do is to commit you all to Him who loves you better than I do. Who considers you more His own than I ever can call you mine, and thus in faith to trust that the committing of you to Him is something real, a trust of which He accepts, and which He will faithfully discharge. And I have been praying for you that the Lord would give you just such a birthday blessing as you need. I think I know some of the things you need, but He knows better, and He knows above all by what ways to reach your heart, and open it for Himself and His blessing. Let me give you a birthday text for this year, *Rom.* xii. 1, 2, ' Yield yourself a sacrifice to God, and then be renewed day by day to know God's perfect and acceptable will.'

" Many young Christians and old ones too think that if they have said to God that they do indeed give themselves entirely to Him, that this is all He desires of them, and that they earnestly desire now to do what is right they will be pleasing and acceptable in His sight. And yet this is not the case. With all this desire to please God, we may be trying to do it *in our own way* and not in His way, and so not at all succeed in pleasing Him, though we have honestly and heartily said ' we want to seek only His glory and His work.'

" I think this is one of your dangers, my dear child, and, therefore, I want you to take this most blessed teaching of the second verse.   If you want to be a living sacrifice, remember that you know, as yet, but little of God's will —that reading of the Bible will not teach it you, that trying to do right will not secure it you, but that you must be taught it by the Holy Spirit and that He will teach it you by transforming you and renewing your mind, your character, so that you can spiritually find out and know what God's will is.   God's will for us individually is something spiritual that the Father will teach us.   It is for this He has given us the Holy Spirit as our Tutor to take our training into His hands, and if we but in a childlike spirit give ourselves daily to Him and say that we do want not to serve God in our way and in our will, but to know what His will is, we can be sure He will teach it us.   And His teaching not only tells us what we have to do, but makes us willing to do it."

In 1885 during Mr. and Mrs. Murray's absence on a six months' preaching tour, his eldest son died, when the following letter was penned : " MY DEAR BOYS—Here we are all ready to start for Middelburg and Lydenburg, but just waiting to have a funeral service from 4 to 5, at the same time as you.   Dear Howson ! he was not a man of strong mind or will, and yet he did amid all failure cling to his Saviour.   He did seek to know his own weakness : how often he has, with a most childlike simplicity, told me his faults ;   and his very last letter to Mary expressed his desire to be humble and Christlike.   And now—we do bless the Lord for the hope that He is in His presence, without fault before the throne.   We gave him to his God in the covenant once, and gave him a thousand times since that, and now we do lovingly give him up to Him who will keep him for Himself and for us too.

"And now, dear Boys, we give you up to Him too afresh. Oh, boys, be wholly His; live for Jesus and Eternity. You have the Eternal life in you I trust, oh, live it out, let it work in you, it makes holy. Let Jesus live in you.

"Haldane! You will feel Howson's absence day by day. The Lord will make it a blessing. Just throw yourself more entirely into the arms of Christ as your own personal friend and companion. Dear John and Charlie! ask the Lord Jesus to make you altogether His very own holy, happy, loving boys, to whom His love is their delight. He can do it.

"Say to Emmie, Kitty and Annie to take care of you, to believe that the Lord has come into the house to bless it—to believe that He is going to fit them doubly for staying in the world and working for Him—doing down here what our Howson is doing above, in glorifying the Father. And let His going be a new bond of love to make us all gentle and very loving as if we were going to part very soon.

"And now—you go to the funeral and we to a little service of love and faith—entrusting our child to the keeping of Him who is the Resurrection and the Life.

"Good-bye. Good-bye—dear children. The Lord bless you, the Lord comfort you, the Lord keep you."

To a daughter in trouble, he writes: " I accept your statement of your impressions in a spirit of love, and under compulsion of what you think it right for me to know. . . . There is something far more important, the question what is the right attitude for us to take before God, so that in the trouble we may have grace to bear it in the way He would wish, and so as not to lose the perfect peace and rest in which He has promised to keep us. You know the thought I have so often insisted on. I was preaching on it last Sunday evening, and I know it was profitable to some. It is this: Every trouble is God's will for me. I have to accept it as His will. That helps me to be sure. That as He has placed me in it, He will give me grace and wisdom to behave in it as He wishes. He is responsible for bringing me into the difficult place, He is responsible for teaching me how to behave in it. He will make it work out blessing. Count it all joy when ye fall into manifold temptations. The trial is the loving Father's message of love—do let us believe He will not only keep us in it, but make it a rich blessing. He will show us the way out. Before we think. He can change everything. I know, dear child, the flesh is weak, and the nerves give way. *But* God is strong and God is near, and God can keep heart and mind by the Peace which passeth all understanding. It is painful to look at the human sin or weakness, it disturbs our rest, it sets us wise to have it otherwise, and attempting to make it otherwise. And we fail. Let us see and come to God in the trial ; it will be a blessing to us, and in His time deliverance will be sure to come.

" In this spirit we shall have much more power to pray heartily for those who grieve or hurt us. In every way the trial will bring us nearer and closer to God. . . .

" I often feel as if I am beside you in prayer, and I ask God to enable me in faith to help you. Be sure, my dear child, God is as near and as loving as in time of prosperity. He will not fail nor forsake you. Just be still every now and then, and say : ' It is all right, Father is watching and working.'

> ' And all is right that seems most wrong
> If it be Thy sweet will.' "

" Believe that *perfect* love is a thing God speaks of in His word not to disappoint us, but to give what it wakens the expectation of.

" Love is a living power that works free, naturally, unceasingly—we know this in our human loves. How sure that the Divine love can be a never-ceasing fountain.

" We are all well—all except my back—I think God is keeping me down so quiet for gracious teaching He has for me.

" Let every trouble be God stirring up the rest to push you out to trust Him, to rest on His shoulder, to use our wings of faith boldly, because He is near to support when you are weary. Wait on Him : He gives strength to the faint and to him that hath *no might* He increaseth strength. Wait on Him in deep quiet rest—He will bless."

This letter from Dr. Andrew Murray to a son and daughter-in-law whom he loved deeply, shows how earnestly he desired that God should have the first place in their hearts and home.

" MY DEAR (CHILDREN),

" A. was disappointed at not getting a birthday letter from me so I write one to-day which will do for you and her together. My heart goes out in great longing and prayer for my dear ones that they may be God's own, His very own, a peculiar possession, with which He is free to do what He wishes. You know God is not left free to do with us what He likes when we bind and hinder Him by giving ourselves and our powers in part to the world. And I feel more and more that our own need is just to see this great God, this Invisible Being in His claims and in His worthiness to have the control of our whole being. The great power that contests God's claim is *the world* in its thousand shapes. And the Shape in which you both are tempted to give your interest and delight and power in love to it, more than to God, is its literature. Do pray amid your Studies, that you may be *kept* by God's Spirit and Grace in entire consecration to Him. Study at times, as you meditate, or read God's Word, or pray, to let the central thought of God's revelation in Christ get possession of you—God has bought you for Himself as a piece of property in which He wants to have joy, and to show forth His glory and power.

And all He wants on our part is a going out of the heart after Him and yielding and sacrificing ourselves in devotion and obedience, so that He may come in and take possession. God wants *to have you for Himself, let Him have you, let Him have you wholly*. Do believe that this living, personal God is a friend whose love and company are worth more than all the World and that the apparent difficulty of cultivating and realizing the Divine friendship will be overcome by Himself in the path of simple obedience and faith. Do what God says in all simplicity, and then cultivate a large faith that He is going to act by you in a Godlike way—in a way surpassing all we can think. I shall to-day make this a special prayer for both of you.

" I see A. studies Shakespeare and other English writers very specially. You know how I have always said this may have its use. But it has its dangers too. It depends upon what becomes the most marked feature of our life, as that is made up of what we are interested in and take as food into our Spiritual being. Do let the thought of God by His Holy Spirit working something holy and of heavenly beauty in us, something approaching to the life of Christ on earth in His devotion to the Father and to men, in His power of influencing men for eternity, be the deepest and most cherished hope of our daily life—this will lead us to give the world and its literature their right place. One thing that will help us in this is a distinct course of religious reading. Let the literature that gathers round God's Word, His Kingdom, and the religious life, have a distinct place in our voluntary studies. The fashion, the conversation and example of others will not help us in this—but just a measure of separation from others is one of the great means of building up a strong individual character. ' Go out from thy father's house, to a land I will shew thee—forsake thy friends on earth and come into fellowship with Me.'

" H. may get himself as a birthday present from me Luthardt's *Moral Truths*, it will be to some extent in the line of his reading on ethics, filling up what is so entirely wanting in the philosophical systems. I wish I knew a book that Annie would like in that style, I would send it. But it must now wait till she comes up. I think, if God allows us, to spend a month quietly together at the seaside. We will make it a blessing and refreshment to us all.

"With most affectionate love and prayer,
"Yours,"

The following letters to his sister are interesting not only because they reveal the intimacy and affection of the relationship existing between them but because they are rich in Spiritual truths of the greatest importance, and few of those who are longing after the life of full surrender to the Lord will read them unmoved or unhelped. They are worthy of the deepest study and of being read and re-read till the experience of which they speak is known personally to the reader. In them truly " he being dead yet speaketh."

" MY DEAREST SISTER,
"Many thanks for your letter and its contributions to our Seminary and Training-school. I accept them as a pledge of your prayer and love.
"I can understand your difficulty in spiritual things. We are so accustomed to look within, and *feel* our spiritual life and to think that that itself, right feeling, is the true test of life and growth, that when God calls us to use up the feeling in work—and we have grace to do it, we get frightened that work has taken the place of Christ. It is not so, my dear Sister. Now that you are starting in business you have to draw heavily on the capital you have been accumulating these past few years, and your purse looks empty. Be not afraid. You have united with a Partner who delights in self-sacrifice—even spiritual self-sacrifice. Thy enthusiasm for winning these young souls for Jesus has run away with all your spare feeling, and it is as if you had none for personal intercourse with Him. But it will all

come right. Only maintain your loyalty—say that you are His, and that you do trust Him most fully to watch over you in the work. He will do it, He does not love you less now you are working for Him than last year when you were praying to be prepared for work. He loves you more. And He just wants you to *rest* in Him. So you see my advice is, No self-reproach, no self-castigation, no attempt to get up the former spiritual experience—but just unbounded trust in His Graciousness. In the course of a little while when the novelty of the new affection has worn off a little, the old experience and feelings will come up again and get adjusted and harmonised without you knowing how—You must just *rest*—not always the repose of a luxurious enjoyment, but the quiet invigoration that comes from just leaving Him to see that you come right, and saying that after the year of fellowship you have had you do not expect Him not to watch over you in your work. Be not careful but leave it all to Him—it will come right—for He is your Lord."

" DEAREST HELEN,

" Your letter would require a longer answer than I can give just now. In the case of the croquet I think the fault may lie in this—that you are not conscious how your presence gives pleasure to a party of young people. They count it a privilege to have Aunt Helen with them. I think this is the side of your character that wants perfecting —the throwing yourself wholly into the interests of others even when they appear insignificant or at variance with your own. The cultivation of this additional grace would give your character a geniality which it is in danger of losing as long as your enthusiasm only runs in the line of school and conversion work.

" As to the mourning. I could quite approve of your not putting it on, on the ground of expense, but you complain of the want of rest after deciding. You remember what I wrote to you about your difficulties with too much delight in active work—the Soldier on parade and the Soldier in action.   Your difficulty now is the very opposite. You have been so much in action when for the sake of others your decisions must be ready and where you had no time for reconsidering that your present inactivity with too much time for doubting becomes a trial.   It is needed for the perfection of your Christian character the cultivation of the more passive grace of restfulness and trusting in God's leading in little things even when there is not the excitement and unceasing activity—to prevent turning in upon self.   It will give you sympathy with others who are not in work as you are.   It will lead you to see the truth —I know he is guiding me.   You now find it more difficult to be a good soldier in the barracks than on the field. Hesitation before deciding is more difficult to deal with Its cure is, I think ' Return unto thy rest O my soul.' There is no promise that you shall be able to decide at once between the 5th and the 12th.   Only do not let the hesitation disturb you.   Quietly trust that in your weakness He is guiding.   I do not know whether what I write will be any help.   Blessed is the man who waiteth on the Lord—God has to teach us waiting in little things.

" With much love,

" Ever Yours,

" ANDREW MURRAY."

" My Dear Sister,

" Thanks for your letter.   If I could have put down on paper the letter I thought out to you in the brain you would have had sheets full.   My letter to C. will have told you that I felt the abrupt termination of our intercourse but found it difficult to find time to write.   I have not seen your letter to Miss F. but write at once as I have a meeting this evening.

" Now as to your questions.

" As to prayer, I think your disappointment about this ought to teach you a very sober lesson—that there is a great deal of what we fancy to be faith which is not faith.

Do not say at once—But how can I know ? That is not the first question. The first and most important lesson is to realize fully looking it full in the face—I have been deceiving myself with a great deal of imaginary, very beautiful looking and happy making faith which has now shown distinctly was not faith. Let this become a deep conviction —it will prepare the way for the further teaching that true faith is something more *spiritual*, more directly God given than the persuasion we work in ourselves. There is no building up in our spiritual life without breaking down— let the old foundations be thoroughly cleared away. After that you will find the teaching as to what faith is and how we can know what is really given us to believe in the School of Prayer—not mine but God's. All schooling needs time and trouble—only be willing to pray on in the dark in the faith that He Himself will teach you. I would not have time now to say where I think the answer to your question is to be found. In general you know it yourself in the teaching of the Spirit as to what is according to the Will of God.

" Now as to the transition from the question about prayer is very important. Note, it is by His crucifixion that Christ won the place of all prevailing Intercessor. Crucifixion is the path to mighty intercession. I don't know whether you noticed my communion address at G. R. on ' Making the Cross of none effect by the excellence of words ' the cross which is the power of God, the cross by which I am crucified to the World. It has been the central thought ending on Good Friday with ' I have been crucified with Christ—I live no longer Christ liveth in me.' This is the cure of pride. As long as I do a thing, *with God's help*, I must get the credit. He who does a thing must have the honour. It is a necessity. It would be a false humility to say I did not do it. The only cure for pride is to cut away the roots—to become nothing—to die so as to live as Christ did (*Jno.* xiv. 10-12). ' The Father abiding in me doeth the work.' When ' I ' is out of the way, God works and will, as a natural thing, have the honour. The Lord teach you my dear sister. Your confidence in His teaching you say is strong, only *beware of not trusting in this confidence*. I would not say this to many. But be sure and get the lesson of faith. I may mistake for a strong faith in God what was really a *faith in my prayer*, and not in the living God. May we go very softly and carefully.

> " With very much love,
> " Your brother,
> " ANDREW MURRAY."

This chapter may be fittingly closed by giving some extracts from Dr. Murray's more general correspondence, the value of the extracts being independent of either the date or the person to whom the letter containing the extract was written. An exception to this is the first extract which is taken from a letter he wrote as a dutiful son to his father on his birthday in 1853. For the sake of readers who are not familiar with South Africa, it may be explained that among the well-trained children of Dutch-speaking South Africans, it is not considered respectful to address parents too familiarly, nor too directly. So most of the letter, although addressed to his father, is in the third person. It is a striking production for one who was then only recently out of his teens.

To His Father.

" 1853. Birthday letter. It must indeed be a long retrospect. Eternity will reveal the additional glory which I trust such a long life has been the means of treasuring up. I know how often Papa wishes to be speedily removed —the prayers of your family and people may detain you long here—may it be so ! I trust it will be to sow so much additional seed, that the harvest may be all the more abundant. I pray that each succeeding day may bring increased grace to live entirely to the Lord. May the close of my dear Father's life be the most instrumental of good to others as he is enabled to reflect the beams of that heaven, to which he feels himself so near, and he may yet find cause for thanking his God that those days were added to his life, which he at times, almost unwillingly, spent upon earth. I sometimes have felt almost ready to murmur at the prospect of a long life for myself. I think I can now feel grateful for each additional day as so much seed time of which the value can only be appreciated in eternity."

Extracts from various letters :

The State of the Church.

" When I do not write it is not that I forget you. I sent you that book ' Love Revealed ' because I wanted you to share what I had enjoyed in reading it. I cannot say how highly I esteem it. Its thoughts on the call to love in the words of Christ and on the blessedness of keeping those words ; on the promise of the Spirit and the ignorance of the Church in regard to what that promise means, are, I think, most true and suggestive.

" I cannot say how painfully I feel it all round—in the Christian literature, in the mission work of the Church, in the life of the believer—that the presence and the power of the Holy Spirit are so little known, and the absence of the Power is so little felt ; that people hardly even enquire what the cure is to be. Let us ask the Lord Himself to show us what is needed that we may be yielded up to Him so that He can really use us freely. And while we do not see Him at work, let us trust Him to carry on His unseen work within us. I have been much struck with the thought of the hiddenness and slowness of God's workings. It must be a matter of distinct faith. If we do not understand this it will make us impatient. If we understand it will teach us to rest in God and to yield ourselves all the more joyfully to Him to work out His purpose. In all creation time is the great perfecter of growth. In us it is needed too. Our prospects are bright

because every day will be better than the one before.
God will be perfecting that which concerns us.

" I go to-morrow for special services—they will be
specially difficult but we will look to God.

" Good-bye, God bless you. Be of good courage, be
patient, trust God to be making you *in secret* every day
fitter for His blessed service."

Daily Dying to Self.

" I pray God that you may have a place selected for
you suitable to your powers, and that you may have
special grace for the place. The Lord is so willing and
sure to give it if we are in a right position to receive it—
that emptiness and lowliness. The experience of dying
daily we shall find not only in outward acts of self-denial,
but specially in ignoring our own wisdom, and yielding
ourselves to be taught from on High. May the Lord
grant this, and with it the Spirit to love and labour, to
fight and conquer."

Indwelling Christ.

" Now if you are to have a full toned healthy spiritual
religion this idea of Union with Christ in His life is essential.
The Church thank God has never denied it, or refused it a
place in her system—but has not given it that prominence
which is essential to the healthy development of the
Church as a whole. Every believer needs the teaching
of the Resurrection life—as his strength and portion.

" As to the secret—I do think one great step the
consciousness and admission of the deficiency of our own
and other Churches' views, as the cause of the deficiency
of life. Now correct spiritual knowledge is what we
need (*Ecc.* i. 17). And then if this need be felt the Spiritual
teaching will show the *living Jesus personally communicating and personally maintaining each moment the life
in us.* Not a new Christ or Christology—but *Christ in
a new* (way) *and nearer aspect.* The Lord teach us the
blessed secret an open secret when He teaches."

Birthday Wish.

" May the Lord's Resurrection power be the power of our inner life and our visible works—all as proof that the Lord truly lives, and to the glory of His Name."

Birthday Wish.

" The birthday recalls a year of many experiences and many deliverances. With you and your house I thank the Lord. And He give you the incomprehensible and irresistible working of His Spirit which He sends from above with the beginning of a New Year, in the midst of the joy and gratitude the deep tenderness of spirit before Him to which He can give His blessing, and in which a deeper consecration to Him can have its roots. This year be for you ' God all and in all.' "

Graceful Old Age.

" ' Difficult times.' ' Trying and dark days,' you write. May the Lord give us grace to understand our place. There was a time when we were leaders. The time is past. We must give the reins to other brothers Japie and Eppie. To do this quietly and cheerfully is great wisdom. We cannot prevent the storm. There will be a change one day. There will be an end. This will come sooner and our influence will be greater according as we now know how to stand aside till the storm is over. The Lord give us wisdom and understanding in all things."

The Lord graciously answered this prayer and taught His servant how to grow old graciously—Indeed, in one sense he never did grow old.

CHAPTER XVI

STILL BRINGING FORTH FRUIT IN
OLD AGE—FULL OF SAP
(*Psalms* xcii. 14. *R.V.*)

1905—1916

Missionary Enthusiast

ALTHOUGH Dr. Murray had retired from the work of the ministry as far as being responsible for a congregation is concerned, he by no means ceased his activities. Just after Mrs. Murray's death it seemed to many that his working days were over.

> But they forgot the mighty God
> Who feeds the strength of every saint.

On May 9th, 1908, Dr. Murray's Diamond Jubilee was celebrated, and in view of the work that he was enabled to accomplish during the succeeding eight years, the sermon he preached on the following day, Sunday, was prophetic. He took for his text *I Thes.* i. 5 " Our Gospel came unto you . . . in power."

His divisions were :

i. God's people need evidence of His Power.

ii. God's power is revealed in His Word.

iii. Faith is the means of receiving that power.

iv. Full Surrender to God the condition of experiencing it.

He commenced his sermon by saying : " I am an old man, as I have grown old I have prayed that God would let me show forth His *power* to the generation to come." God granted his request and satisfied his soul, for in the coming years he was enabled to prove afresh that the God of Abraham still responds to the prayer of faith, and he who had no reserve of strength, and who was crippled by an injury to his back, through a fall from a cart, did work which would have tried, if it had not been beyond, the power of many a young man. And he did that work with mighty energy, and moved multitudes of people to put forth efforts in connection with the work of God who had never before been so moved.

A serious crisis in connection with the missionary work of the Church called for a powerful leader, and God's aged servant responded to the call, and God responded to his call of Faith. The story of the missionary work of the Dutch Reformed Church is full of interest. It has been already recorded in this story how in the old Graaff Reinet home Andrew Murray the elder had trained his children to take an interest in the missionary movements of the Churches in Scotland and England, and also on the Continent of Europe. As a student, Andrew the younger had had his interest greatly stirred in this way while in Holland, and the impressions then made were never effaced. But among the people of his congregations generally in earlier years there was little sense of responsibility towards the heathen by whom they were surrounded. This is not to be wondered at, for the first contact the early " voortrekkers " (pioneers), had with the natives was in constant strife and in much bloodshed. It is easy for those who live in these peaceful times to blame unsparingly those hardy men who were laying the foundations of the civilization we now enjoy. But apart from the fact that these natives had been the slayers of friends and relatives of those who survived, is the further fact that the true Missionary Spirit is the result of a quickened and vigorous life in the believer, and no one pretends, that, as a rule, the voortrekkers were spiritually minded men, beyond the ordinary. Many of them truly feared God and it was this fear that kept them from falling into open forgetfulness, and neglect of the ordinances and Word of God. We may not measure them in our measures. They lived in another world, a different world from ours. But contact with the savages of heathendom did not so affect Andrew Murray, and in his Free State days he was feeling the need of doing something for them. But his people were living in the pre-missionary age of the 17th century.

In the chapter dealing with his pastorate at Worcester, mention was made of the fact that Mr. Murray accompanied the first missionaries sent by the Church to begin work in the north of the Transvaal. But the years passed and little or nothing further was done. All that had been done, however, centred round Andrew Murray, and when his own children began to offer themselves for the work a very important step forward had to be taken, and now in a new sense Andrew Murray became the Father of the missionary work of the Church.

In 1881 the second daughter felt called to mission work. When Mr. Murray was in England he made inquiries whether she should join the China Inland Mission, for there seemed then no opening in connection with his own Church, but he finally decided it was better she should remain in South Africa. This fact gave a new interest in missions to a large circle of relatives, and she was the first of a band of about 30 cousins, who, later on entered, the mission-field. Dr. Murray, Miss Ferguson and other friends in 1885 united in praying for twenty missionaries for home and foreign work, during the following five years, *and God graciously granted their request.*

In 1886 a Ministers' Missionary Union was started at the suggestion of a young minister, Rev. H. C. de Wet, Dr. Murray immediately took it up, and others united themselves with him. They made contributions from their own allowances. Dr. Murray's contribution was £25 per annum. When he retired on pension he continued to pay this amount. Once on his forwarding it, the Secretary returned it saying it was surely a mistake, it was too much, but it was sent back with a note stating there was no mistake.

In this year the first two ministers offered their services as missionaries. The one was sent to Mashonaland, the other, Rev. A. C. Murray, nephew of Dr. Murray, went to start a new work in Nyasaland in 1888. The newly formed Missionary Society consisted of 50 members, and some well wishers, and its income was £350 per annum at this time, an average of £7 per member per annum.

In Nyasaland there had been during the first ten years considerable growth, the workers numbered fourteen in 1899. Doors were opening on every side. In whatever direction the missionaries journeyed they found the natives eager to listen to the Word. Rev. A. C. Murray wrote : " You have been praying that God would open the door for His word. That is no longer necessary. There are so many open doors that we are thrown into a condition of great perplexity."

Recognising the importance of this crisis, the committee was summoned to meet at Dr. Murray's home, " Clairvaux," where, after much prayer and conference, the following circular was drawn up :

" To Friends and Supporters of the Nyasaland Mission.

" DEAR FRIENDS,—We are in special need of your assistance in prayer. The call for more workers is most insistent. The need for more money to continue the work makes itself continually felt. Moreover, there is greater need for the powerful working of the Spirit of God, as congregations are being formed in the mission field.

" We therefore invite you all to set aside a portion of your time, though it were but half-an-hour, on Ascension Day, May 11th, 1899, in order to seek the Lord's guidance.

" Pray specially,

" 1. That the Lord, through His Holy Spirit, may graciously work in the hearts of His children so that more labourers may offer themselves, and that His people may come forward willingly to support the work financially in the spirit of true self-denial.

" 2. That the Lord may fill with His Holy Spirit all our missionaries, evangelists, teachers and converts in Nyasaland.

" 3. That in the course of the next five years the workers may at least be doubled.

" If we pray sincerely, asking at the same time what God would have us do, the blessing both for ourselves and Nyasaland will be sure.

" In the name of the Committee of the Ministers Mission Union,

" ANDREW MURRAY,
" and others."

The answer came quickly. During the next four years, although the Anglo-Boer war raged and left its aftermath of sorrow and commercial depression fourteen new workers were sent out. To quote the larger biography, " Gifts of money, frequently from unsuspected sources, and sometimes in comparatively large amounts streamed into the treasury." The Nyasa Mission has grown rapidly, and in addition to it the Free State and Transvaal have now each their own Mission, the one in Northern Rhodesia and the other in Portuguese East Africa.

In 1899 Dr. Murray received an invitation to speak at the Ecumenical Missionary Conference to be held in New York in 1900, he did not, however, feel that he could leave South Africa then. But as the Committee of this Conference was so urgent in its wish for him to attend, and as he still could not see his way clear to go, he wrote : " The Key to the Missionary Problem." He says : " I found in the Report presented to this Conference many important suggestions as to how interest in Missions may be increased. But, if I may venture to say it, the root evil, the real cause of so much lack of interest, and the way it should be met was hardly dealt with." The message of his book is: " The Missionary Problem is a personal one ; every believer ought to be a soul-winner ; every minister holds office under the great Commission ; the Missionary Enterprise is the work not merely of all, but of each."

Of this book, Dr. Horton says: " I want the people to read it, too, because it seems to me the most inspired and inspiring book written in 1901—the true note of the new century." Dr. MacLaren says: " I hope that Dr. Murray's heart-searching book may be widely read and prayerfully pondered. It is the Key to the Missionary Problem indeed, but it is also the Key to most of our problems, and points to the only cure of all our weaknesses."

In a little pamphlet entitled " The Kingdom of God in South Africa " he makes this appeal: " Prayer is the life of missions. Continual, believing prayer is the secret of vitality and fruitfulness in mission work. God has taught us, in the history of missionary revival that it was in answer to half a century of prayer for the outpouring of His Spirit that the awakening came. God calls us now again to unite in fervent unceasing prayer for the power of His Spirit in the home churches, if our Missionary Enterprise is to be carried on under spiritual conditions of the highest force. . . . Brethren ! Let us pray in the Spirit of faith and joy and love."

Just at the time Dr. Murray preached his sermon on the Power of God, already mentioned, the prospering Mission work of the Church was faced by a serious financial deficit of £2,500. The Committee issued a request for special prayer at Whitsuntide in regard to this matter, and Dr. Murray preached at Wellington on *Exodus* xiv. 15, and impressed the congregation with a sense of the seriousness of the crisis in their Mission Work. Miss Murray describes it as a never-to-be-forgotten sermon. The

words were those God spoke to Moses in his hour of trial :
" Speak unto the children of Israel that they go forward."
Even if there is no way through the sea and the enemy is
mighty and near at hand. Tell them to go *forward*.
There is a time to pray and also a time to work ; a time
to exercise faith ; to believe that the prayers that have
been offered have been answered, and a time to arise and
do what God commands us to do. Like a General with
his Army or an Officer with his battalion, he sees that the
moment has come for action, he inspires and speaks
courageously, ' Forward : Men, Charge ! ' So God calls
you. God often speaks to his people : ' Forward : Men,
Charge ! ' in this battle against the hosts of hell and its
forces, against Sin and the World. I have heard the
voice of God calling his people to go forward with new
vigour and new hope, to bring out new forces for the work
of extension. I have heard His voice calling on his people
to renew their vows, to redouble their efforts in advancing
His Kingdom upon earth, His voice is calling on every side.
Three months ago Dr. Jacob Chamberlain died in India
at the age of 72. He was one of the most gifted preachers
of the D. R. Church in America. In his last address he
said this : " The time has come when the whole Church
must redouble her efforts and understand that the reason
why the Church exists is to go and preach the Word to
every creature." I still hear the cry of Forward ringing
in my ears."

As a result of this appeal Wellington Consistory made
arrangements for the holding of a Congress to consider
the matter, and out of this Congress came the establishment
of a Laymen's Missionary Union, and money was pledged
to cover the deficit, and together with £2,500 for further
extension, and a provisional annual increase of 25% ;
lastly a Missionary Crusade was initiated which proved a
great blessing to the Church and work.

This Missionary Crusade was not only inaugurated by
Dr. Murray, but the weight of the responsibility and work

of carrying out the scheme fell upon him as he entered his 80th year. He travelled through the country far and wide, speaking at many of the chief centres of population, and giving rousing addresses on behalf of the Mission Cause. Old as he was, he found his experiences as a Crusader most interesting. The people often wondered how he, such an old man, could stand it. His daughter Mary once said : " Father, you will die in the train." " No, my child," he answered, " I shall not, I shall die in my bed," and this also proved to be true.

It was another opportunity of proving God's faithfulness for when the Crusade closed, £10,000 had been raised for missionary needs. The following account by his daughter of a small portion of his tour shows how full of vigour God's old servant was. She says : " We arrived by train at Kroonstad at 2.30 a.m., where the carriage was disconnected from the train and stood in the station yard. At 6.30 the Dutch minister, Rev. Mr. v. d. Lingen, met us and took us to his house where we rested till breakfast at 8.30. 10—11 a.m., ministers' meeting ; 11.30—12 noon, he visited all the old members of his Wellington congregation resident in Kroonstad. After dinner rested till the Convention meeting at 4 p.m., which lasted till 5.30, and Dr. Murray gave the principal address. Evening meeting, 7.30 till 9.30, when he again gave the chief address, retired at 10 p.m., rose at 1.30 a.m. to catch the 2.30 a.m. train to Bloemfontein, where we arrived about 11 a.m., and after resting Dr. Murray attended all the sessions of the Congress for the next two days, and gave the chief addresses. It was wonderful how fresh all the addresses were, one of his brethren remarked, " he never repeats himself." One secret of his power was that every message was newly received for the occasion, he did not offer stale bread to hungry souls."

She adds further : " During the next six years he travelled much up and down the country, usually taking one long tour each year, lasting from three to five weeks, and then shorter journeys as opportunity offered. The winter tour almost always included the Annual Conference of the Christian Students' Association where he usually gave several addresses. He generally attended other Conferences also, such as the Laymen's Missionary Union. Often he was invited to take part in the Services connected with the opening of new churches, and Communion Seasons often gave him the opportunity for preaching two or three sermons. Going to Johannesburg for a ' Keswick ' Convention and Missionary Congress, and the ten days of prayer at Pentecost he preached twenty-eight times in twelve days, and it was *preaching ;* from a full heart he would pour out praise and thanksgiving for travelling mercies, and intercessions on behalf of the work, and for the friends he had met as we drew near home after these tours.''

In his home he was just as energetic as when on tour. He usually dictated letters and books both in the morning and afternoon, but he was always ready to meet any friends who came to see him, and would have prayer with them. Often friends came from Cape Town to stay for the day. He took much interest in the grandsons who lived with him.

When not writing he spent much time on the broad stoep (verandah) in front of his study. There he would sit and pray and meditate. Once asked what he was doing, he replied, " I am asking God to show me the need of the Church, and to give a message to meet the need." "Children, remember to bask in the love of God as we bask in the sunshine," he would say on a winter's day when enjoying the sunshine on the stoep. One day one of the Convention speakers came to see him as he sat there surrounded by several friends. " Well, my brother," said he, " what news ? " He replied : " I have brought you a pamphlet to read which has deeply interested me." " What is it ? " he asked. " Oh ! it is an exposure of the damage Spiritism is doing, and its title is ' Satan Among the Saints.' "

With a twinkle in his eyes he took the book and said:
" But I want to hear of God among the Saints."

In 1911 political feeling ran very high, and it was affecting
church life. It seemed to call for some special effort to
counteract it, so early in 1912 the theological professors
at Stellenbosch sent out invitations for a Ministerial Conference at which about 200 ministers, missionaries and
students were present, in response to the call. It was a
solemn time as they sought in God's presence to search
their hearts, and God dealt with many. Dr. Murray was
emphatic in his expression of the conviction that one chief
cause of weakness was the lack of prayer, and his
addresses on this subject which were first published in
Dutch were later translated into English, and published
by Morgan and Scott under the title, " The Prayer
Life."

Before and after the Stellenbosch Conference his mind
was engaged on the subject of prayer, and as a result he
wrote twelve little books of short meditations on the
subject during the last five years of his life. A book written
previously in Dutch was translated by his daughter under
the title of " Thy Sun shall no more go down," and was
distributed by hundreds in the Navy.

Closely connected with the missionary movement were
all the societies at work among the young to lead them
to a full surrender of life and its powers to the Lord Jesus
Christ, and these had his warmest support.

Miss Bliss had been the means of establishing the
Christian Endeavour Movement in Wellington. The first
convention represented only seven societies. In 1897, a
visit from the founder of the C.E. Movement, Rev. Dr.
Clark, gave a fresh impetus to the work. Dr. Murray
much enjoyed meeting such a kindred spirit and did all he
could to make the visit a success. He became, and
remained President of the Society to the end, and took a
deep interest in the work. Beside the English branch
there is now a large Dutch branch of about 5,000 members.

To this Society, Dr. Murray dedicated his book on " The Mystery of the True Vine."

Another society for young people which had a warm place in Dr. Murray's heart and prayers was the Students' Christian Association. Two small Missionary Volunteer Students' bands had been formed in connection with the Theological Seminary in Stellenbosch and The Missionary Institute in Wellington respectively. Later on these became united with the Students' Christian Association and formed the nucleus of the Volunteer Movement in which were enrolled those students who felt the call of God to devote themselves to mission work. Great was Dr. Murray's joy when his youngest son and two nephews, three student volunteers, left together for Nyasaland. In 1896 Mr. L. Wishard and Rev. Donald Fraser, who was on his way to Nyasaland as a missionary, came to Cape Town in the interests of the S.C.A. They were warmly welcomed, and Dr. Murray threw all his influence into the movement they represented. He was almost always present at their Annual Conferences and usually gave several addresses of great power, and yet so simple that the youngest present could understand him easily, and he was so full of vigour and life, and made the service of Christ seem so attractive that no speaker was more acceptable than he.

One secret of his ever abiding influence with the young was that he was intensely interested in them and the students who came for a quiet talk in the study never went away without being the better for it. Once, after revival services, he made particular inquiries from a student concerning two schoolboys, who professed conversion.   The student said : " I do not know how they are spiritually," to which Mr. Murray replied : " A nurse always knows the state of her patient," implying he was the spiritual nurse of these babes in Christ.

One other fact has to be remembered. Writing about Dr. Murray after his death, one of the younger members

of the family said : " Uncle Andrew never grew old."
One who was for long closely associated with him said he
always reminded him of the man described in the xcii.
Psalm xiv (R.V.). " He shall be green and full of sap." The
charm of Andrew Murray was that in him so much of the
character and life of his adorable Lord had been worked
out and young men and maidens felt, as well as older
people, the power of an endless life in him. Once more, to
God be all the Glory !

Chapter XVII

"HE FELL ASLEEP."

Acts vii. 60.

"IN SURE AND CERTAIN HOPE."

I Thes. iv. 14.

Mark the perfect man and behold the upright for the end of that man is peace.—Psalm xxxvii. 37.

THE closing years of Dr. Murray's life were spent in the midst of the sorrows and turmoil of the World War, and he, like so many others, was called upon to realise its bitterness, by the loss of his fine, noble son, Haldane, who fell in South West Africa in seeking to save a comrade. But in spite of all this tumult and sorrow his own spirit was entering into a deeper and sweeter peace in God as the days passed.

One of the family writing at an earlier period says : " Father speaks very quietly now, with very little exertion, but with great spiritual power. It seems like a voice on the verge of eternity, of one, just ready to go on living while God wills. Glad to live to deliver God's messages, but he talks little, and spares all his strength for work, yet he was never more bright and joyous in his whole life, so restful, and peaceful. The world and all its interests are in abeyance, God's kingdom and its interests absorb his thoughts and heart."

While this is a true testimony both at the time it was written and later on as well, yet he never lost touch with the life that was round him, and one of his visitors during the war was filled with wonder at his intelligent interest in aeroplanes, and frequently he relieved his mind by reading some article in an Encyclopædia or magazine, but his " life was " truly " hid with Christ in God."

He was deeply interested in the war news as it reached him day by day, and he learnt many lessons from it.

Here is one : That which is impossible with man is possible with God. How many impossible things have been made possible. We see that in the present war. Who, some years ago, would have believed in the possibility of ships being able to carry crews of men, for hours at a stretch, under water, and to shoot under water ? Who would have believed in the possibility of fights in air-ships ? Yet, to-day, they are realities.

What has made these things possible is the patient, persistent, watching, and *waiting on nature to reveal her laws*, such as Edison and Marconi have exercised, in the faith, that the secret would be wrested from nature some time. Everything was surrendered to the one purpose of finding out the secrets of the laws of nature.

It is the same with all God's laws. His workings are hidden and not generally understood, but to him who surrenders himself fully and completely, to wait for God's revelation in the soul, the secrets of what is possible with God will be revealed. There are possibilities of sanctification and of the application of God's power in the soul that can only be proved by those who in faith wait on Him to make possible what is impossible with man.

A further illustration of his interest in current events may be given :

Immediately after the outbreak of hostilities a number of German professors and ministers of religion issued a manifesto justifying the German Government in declaring war. A copy of this manifesto was sent to Mr. Murray, who prepared the following reply which was never sent. But it is worth inserting here, for the revelation it gives of a truly catholic spirit—with no closing of the eyes to facts :

" To the Brethren who sent from Berlin a letter to ' The Evangelical Christians abroad.'

" BELOVED BRETHREN—I am in receipt of your letter

of August, and desire to send an answer, expressing my sense of the deep and divine unity which exists among God's children in the nations that are now at war. They know that they are members of one body in Christ Jesus.

" In regard to the contents of your letter, there will be, of course, very great differences of opinion. But this is not the time, or the occasion for entering upon them. It is our great duty, as beloved in Jesus Christ, to love each other through all the misunderstandings and estrangement that a war causes. You speak of the fellowship and co-operation inaugurated in the Edinburgh Conference, for which you and others have since that time been striving so earnestly. As far as that union was human, it will not be able to stand the strain of the war, with all the bitterness that it rouses in human nature ; but as far as it was a unity in the power of the Holy Spirit, uniting us closer in the person of Jesus Christ, there is in it a divine life and energy to surmount every difficulty that endeavours to break it.

" And my one object in writing these lines is to send you my brotherly greetings in Christ Jesus. The members of the body of Jesus Christ, whether in Germany or England, are bound in the love of the Eternal Spirit. For a time, national or personal differences may stir up unholy feelings, but the moment we return again into the secret of God's presence and hide ourselves under the shadow of His wings, we are brought back to the place where we are really one, and our love and prayer pours itself forth on behalf of all who are one in Christ Jesus.

" Accept the assurance of my continual daily prayer that God may help me and you, dear Brethren, and all who are apparently utterly separated from each other by the war, ever to take refuge in the High-priestly prayer of our beloved Saviour, and in the Power of His grace to pray in the fulness of faith and love, with our Lord Jesus : ' That they all may be one as Thou, Father, art in Me and I in Thee—I in them and Thou in Me—that they may be one even as We are one, that they may be made perfect in one.'

> " In this love,
>> " Ever yours most faithfully,
>>> " ANDREW MURRAY."

In June, 1916, Dr. Murray preached in Wellington for the last time, but none seemed to realise that it was the last. The following week he at the age of 88, together with his brother aged 70, made a six days' tour of Somerset West, Caledon, and Villiersdorp, holding five or six services at each place. It was a touching sight to see these veterans so full of zeal and life.

On his return he said to his daughter Annie, who ever acted as his amanuensis : " As a result of my visit to Caledon I must begin a new book, I can't help it." He then dictated the titles of eight chapters and the whole of the first two chapters of the new book.

For some years Dr. Murray had been suffering from a hardening of the arteries, a common accompaniment of old age, and the end was drawing near. In August he had an attack of Influenza from which though he rallied, he never fully recovered strength. God was gently taking down the pins of the earthly tabernacle.

Miss Murray records scraps of conversation at Patmos. Sitting on the stoep and looking out over the sea, he said : " Just look at the sea what beautiful waves. How full the sea appears to be to-day, just like the love of God, so boundless, so vast, so free, so full. Can we look upon this beauteous ocean and doubt the love of God ? Does not each wave seem to say to us ' Have faith in God. He is so wonderful, so mighty. He is the Almighty.' Annie, where is Annie ? I want to write so that all may know about this wonderful mighty God so loving, so tender, so unutterably worthy to be trusted and believed in by perishing mortals who are so unable to grasp His greatness and majesty and might."

In December they returned to Wellington, for his weakness increased. His mind often wandered, but during the night when he could not sleep he poured out his heart in prayer for ministers, for God's people, for the country.

To one of his daughters on her birthday he said : " I give you as a birthday text *Psalm* xx. especially the words ' The Lord fulfil all thy petitions.' For a birthday present I will give something for your mission in Annam. I have been thinking much about the Armenians, and can give something for them, too."

On another occasion he said : " Pray, Pray, Pray, for the nation that it may be a righteous nation. What our people need is the spirit of self-sacrifice. There is a need of those who would be willing to give their lives for the nation, to sacrifice themselves for the sake of Education and of the poor whites."

His mind was still on the book he wanted to write. In a letter from a friend about the death of a little child, the word PROMOTION was used. He said : " that word PROMOTION has given me a thought for the new book. Promotion is the favour of God. So I will write how we may obtain it, very simply, so that the most ignorant can understand it. First I will write about the favour of our Great God. Second, We obtain it only through Christ, and lastly, It is applied by the Holy Spirit."

On the day after Christmas Day he thought it was New Year's eve, and so wished to hold a meeting, asking them to sing " *Open uwen mond.*" He said : " God loves to give, and we should open our hearts wide to receive Him. We have now to close the book of the year. On one side, which is full, we have the record of the prayers offered, and the answers of help or grace supplied. The other page is blank, and there are two columns. Above one is written ' Prayers not offered.' Above the other ' Graces not received because not asked for.' Oh, how much we have missed of blessing this year, because we have not

opened our mouth wide for God to fill. Let us seek in the
New Year to have our hearts open, and our prayers, our
petitions made deep, to ask and receive more from God."

Later on, he said : " This great and wonderful God of
ours wants to live out His own life in us. He can do so
only as we dwell in love. We can dwell in love only as
Christ lives out His life in us, when we are fully yielded
to him. Let us then surrender ourselves to Him that
more of God's great and wonderful life may be lived in us."

On the last evening of his life he paused as he was
preparing for bed, and said : " We have such a great and
glorious God we ought to be always rejoicing in Him,"
and then he prayed " Oh ! ever Blessed and glorious God,
satisfy us with Thy mercy that we may rejoice and be
glad in Thee all our days. Satisfy me that I may rejoice
and be glad always in Thee."

Miss Murray writes : " Early the next morning, at 3.30,
Sister Brown who was nursing him called us and said :
' I think your father is going, his pulse is so weak.' So
we got up and went into his room. After some time he
seemed to revive, and my sisters retired to rest while I
remained watching at his bedside. That was my farewell
to him. He was conscious at times, and would say :
' Have faith in God, my Child. Do not doubt Him,' He
was so sure that God would hear prayer.

" Later on he said : ' Ah, it is my little Emmie, my
eldest child.' He stroked my hair and then relapsed into
unconsciousness. After a while he revived and said :
' God is worthy of trust.' I was kneeling in the attitude
of prayer when he said these things to me. He thought I
was praying, but I was just committing him to God. I
knelt there till 5 o'clock, when I opened the shutters and
said : ' Father, the day is just dawning, and it will soon
be light,' and I retired, leaving him to the care of the
nurse.

" During the day he was restless, but passed away
peacefully into the presence of the Lord, His Saviour,

and the Master, whom he had served so long and so faithfully, at 6.45 on the 18th January, 1917, in the 89th year of his age."

When Charles Wesley was nearing his death, an old man, he dictated words peculiarly fitting, not only his own case but the experience of this aged servant of the one Lord.

> In age and feebleness extreme,
> Who can a helpless soul redeem ?
> Jesus, my only hope Thou art,
> Strength of my failing flesh and heart,
> Oh, let me catch a smile of Thee,
> And drop into Eternity.

Chapter XVIII

" HE BEING DEAD YET SPEAKETH."
Hebrew xi. 4.

" Uncle Andrew never grew old," was the statement made by one of his nephews. In a very important sense Dr. Murray still lives, and will live in his writings. He will never be the chosen companion of those who want to follow Christ with as little trouble as possible, but to those who are willing, as he was, to forsake all and follow Him, he will still be friend and helper.

Probably more has been said and written about him since his death than during all his long life, and while there is no desire to glorify *him*, this short story of his life may well be brought to a close by bringing together a few outstanding testimonies concerning the man and his influence.

First of all however, we are privileged to have a glimpse of his Prayer Life. We know how constantly he insisted on the prime importance of Prayer, and especially of Intercession in the life of the believer. There was found after his death, a small book in which he made notes from time to time in connection with his own Prayer Life. He entered in this book lists of subjects for which he was specially making request in prayer, and the answers also are recorded as God, in His mercy responded to his cry.

In one of the earlier pages he wrote down as matters for special prayer : " For a Girl's School at Wellington ; For Godly Teachers ; For the Children of Godly Parents ; For the Power of the Spirit in all my work, that it be not done in my own strength."

Those who know Wellington see in the noble pile of buildings now standing there in connection with the Huguenot Seminary, the outward proofs of answered prayer. They know that in Miss Ferguson and Miss Bliss and a succession of godly women who followed them, and worked with them there, was a further answer to prayer. And they recognise in the long continued line of students who have gone out to bless the land, a further reason for glorifying God for His mercy. How God answered His servant's prayer for his own work, his whole after life testifies.

In another entry he writes : I need and desire to pray. I am praying for these blessings :

1.—That I may endeavour in preaching to make clear this truth of main importance—CONVERSION is surrender of sin of ALL SIN.

2.—For wisdom in dealing with young converts.

3.—How to act in dealing with the impenitent. Must I go to them to speak ? Father, I am Thine, to do Thy will alone. Thou wilt guide me."

Again : When in the midst of building operations :

" May I have grace to do everything by faith and prayer, and to have everything done so as to cultivate the spirit of love with those with whom I work. And let me, myself, feel that when once I have CAST my cares upon Him, they are His concerns and not mine, and that he will do all for me. May I have grace with STONES and BRICKS, and WOOD, with all the burdens, and workmen, to trust, and pray, and rest in His faithfulness who never fails."

" Unspeakable privilege to cast all my cares upon Him. I can do so unceasingly. At moments it is as if they are too many, but with Him it is nothing to make provision for all my wants. I feel it good to lay them continually before Him and to pray for :

The Architect's plan for the School : Money: Contractor: Boys' School : Men for our Mission : Our old school building : The Paarl.

" Infinite God, Make me empty and fill me full of Thy Holy Spirit and Love, full to overflowing, that then this weary world may see and drink. Full of Thy love to me:

full of love to Thee : full of love to them : full, myself, of love, of loving kindness to every one. Answer me Lord. Why should any perish with such love, such infinite longing to bless them ? "

" How blessed it is to walk by faith in the dark, His right hand holding us and leading us. Blessed to know One Whom we can trust to the utmost, and One Who knows and sees from the beginning, Who has foreordained our work for each of us, Who has made the pattern in the Mount for every part of His Holy Tabernacle. God keep me praising, working, trusting, praying, waiting."

" This morning, thought much on what is God's will as regards asking people for money in the same way as I did for the Girls' School, or has He not still a better way in store ? Reading George Muller."

" Miss McGill left to-day. Let the kindness that sent her here to our School be praised and trusted. May I ask that He should so provide that the School suffer no loss.

> I have no cares, O blessed Will,
> For all my cares are Thine."

Is it not interesting and encouraging to get a glimpse of this devoted and experienced servant of God in the midst of all his various occupations making each new trial a new opportunity of trust and confidence ? The work of Intercession and the life of faith did not come to him any more easily than to those who would follow him as he followed Christ. But the result is worth more than all it costs.

There lies at hand a volume full of cuttings of great interest, taken from religious and secular papers, and writings which show how greatly he was honoured and esteemed by men of good will all over the world. From this storehouse there is room for but a few, and they are given because in a peculiar way the writers were connected with Dr. Murray.

The first is from the pen of Miss Ferguson, D.Lit., President

Emeritus of the Huguenot College for Girls, the first and only college for Women in South Africa. The intention was that only women should attend the lectures or graduate from it, but exception is made in the case of men students domiciled in Wellington. It was due to her and her life-long companion and friend Miss Bliss that the ideals of Mary Lyon were so successfully transplanted to, and took such deep root in South Africa. So that even in these days of multiplied educational advantages the Huguenot Seminary and College hold an unique place. What she has to say about Dr. Murray cannot but be of interest to a very large circle of readers.

She writes :

She calls it : *An Appreciation.*

Dr. ANDREW MURRAY

May 9th, 1828—January 18th, 1917.

It was these two dates beneath the portrait of Dr. Andrew Murray in the morning paper January 19th that told us that an honoured friend had entered into the presence of the King.

What a wonderful entering-in it must have been. The joy of it filled our souls as we travelled out to Wellington. As we looked for the last time at his saintly face, as we saw him laid away in his last resting place. He was with the Lord whom he had loved with all his soul ; whom he had served so faithfully ; whom he had made a living reality in thousands of lives all round the World. What a welcome he had had ! What would it mean to him to be emancipated from the frailties of the body and pass forth his whole being in praise and adoration. He had done this very wonderfully on earth, and we who had followed him, had in some measure entered into the rapture of the divine, but what would it be to him with unveiled face to come into the presence of the King, to be like Him, because he sees Him as He is.

Surely our dear friend, being dead, will yet speak to us ; we will read his books with new meaning, for he has entered into the secret of things, that he tried to make realities in our lives.   And Andrew Murray being dead will yet live and bear much fruit.

It has been a great privilege to Dr. Anna Bliss and myself to be closely associated with Dr. Murray for over forty-three years.   It will be forty-four years in April since we saw his letters that brought us to Africa.

Dr. and Mrs. Murray had read together a few months before " The Life of Mary Lyon " and the story of her pioneer work for the higher Christian education of girls in America.   As they read they said " This is what we want for our girls in South Africa."   They had lost a short time before a little girl of five and a baby boy, and as Mrs. Murray said : " Their hands were empty for their new work for the Master."

With Dr. Murray a vision of possibilities became action. He wrote to Miss Ward, the Principal of Mount Holyoke Seminary asking for one of their graduates to come to South Africa to establish a Mary Lyon School here.   He wrote to others who might be interested.   A few weeks later he sent his private cheque for the passage money of the teacher.   A friend in America, when told of this, exclaimed : " What faith, what wonderful faith to send the money before he knows whether a teacher will come ! "

There were frequent little meetings in Dr. Murray's study to commit the whole matter to the Lord.   He wrote a short sketch of Mary Lyon's life for the " *Kerkbode* " and sent with it a request for prayer that God would choose the teacher and incline her to come.

It was about this time that Miss Bliss and I saw Dr. Murray's letters, and were made willing to come, constrained as we believed, by the prayers of God's children in South Africa.   Dr. Murray had asked for one teacher, but those to whom he had written in America felt that one should not go alone.   It was a work for two.   They wrote to Dr.

Murray to this effect. His answer was, " I asked the Lord for one, He has given me two. It is like Him to give me double what I ask for," and with this answer he sent the passage money for the second teacher. Dr. Murray took his people at Wellington into his confidence, told them all the desires of his heart, and the answer that had come, and never did a people respond more heartily. He sent out a call to the girls of South Africa, telling them his desire that they might have a training that would fit them for the Master's service, and they came, forty of them that first term.

And now we look back over forty-three years that it has been our great privilege to be co-workers with this man of God, entering into his plans, helping him to attain his ideal in one department of Christian work, that God had laid upon his heart.

There were many consultations over the detail of the work and all was brought in prayer to the Master and laid at His feet with the earnest desire that in all things we might know His will. He was very eager that our girls should be trained as teachers and be prepared when they were able to take up this work, and when the Teachers' Class developed into a Teachers' Training College under Mr. Harvey's efficient leadership, there was special gratitude.

The Huguenot College he looked upon as the natural outgrowth of the Huguenot Seminary. The child must grow up. Our daughters must be fully equipped for the positions of responsibility they were to occupy. Because the work was for the Lord, we must give Him the best possible for the development of life and character.

The highest efficiency was to be able to pass on to others the good gifts received, to help others to their best, body, soul and spirit. Living in such close fellowship we were interested in the many Christian activities that occupied Dr. Murray. He was keen to help the boys as well as the girls. The Missionary Training Institute with its bands of young men, going out into missionary work was a great joy to him. The whole wide field of missionary work appealed to him. How South Africa might reach out the helping hand to the regions beyond was his constant study. He was ever ready to turn aside from the wider fields to our little corner and show how we might help.

It is through his books that he has reached tens of thousands, and testimony has constantly come from one and another as to the transformation wrought in their lives through his message. His last pocket series of books on the Secret of Intercession, of Adoration, of the Faith Life, etc., are full of fire and inspiration and we who love his Message will keep them by us and let him speak to us through them.

He loved to gather God's people about him in Conventions and wait with them before God for His deeper teaching, and for Him to reveal himself in answer to prayer. He has shown me, as no other person has ever done, what it is possible for God to do in and through a life, wholly yielded to Him where God is given right of way.

A. C. FERGUSON.

This may well be followed by an extract from an article written by the Rev. Henry Vicars Taylor, M.A., for the *British Weekly*, describing Dr. Murray as he appeared to him. Mr. Taylor was at the time Minister of the Presbyterian Church in Wellington, and although he represented a different school of thought from that of Dr. Murray he recognised the unique place Dr. Murray filled in the religious life of the age. Many who knew the old saint intimately, would not have expressed themselves as Mr. Taylor has done about his oratory for they would feel that the over powering weight of his words at times was due chiefly, if not wholly to the power of the Holy Spirit within him. They like Dr. Murray himself believed that it was the power of that Spirit alone which made any preaching effective and Andrew Murray dreaded the use of other power in the preaching of the Word. But Mr. Taylor's graphic description of this servant of God is full of interest.   Mr. Taylor says :

" He seems wrapt about with a mantle of adoration. When preaching or conducting a service his whole being is thrown into the task, and he glows with a fervency of spirit which it seems impossible for human flesh to sustain. At times he startles and overwhelms his listeners.   Earnestness and power of the electric sort stream from him, and affect alike the large audience or the quiet circle gathered around him.   In his slight spent frame, of middle height, he carries in repose a volcanic energy which, when he is roused, bursts its barriers and sweeps all before it.   Then his form quivers and dilates, the lips tremble, the features work, the eyes spasmodically open and close, as from the white hot furnace of his spirit, he pours the molten torrent of his unstudied eloquence.   The thin face and the emaciated body are transfigured and illumined.   The staid, venerable minister of the nineteenth century with the sober clerical garb and stiff white tie, which is *de rigueur* among the Dutch clergy, disappears, and an old Hebrew prophet stands before us—another Isaiah with his glowing imagery, a second Hosea with his plaintive yearning appeals.   Audiences bend before the sweeping rain of his words like willows before a gale.   The heart within the hearer is bowed, and the intellect awed.   Andrew Murray's oratory is of that kind to which men willingly go into captivity."

Dr. Wilbert W. White of the Biblical Seminary, New York, tells in *The Christian* of May 1st, 1924 : how he was influenced by Andrew Murray's book " In the School of Prayer."   My life was revolutionised by Andrew Murray's " In the School of Prayer."   As far as I can discern without this prophet's message, there never would have been release from the routine order of things to which I was then committed.   It was in this wise.   While Professor of Hebrew and O. T. Lit., in Xenia Theological Seminary, the Secretary of the Y.M.C.A., asked me in January '93 to lead a series of meetings in Prayer. About a year before my brother, Campbell White, had recommended Murray's book to me. Examination must have been superficial for I found nothing particularly striking in it. Probably I was not then properly tuned up to " listen in." The book being to hand and suggested by the secretary, it was selected as the basis of study for the meetings which were duly announced. A week's programme was printed.

The Meetings began on the following Monday. We took a chapter of Murray each day . . . Almost every sentence challenged me, and sent me to the Bible. Herein was Murray's great contribution. He challenged me to study the teaching of the Bible about prayer . . . On the 3rd day I was led in the meeting to say, "If Murray's teaching is true, there is more in the Christian life for me than I have ever experienced and I am going to get more out of it or know the reason why." I soon learned the reason why. Those meetings from the very opening of the series were unusual. Before the end of the first week it was clear that we should continue. Thus we proceeded for five consecutive weeks. A marked revival resulted in the community. In the midst of those weeks there came a personal revelation of the love of God which I cannot describe. It surprised and astonished me. It quieted and rested me. I shall never forget it. As I now interpret it it was my Pentecost. I have been different since. I do not know how to make plain the difference. Perhaps for one thing I was headed too exclusively before for high intellectual attainments. Since then I believe I have been more clearly and distinctively ambitious for the least possible thinking in everything, but there has been a blending of the intellectual with the spiritual and the practical, in other words a balancing of parts which has made things distinctly different.

One of the most striking reminiscences comes from the pen of one well known in South Africa, Dr. F. C. Kolbe, now a Roman Catholic priest, occupying an important and prominent place in the Ecclesiastical circle in which he now moves. He is well known also in literary and social life in Capetown. There is a romantic story told in connection with his turning from the Protestantism in which he had been brought up and entering the Roman Catholic priesthood, but the fact remains that such a change has taken place. He was at one time an inmate in Dr. Murray's house and family. The article from which these extracts are made was contributed by him to *The Cape* soon after Dr. Murray's death. He writes :

" The name of Andrew Murray is graven with an iron pen and lead on the rock of South African history, and there it will stand for ever. But it is also written in softer characters on the hearts of many, and in that gentler form of survival it will endure far beyond the ordinary lot of human names. I have known only one unkind word ever said of him, and that was (strange to say) in the Synod of his own Church. He had written a piece of advice (never mind what ; it was his, and it was wise) and one member not liking it said that Mr. Murray was growing old. Old ! of course he was, but with an age more full of honour than of years, and more full of wisdom than of honour . . .

" When Dr. Murray was in Capetown he had the characteristic and kindly thought of always having in his house as guest, as a son indeed, some young man studying for the ministry. At that time I was destined for the Theological Seminary at Stellenbosch ; so when Mr. Bosman (now Rev. Dr. Bosman of Pretoria) left, this enviable privilege was offered to me. . . .

" That was the time I saw Andrew Murray at the closest possible quarters. I may have been shy, but I certainly was observant. He was a very highly strung man. His preaching was so enthusiastic ; his gesticulation so unrestrained that he was wearing himself out and the Dr. ordered him to sit while preaching . . . Now, such an output of nervous energy might well mean some reaction at home—some irritation with his wife, some uneveness towards his children; some caprice with the stranger withing his gates. But no; I never knew him thrown off his balance. . . . He was solid gold throughout. . . .

"When I came back from Europe of course he did not like my change to Catholicism; but I went to him and we both spoke frankly. There was no quarrel. There was no bitterness in Andrew Murray, his nature was sweet to the core. . . ."

"There can be no sorrow over his departure . . . There was no mid-autumn spoiling of the crop; but the whole matured harvest fully gathered in without shortcoming and without loss. And, what a harvest . . ."

The following letter was written by a friend of the family giving some intimate recollections of Dr. Murray. It was addressed to Miss Mary Murray. The writer says:

" My dear Mary,

"I am very grateful to you for writing me something of the last days of dear Father. Such a feeling of loneliness came over me, when I heard of his death ! You know he used to pray for us and for our work here, every day, and my first thought was, what a loss to us and the Congregation. . . .

"You ask me to write down what I remember of your Father's life. . . . His was such a full and blessed life, his books more than anything else will testify to that. I remember his telling me one day that some people thought there was too little personal testimony in his books. I said to him : ' Oh Mr. Murray, I hope you will not listen to them. I think the great power in your books consists of just that that there is so little of yourself in it and Christ is always in the foreground.'

"Do you remember the time when he was not allowed to preach ? A great change came into his life after that. He used to be rather stern and very decided in his judgment of things—after that year he was all love. His great humility also struck me very forcibly at that time. I remember his coming home one day from a walk with his face beaming;

he had conversed with an old coloured woman on the road and had learnt so much of God's love from her. His faith in God was marvellous, and I learnt many a lesson from him. I remember once going on a difficult journey alone with seven little children. When I went to bid him good-bye he prayed so earnestly for me, and when he was finished he put his hand on my shoulder and said : " Now my child be perfectly still and know that God has taken everything in His hands." I did it, and the way God undertook for me was marvellous.

" His power for work was something unusual. One day your mother said to him : " I think we ought to go home now, we are getting old.' He said, ' Speak for yourself only, Mother, I don't want to die, there is much to be done still.' I was often astonished at the amount of work he got through, even when travelling or having special services.

" He had a wonderful memory for faces and also for things that happened long ago. I was often surprised to hear him tell of what happened 50 years ago, when he was preaching in Zoutspansberg or Lydenburg. The old people in the Transvaal used to tell the most wonderful tales about him, his power of endurance, his great earnestness in preaching, and how frightened people often were of him, though he looked a mere boy. I often look back to the days he spent with us, it was a benediction to have him in the house. What made a great impression upon me at such times was the perfectly natural way in which he would take everything to the Lord in prayer. One day there was an argument with another man who was helping with special services here ; this man was rather bent on having his own way ; we were at dinner, and all at once Mr. Murray said : ' Let us ask God ! ' and we all knelt down at table while he prayed. It seemed to me that the man looked rather ashamed of himself when we got up, at least he did not continue the argument.

" This was surely an unusual and evidently very effective

way of dealing with an over-bearing brother. Dr. Murray had wonderful tenderness and skill in dealing with such persons and his patience seemed never to fail."

The following article which the writer calls "AN IMPRESSION," was written by one whose closest acquaintance with Dr. Murray was while a girl at school and Training College in Wellington who later on went to the mission field.

"Sometimes one can know people for years and yet not *really* know them. That was my experience in regard to Dr. Andrew Murray. For years as a school-girl and teacher at Wellington, I looked at him but never really saw him, just like Thomas who for years associated with Christ, and then a moment of revelation came, and with it the declaration, 'My Lord and my God.' Well my hour of revelation came one Pentecost Sunday at Wellington, seventh of June, 1908. There was a deficit, an alarming deficit in the funds of the D.R.C. Mission. Missionary leaders in the Church had been deliberating what to do in regard to retrenchment. At the same time a crisis had arisen in the field which demanded immediate extension. The Macedonian Cry was 'extension, more money, more missionaries.' At the home-base people were considering whether there would be a forward or a backward movement. The decision came on Easter Sunday. Dr. Murray, frail in body but magnificent in command and spirit, gave his marching orders *Exodus* xiv. 15, 'The Lord said unto Moses, Wherefore criest thou unto me? speak unto the children of Israel, that they go forward.' He spoke as one having authority, as though the command had come straight to him, for the Church, from God Almighty Himself. The one word 'forward,' was like a clarion call, there was a note of triumph, as though he was assured of victory. I felt Dr. Murray had faced the whole question not only materially but spiritually as well, he had battled his way through the doubts and questions of man, through the onslaughts of the powers of darkness, right into the presence of God. He had prevailed with God, and was now prevailing with man. It was truly like a general marshalling his forces, urging them on to victory, sure of the ultimate issue. This was the hour of my revelation when I beheld not Dr. Andrew Murray, but the Almighty God in and through Dr. Andrew Murray. As a result of that Pentecost message a Congress was held at Wellington in August of the same year. Inspired by such a leader there was boundless enthusiasm and truly ' His people were made willing in the day of His power.' The Laymen's Missionary Movement in South Africa was started, daring resolutions were passed, such as wiping out the disgraceful deficit before the end of the year, finding money amounting to some thousands of pounds for the forward movement of the mission enterprises of the Church, securing the needed missionaries for extension purposes, trusting in Him Who is more than able to supply all this. These resolutions became realisations before December of that year. The intervening months between the Congress and that time were spent in a Missionary Crusade throughout the land. Many startling and interesting stories can be told of this crusade. It was then for the first time that people were led to give generously in our country and Church. Instead of the usual silver missionary collections, golden offerings were demanded and given, individuals giving lump sums amounting to £50 and more.

Sometime after this I was at Woodstock Hospital, preparing as a candidate of the S.U.M. Dr. Karl Kumm was in town. A big meeting was held in the Wesleyan Metropolitan Church, people who in the ordinary course of events do not go to religious meetings, and did not know Dr. Andrew Murray, went to this meeting to see and hear the traveller Dr. Karl Kumm. Dr. Murray was there too, in his humble way, to welcome the man of the hour. A lady was sitting close to me, and as Dr. Murray went up the pulpit steps, frail and grey and old, she asked : " Who is that old man ? What a shame to make him go up those steps to preach." I smiled inwardly and thought: "My dear lady, you will be surprised to-night." Dr. Murray got up, he seemed to grow tall and majestic. In regard to the new work in the Sudan he once more spoke according to the oracles of God. "Forward" was his cry. Well, my lady was surprised, and more than surprised, pity made way for reverence. "What a voice for such a body!" she exclaimed. Clear as a bell, irresistible in its power and command, the all victorious *forward* rang forth in tones which knew no hesitation or defeat. And like Mary who through the one word "Mary" that resurrection morn knew and worshipped the Christ, so through that one word "Forward" Dr. Andrew Murray was revealed to me, and I bowed and worshipped the God he served and loved!"

And now the writer's task is finished. The compiling of the facts recorded in these pages has been a means of greatly quickening and strengthening to his own spiritual life, and his prayer has been, and is, that the reading of the record may be blessed to many. Andrew Murray is not a writer to be read through quickly. A little at a time is all that is possible for most students. One night at Clairvaux the old Dr. was going to bed. He had under his arm a copy of his book on "The State of the Church," and drawing it out he said: "Many a minister or other friend has said to me 'I have read your book on "The State of the Church."' Yes, they have read it through, and then put it on their study shelves among other books they have read through. Now I have written that book, and yet I have to read it, and re-read it myself, so that I may be able to take in the true state of the Church and be suitably moved by it."

Most of this book is Andrew Murray himself speaking, and after perhaps it has been read through to get the connected story of this life so full of God, and so full of miracle, it would be well to go through it again, and yet again, so as to benefit by the important message he has left behind him for less experienced travellers on the way to Zion. It will be helpful to read and think and pray over it " till we all come to the unity of the faith, and of the knowledge of the Son of God, unto a perfect man, unto the measure of the stature of the fulness of Christ." *Ephesians* iv. 13.

CHAPTER XIX

ANDREW MURRAY'S PRAYER LIFE

The following extracts have been taken from a private note book of Dr. Andrew Murray which became available for the writer only after the Life had been written. Here a glimpse is given of the inner prayer life of this devoted servant of the Lord Jesus Christ. It is all in his own handwriting.

On the opening page he writes :—

" God's words are a seed which He sows in our hearts. This seed becomes fruitful in the words which we speak to God. Our words ; our prayers are seed which we sow in God's heart. God watches over His Word to see if it matures and fructifies, and we must watch over and take notice if our prayers, which we have sowed, bear fruit. The Believer must not forget what he has prayed for, so that he may be able to notice God's answers.

This then is my account book with notes of the desire which He has awakened and of the reward that may be expected :

I. A Minister's Prayer.

" Give . . . Thy servant an understanding heart to judge Thy people."—*I Kings* iii. 9.

What a power lay hidden for thousands of years in water : the power of steam. What an influence it exerts to-day. So there lie hidden in the Church of Christ powers that are not used. The Spirit of God can teach us to make use of some of them ; but He must first give us some conception of the present unsatisfactory state of the Church. He must give us an insight into what is possible with HIM, THE ALMIGHTY ONE ; above all He must show us what is the calling of the Church, and then He can by His Spirit teach us how to reach a higher state . . . The Lord can cause such light to shine upon these things—His Light—that we may see them and obtain them.

" Give the servant an understanding heart to judge the people."

" Thy servant " for THY work, among THY people.

" An understanding heart." Not understanding without the heart, but heart understanding. " Give "—Thy divine and efficacious gift.

II. Evidently written on the eve of a holiday : A Minister's Holiday :
    " Behold I send an angel before thee . . . to bring thee into the place which I have prepared." *Exodus* xxiii. 20.

A place of rest chosen by the Lord for his people. May the place of rest be a place of prayer. Rest which is the result of true prayer ; Prayer for which rest gives the opportunity. Lord let the time of rest be a time of prayer. Prayer for the work that lies at hand, but above all for the effective revelation of the great gift of the Spirit.

III. Meditation on *John* vi. 37–40. The Minister and God's Will.

The work of Jesus has its value not only in WHAT he did but in the SPIRIT in which it is done. He did all as the will of the Father. He would not be simply a Saviour but desired to fulfil the will of God for Salvation. The Divine will in the Father is the foundation of our salvation, carried out by the SON, and imparted to the Believer. By the which will we are sanctified.—*Heb.* x. 10.

As I meditate on the will of God sometimes it seems to me as if I shall be hindered and circumscribed in my work if I devote myself with fervour and strength to prayer : that I shall be drawn off from my work, if not hindered, by the thought of what God, perhaps, wills.

This is folly. The Son of God found his comfort and

power in the will of the Father. . . . It must be so also with me. The surrender of myself to the will of ETERNAL LOVE so that through me He may fulfil His Counsel is my *safety*, and the *assurance* that my work will not be in vain. . . . I shall in fellowship with Him be a channel through which His fulness of love can flow out. Oh that I may preserve in my inner being the spirit of intercession, love, singleness of heart, trust. May I trust Him Who can keep me.

Eternal God Thy will rules everywhere. Inanimate creation serves Thy will: it is its beauty. Angels accomplish Thy will: it is their glory. Thy Son on earth did only Thy will. I, also, O my God, wish to accomplish Thy will. To this end I desire to yield myself to Thee. I do it now. Here am I Lord, O use me to further Thy Divine purpose. Thou dost accept of me, Lord, I believe. Give me the assurance. I rejoice in the will of God which is LOVE, and Infinite power and always attains its end. He will accept of me as His workman and servant. I accept Thy Divine power, so that Thy will may be done in me and by me.

IV. Meditation on *Col.* i. 9–10 and iv. 12 : THE WILL OF GOD.

The difference between a life of self-reproach and a life of peace seems to consist in this :—In the first the Believer intends to do the will of God in all things. It is for him an unbroken chain of difficult duties, of heavy burdens which must be carried, and in each case he has a conflict to wage and defeat to suffer. In the case of the other, he accepts the will of God as the POWER by which the Divine life as it was revealed in Jesus may be attained. He understands that he must just surrender himself to God's will and God will bring it to pass in him. The Lord Jesus as surety for his people accomplished that will in his sacrifice of himself when he said : " Not my will but Thine be done."

There are for the Believer four steps in the Will of God :

    (1) Suffering God's will

    (2) Doing God's will

    (3) The knowledge of God's will. *Col.* i. 9 and 10

    (4) Perfect in the will of God. *Col.* iv. 12.

Restore unto me the joy of my salvation, *Ps.* li. 12. This is the will of God, even your sanctification, *I Thes.* iv. 3. " The Will " : It is not just the life, but the power of God, The Almighty Will. And so I must surrender myself in the sure confidence that He will see that His will is accomplished. The Eternal Will is my sanctification. This Will is conditional and for its fulfilment is dependent on my free co-operation, my free consent. But now I have learned to trust. How blessedly can I now say : God wills my sanctification !

CHAPTER XX

THE MAN AND HIS MESSAGE

The Message of Andrew Murray to the Church of God as given in his various writings by his friend Rev. Walter Searle, of the S.A. General Mission.

DR. ANDREW MURRAY.

Beloved Seer, how sweet the memory now,
  That in a favoured hour this hand in thine
  Was clasped, that we beheld the glory shine
In thy clear eyes and o'er thy saintly brow,
What time thou cam'st to tell God's weak ones how
  Thro' potency of prayer the life divine
  Could from a snaring world their love intwine
And make them fair and fruitful—even as thou.

Like Alpine traveller, strong of lung and limb,
  Who scales the summit hitherto untrod,
  So didst thou climb to dwell with Christ in God,
Thro' faith transcendent, vision never dim ;
Then spoke alluring words to saints of Him,
To saints who linger on the earthly sod.

Samuel S. McCurry.

ANDREW MURRAY once explained to a friend what he considered the practical difference between his own style of preaching and that of his brother John, then Professor of Theology in the Dutch Seminary, Stellenbosch. He said : " Whereas my brother considers most Christians are merely feeble and weak, and need to be strengthened by wholesome food, I, on the other hand, regard the Church generally as sickly and spiritually diseased, which is the real cause of their feebleness. Accordingly, I think the first thing, in order that the doctrine may nourish, is to skilfully administer suitable healing medicine." " As many as I love I rebuke and chasten."

This conviction on his part and practice will explain

his method and purpose in his writings. In " The Ministry of Intercession," the opening sentence in the eighth chapter is : " Feebleness in prayer is the mark of disease. Impotence to walk is in the Christian as in the natural life a terrible proof of some evil in the system that needs a physician." Then follows through many earnest pages the pressing home of Christ's tender question to the paralytic at the pool : " Wilt thou be made whole ? "

A striking illustration is given in his preface to " The Inner Chamber," one of his most valuable helps in the prayer life, with its solemn warning against the subtle danger attending our regular Bible Study. Speaking of our Sunny South Africa and the various diseases that affect our orange trees, he says : " One of them is popularly known by the name of the root-disease. A tree may still be bearing, and an ordinary observer may not notice anything wrong while an expert sees the beginning of a slow death. Then again, the phylloxera in the vineyard is nothing but a root disease, and it has been found that there is no radical cure, but by taking out the old roots and providing new ones. The old sort of grape is grafted on an American root, and in course of time you have the same stem and branches and fruit as before ; *but the roots are new* and able to resist the disease. It is in the part of the plant that is *hid from sight* that the disease comes, and where healing must be sought.

" The Church of Christ and the spiritual life of thousands of its members suffers from the root-disease ; the neglect of secret intercourse with God."

Then again, in " The Full Blessing of Pentecost," where from the first page to the last, the fire of an intense passion to get the Church filled with the Holy Ghost is always burning on his heart, he reiterates it again and again that the Church of to-day is suffering from the lack of one thing only, the heavenly enduement of power which made the Apostolic Church triumphant—the Pentecostal Spirit. Mark that word, " suffering "—yes, suffering as from a deadly crippling disease. And once more in his book, " The State of the Church," a book too faithful to be popular, and yet as remarkable in our day as the " Reformed Pastor," by Richard Baxter, was in his time, who notices in his preface that the ministers wanted it to be published in Latin so as not to expose their sins before the public. The answer was brief and blunt : " You have sinned in English, and you must be exposed in English." It will be noted that in this book Andrew Murray devotes one chapter to show that what is wanted is a Holiness Revival, reminding us that such was the Evangelical Revival in England through Whitfield and Wesley.

Andrew Murray shows it is no use crying " Peace where there is no peace," or attempting by palliatives to heal the wound slightly ; and, speaking of the lack of conversions and the terrible decline of Church Membership, says : " *The disease is becoming chronic.*" To speak thus is not to disparage the Church, no more than the surgeon's diagnosis of the wife's deadly disease, and his announcement to the husband of the necessity of an immediate operation with a view to a speedy cure, would be a disparagement of her.

In reading over the complete list of his published writings as furnished by his biographer, Professor du Plessis, we find there are nearly 250 in Dutch and English. And, although some are small booklets and pamphlets, yet most are of a substantial size, showing what a voluminous writer he was, as well as the vigorous worker, the flaming evangelist, the organiser of educational institutions, the missionary statesman. To us who knew him best his sane mysticism, instead of being an excuse for effort, was the very main-spring of his ceaseless activity, and those whom he could not reach by his voice he inspired by his anointed pen.

On the granite monument placed on his tomb, his grateful congregation commemorate his fruitful ministry to them, and to the whole Dutch Church in South Africa; and, regarding Wellington as the radiating centre of his influence, they recognise that through his books—some published in several languages—he has enriched the whole Church of God.

To estimate his spiritual influence would be utterly impossible, but countless testimonies could be furnished from all parts of the globe. As one whose life has been enriched, and whose ministry was transformed largely by his books, thirty-five years ago in England, I would to the glory of God Whom he served so faithfully claim the privilege to add my own personal grateful testimony. There are some authors that you wish you had never seen but I can say that, from the first hour I met him in Cape Town when he came from Wellington, as President of the S. A. G. M., to welcome me to South Africa, and to pray that I might " bear the transplanting," until the last farewell, five months before his death, when his venerable face shone like Alpine mountains with the glow of setting sun, so radiant, so benignant with the purity within, I have never heard a word, nor seen a look, nor known a deed, inconsistent with his holiest teaching, and I have had ample opportunity to judge, I have been his guest on many occasions, and once he was my guest in Natal. I have travelled with him to Conventions, and have also met him at Council and Committee meetings under trying circumstances, for he came regularly to Cape Town to preside at our Council's monthly meeting, but I have never seen the slightest impatience, irritability or anger. To me he has seemed the loveliest, holiest and humblest of men, the embodiment of holiness as well as its public exponent. Through a long friendship I have learned to love the man increasingly and to admire his humility, consistency and exalted spirituality, and through unceasing study of his books I have come to honour him as a unique teacher with rare insight into the visions of God, who delivers his message more like one of the old prophets, in the power of the Spirit and with the authority of God.

It may be desirable to summarise his writings under three main heads :

1. THE MINISTRY OF INTERCESSION.

2. THE ATTAINABILITY OF HOLINESS.

3. THE NECESSITY OF PENTECOSTAL POWER.

1. *The Ministry of Intercession.*

" Men ought always to pray."   *Luke* xviii. 1.

" Prayer is the Key of Heaven : the Spirit helps faith
to turn the Key."   *Thomas Watson.*

" Happy man," wrote Dr. Alexander Whyte to Andrew
Murray, " You have been chosen and ordained of God to
go to the heart of things. I have been sorely rebuked,
but also directed and encouraged by your *With Christ in
the School of Prayer.*"   And far away in lonely Mongolia
the brave solitary missionary Gilmour wrote thanking
God for this book and *The Holiest of All.*

This, his first great book on prayer, was written after
thirty-five years of wide and deep study, and the experience of a fruitful ministry. It was the outcome of a
Ministerial Conference at George on prayer, and was
prepared while travelling.   It was followed by *The Ministry
of Intercession, The Inner Chamber, The Prayer Life,* and
The Secret of Intercession, one of the series of Pocket
Companions which have reached many who are not familiar
with the larger works. A young soldier in the Great
European War always carried one of these with him on
the battlefield.

In *The Ministry of Intercession,* containing the substance
of addresses delivered in Africa at a series of Conventions,
these truths are just as strongly emphasised, but two
others are added to them, which the author confesses he
did not formerly fully understand. " The one is," he

tells us, " that Christ actually meant prayer to be the great power by which the Church should do its work, and that neglect of prayer is the great reason the Church has not greater power over the masses of Christendom and heathen countries. The second truth which I have sought to enforce is that we have far too little conception of the place intercession, as distinguished from prayer for ourselves, ought to have in the Church and the Christian life."

With these two convictions pressing upon him with all the weight and authority of a Divine revelation to his own soul, there was begotten a desire to raise believers to a sense of their high calling as kings and priests, the vice-regents of God, Who purposes to rule the world by the prayers of His saints.

" And so," he says, " this book differs from the former one in the attempt to open a Practising School, and to invite all who have never taken a systematic part in the great work to begin to give themselves to it."

At the end there is an Appendix with daily directions for one month's prayer. Each day there is the subject : " What to pray for," and " How to pray." A marvellous exhibition of the fertility and freshness of the author's mind.

The Inner Chamber, which appeared as a series of papers in the " South African Pioneer," differs from both these books in that it lays stress on the necessity of having a secret place for the daily renewal of the spiritual life. The Morning Watch is not an end in itself, but means to an end, and that is to secure the presence of Christ through the whole day. The means used are the devout study of the Word and prayer. Here is a striking sentence which should be written in our Bibles, " In the Word of God His omnipotence works ; it has creative power and calls into existence the very thing of which it speaks." " All the infinities of God and the eternal world dwell in the Word as the seed of eternal life." But, wonderful as the Word is, we must be warned in reading it of the same

danger besetting our secret chamber that found its way
even into Paradise. " If Adam had eaten the tree of life,
he would have received and known all the good God had
for him in living power and experience. But Eve was
led astray by the desire of knowledge." And since that
day man has ever sought his religion more in knowledge
than in life. It is only as Scripture is received out of the
life of God into our life that there is any real knowledge
of it. " However delightful our Bible Study may be there
is no true knowledge gained farther than spiritual renewal
is experienced." There are three chapters devoted to
this important subject, the Daily Renewal of the spiritual
life in the Morning Watch. " The renewing of the Holy
Ghost becomes one of the most blessed verities of our daily
Christian life." But there is its uncompromising cost,
" All we have by our birth from Adam is to be sold, if we
are to possess the pearl of great price." And again, " It
is a solemn thing, far more solemn than most people
think, to be a real Christian."

In *The Prayer Life*, a volume published in his ripe old
age, he reiterates more strongly than ever the paramount
importance of the *Inner Chamber*, especially for the
minister, and devotes a third part of the whole in exhorting
to its faithful habitual use. The book consists of addresses
delivered at a Ministers' Conference held at Stellenbosch,
1912, attended by over two hundred ministers, missionaries,
theological students and their professors. Published first
in Dutch, it was translated into English by Rev. W. M.
Douglas, B.A.

In the Epilogue, Dr. Murray says : " It is with a feeling
of deep unworthiness that I venture to offer myself as a
guide to the Inner Chamber, which is the way to holiness,
and to fellowship with God." He warns us of the arch-
enemy who hinders. " Satan endeavours to become master
of the Christian's Inner Chamber, because he knows that,
if there has been unfaithfulness in prayer, the testimony
will bring little loss to his Kingdom." In another part

he says : " As far as the minister is concerned, everything depends on whether or not he is a man of prayer and one who in the Inner Chamber must be clothed each day with power from on high. Be faithful in the Inner Chamber."

The first Chapter is entitled *The Sin of Prayerlessness*, and here he speaks in an entirely new strain. The physician of souls, dealing with our infirmity in prayer, has become the prophet, like Nathan going to David the man of God, coming even to ministers of the Gospel, to show that there is sin, for which we have no excuse. Like all sin it must be confessed as such, repented in sackcloth and ashes, and for ever put away. A young minister at one Wellington Convention cried out in agony : " O God, it seems as if even the Atonement could not cover the iniquity of our neglect of prayer." And even Andrew Bonar although it was his habit to spend not less than three hours daily in prayer and meditation on God's Word, and one whole day monthly in prayer and fasting, records in his diary : " Had some almost overwhelming sense of omission in the days past If I had prayed more——." And again : " Oh, that I had prayed a hundred-fold more."

Why is prayerlessness so sinful ? Because it disobeys the command to pray without ceasing, and despises the abundance of grace that would come upon ourselves first and then on the world in answer to our importunate cry. If God has chosen to limit His working by our praying, it is of infinite importance that above all we should say, as we see our Divine Model praying, " Lord, teach us to pray." This is the exceeding sinfulness of our prayerlessness, that we neither learn of Him nor follow Him in prayer.

There are Four essentials in prevailing prayer.

(1) *The Childlike Disposition.*

The First Lesson we have to learn in the School of Prayer is one that the human mind is dull in learning, namely, that Prayer is to be answered, and that God means what

He says : " The God that answereth by fire let Him be God."

" Next to the revelation of the Father's love, there is, in the whole course of the School of Prayer, not a more important lesson than this, that every one that asketh receiveth." And again, " This is the fixed eternal law of the Kingdom, that, if you ask and receive not, it must be there is something amiss or wanting in your prayer. If, therefore, no answer comes, we are not to sit down in sloth that calls itself resignation, and suppose that it is not God's Will to give an answer. No, there is something in the prayer that is not as God would have it, childlike and believing."

In making these uncompromising assertions, that God's purpose is to answer prayer, and that the fault is wholly ours, if the answer comes not, it must not be imagined for a moment that Andrew Murray, like all devout thinkers, has not felt the mystery of prayer, as involved in the very perfections of the Divine Nature, His sovereignty, His wise purposes, and absolute foreknowledge. He confesses at the close of the very chapter where he has endeavoured to solve the problem, " This perfect harmony and union of Divine Sovereignty and human liberty is to us an unfathomable mystery because God as the *Eternal One* transcends all our thoughts."

The subject of the Chapter is : " Prayer in harmony with the very being of God," one of the profoundest and most philosophic in the book. He shows that so far from the being of God rendering prayer an impossibility, it is this, rightly understood, which proves its very possibility. If the being of God were one as the Deist thinks, prayer could not avail, but God is *Three in One*, and *One in Three*, Father, Son and Holy Ghost, and the contemplation of the Trinity is not only the subject of adoring worship with cherubim and seraphim, it is a study in the philosophy of prayer. " This day have I begotten Thee, ask of Me and I will give." This is the eternal inner relationship of Deity. The Father determined that He would not be alone in His counsels, there was a Son on Whose asking and acceptancy their fulfilment should depend. And so there was in the very Being and Life of God an asking, of which prayer on earth is to be the reflection and outflow. The prayer of the Man Christ Jesus is the link between the eternal asking of the Only-begotten Son in the bosom of the Father, and the prayer of men upon earth. *Prayer has its rise and source in the very Being of God.* In the bosom of the Deity nothing is ever done without prayer, the asking of the Son and the giving of the Father."

Is any one, notwithstanding this, troubled still about the decrees of God ? Jeremy Taylor, the golden-mouthed preacher, asserted that : " Prayer rescinds the decrees of God." Andrew Murray assures us : " The decrees of God are not decrees made by Him without reference to His Son, or His petitions, *or the petitions to be sent up by us through Him.* In the decrees of the Eternal purpose there was always room left for the liberty of the Son as Mediator and Intercessor ; and so, for all petitions of all who draw nigh to the Father in the Son, God's decrees are no iron framework against which man's liberty would vainly seek to struggle." " To sum up : the Father-heart holds itself open and free to listen to every prayer that rises through the Son, and that God does indeed allow Himself to be decided by prayer to do what He otherwise would not have done."

Our *a priori* reasoning may lead us to conclude that God cannot be affected by our wishes or will when asking for rain or healing and other things ; and at one time Andrew Murray experienced divine healing and wrote about it, but, if we are convinced by Scripture and fact that God does grant our requests, then we may perhaps shift our ground and say : " Well, if God does hear prayer, it is surely unreasonable seeing He is infinitely benevolent and has a Father's heart of love, to think that He should require the child's entreaty even to the point of agony."

But our Lord says : " That though he will not rise and give him because of his friendship (Syriac version) yet because of his importunity he will rise and give him as many as he needeth." Bounds, Author of *Purpose in Prayer*, says : " God loves the importunate pleader and sends him answers that never would have been granted but for the persistency that refuses to let go until the petition craved for is granted."

Andrew Murray acknowledges that the need of persevering prayer is one of the greatest mysteries of the prayer world. But after all it is one of the laws of the Kingdom, and one of the hard lessons we have to learn in our Master's School, Who Himself prayed with importunity and fervently even unto blood.

> " Yield to me now for I am weak,
>   But confident in self despair :
>   Speak to my heart, in blessing speak,
>   Be conquered by my instant prayer.
> Speak or thou never hence shalt move,
> And tell me if Thy Name is love."

(2) *The Right Spiritual Condition.*

If we have rightly learned the First Lesson in Prayer, namely, that it is God's Will to answer it, we are now prepared for the *Second Lesson*, a very simple one, but not always acceptable, that the gracious giving on God's part is conditioned by holy living on our part. The Sermon on the Mount where the earliest instruction was given, was the revelation of the Father's heart of love, and therefore prayer is considered as " the simplest form of speech that infants' lips can try." Then follows the natural direction, " Live as a child of God, and you will be able to pray as a child of God," and the assurance that he who lets God be Father always and in everything, will experience most gloriously that a life in God's Infinite Fatherliness and constant answers to prayer are inseparable."

There is only one way to live as a child, and that is in

obedience, and while much will be said elsewhere of this as the *sine qua non* of blessing and an almost forgotten duty, it is enough to see how in this Sermon on the Mount " our primal duties shine aloft like stars." To Andrew Murray it must have been unthinkable how Christ's disciples could by any system of exegesis postpone the observance of Christ's Sermon to another age or dispensation, especially with its solemn climax that not to do these very words is like " building a house on the sands." He says : " The prayer-promises are imbedded in the life-precepts, the two are inseparable. They form one whole, and he alone can count on the fulfilment of the promise who accepts too all that the Lord has connected with it."

The open reward depends on the secret and habitual entrance to the prayer-chamber. " Enter into thy chamber, as my disciple thou must have thine own, and use it." The Lord Himself found His in the desert or the garden, or on the slopes of the mountain ; Brainerd in the back-woods of America ; Hudson Taylor in the crowded Chinese river-boat, long before dawn while the others slept, by lighting his candles which he carried with him as well as his Bible. Praying Hyde once made the church belfry his Inner Chamber. A place for the Morning Watch is as much a necessity for the Christian as an office for the merchant. But this precept to pray in secret is not the only one. " Seek first the Kingdom " is another, that is, make My claims paramount. " Pluck out the right eye "—rather than look on evil. " Be reconciled to thy brother "—for worship with anger within is a mockery. " Exhibit the Beatitudes of My followers— Poverty of spirit, purity of heart, peaceableness of disposition, and you shall be called the children of God." Obedience to " These Sayings of Mine " is as necessary to the prayer-life as a rock foundation to a house. And if these things are conditions of successful prayer, we are now beginning to discover, at least one reason why there are millions of unanswered prayers in the Church like the accumulation of undelivered letters in the dead-letter office.

(3) *The Whole Armour of God*.

David in his contest with Goliath declined the use of Saul's armour and went forth with only sling and five stones. Woe to the prayer-warrior who attempts to wrestle in prayer without the whole armour of God specially designed by Him as protection against spiritual principalities and powers.

> " Legions of dire malicious fiends
> And spirits enthroned on high."

To David the defiant champion and the Philistine armies at his back were plainly visible. To us Satan and the hosts of wickedness are all unseen. St. Paul, however, reveals their existence in the Sixth of Ephesians just as astronomical photography pictures innumerable bright stars which even the most powerful telescope cannot discern.

God's missionaries in heathen lands are painfully conscious of their presence and activity behind hostile chiefs, pagan customs and foulest sins. And readers of Andrew Murray are surprised that such a master in the science and art of prayer as he is, writes so little about this martial aspect of it. He refers to it indeed in his Chapter on Fasting, because he says : " Food may hinder the spirit in its battle with the powers of darkness," and illustrates it in the case of Pastor Blumhardt who, being defeated in his first struggles ultimately obtained an easy victory over evil spirits after thirty hours' fasting. Pastor Hsi, in China, is a modern illustration of this.

At the end of Chapter XXVII, *School of Prayer*, he utters this prayer : " Into Thy hands I would believingly yield my whole being : form, train, *inspire me to be one of Thy prayer-legion*, who as wrestlers watch and strive in prayer, who as Israel's and God's princes have power and prevail." Whitfield said that God's praying legion had never yet been defeated.

Many years ago the guest of a Minister of the Dutch Reformed Church in the Orange Free State, I was taken into his study and amongst other books the host pointed to a collection of Andrew Murray's on the shelves, with this remark : " Mr. Murray sees in the Bible so much more than others see."

This becomes increasingly apparent as we advance in our studies and now come to hear him elucidate and illustrate what is our Lord's Final Teaching on the mystery and the glory of prayer. These Lessons, unlike the earliest which were given in the open air, were delivered in the Upper Room on the last night under the gloom and shadows of the approaching sacrifice, where He became for us the true Paschal Lamb. In the three Synoptic Gospels we read His own explanation of the out-poured Blood, and the Sacred Body broken for us. To St. John is reserved the privilege of reporting His Farewell Discourse. Two great truths are prominent in these three Chapters, the promise of the other Paraclete, and the sixfold promise of the unlimited power of prayer through His Name, and these two conditions, living in the Spirit and praying in the Name, must be inseperably united, as in the first lesson we saw precept is linked to promise.

(4) *The Continual Inspiration of the Holy Spirit.*

" Hitherto have ye asked nothing in My Name. *At that day* ye shall ask in My Name."

These verses clearly mark the contrast between the former mode of praying and the latter. *The coming of the Holy Ghost will introduce a new epoch in the prayer world.* The Saviour was going to the Cross there to gain a victory over the powers of darkness and to accomplish a full redemption. He would then ascend to Heaven to carry out the redemption and victory in His people. For this He would ever live to pray. Then through the Holy

Ghost descending, they are to be drawn up into the great stream of prayer. "Through the Spirit, Christ's prayers become our's, and our prayers become His. To pray in the Spirit is to pray in the Name."

It would be well in this connection to read his book suggested by an old vine stump on his study table, "The Mystery of the True Vine," but first and foremost on bended knee, hushed in the Sacred Presence of the true Vine Himself, let the reader ponder these wondrous words in the Fifteenth Chapter of John, with their deep heavenly mysticism. And when he comes to the verse, "If ye abide in Me, and my words abide in you ye shall ask what ye will and it shall be done unto you," then let him pause and say, "Lord if this is the golden key tell me what it really means to have Thy words abiding in me that I may ask and receive."

One thing we are sure He will say, and that is, it is not enough to have them abiding in the memory only, nor the understanding nor even the affection, they must be in the will as they are literally and actually obeyed.

Bishop Westcott has a suggestive remark, that there is another reading of the Greek which in *John* xiv. 14, makes Christ say, "If ye ask *Me* anything in My Name I will do it," proving what surely is the spirit of all His other teaching that "in thy Name" cannot be a mere talisman and charm which we can use in the presence of the Father. Even when we speak to the Son Himself it must be in His nature, disposition, which really means His Name.

Professor Beck, a favourite author with Dr. Murray, is quoted in the Notes on Chapter XXVI, as saying, "It is idle at the conclusion of our petitions to use the phrase, "For the sake of Thy dear Son as if it were a mere formula attached, out of all relation to our life and conduct." But if we only knew the omnipotence represented by the symbol, "For Thy Name's sake," prayer would achieve all that Christ has promised.

Three illustrations are given to show the use of a name

in daily life. There is the legal right given to a clerk by the merchant in his absence and to be used only in transacting, not his own, but his master's business. Then the life relation between child and father who can use that name so long as he lives worthily of that name. And last the love relation between bride and bridegroom in whose name she can now purchase what is necessary for the home life. " Such illustrations show us how defective is the common view of a messenger sent in the name of another, or a guilty one appealing to the name of a surety." The application is obvious. We have the right to draw upon the bank of Heaven for supplies only as we " seek first the Kingdom." We cannot come as children expecting the Father's gifts without measure unless we live as sons and daughters of the Almighty, nor can we expect to use the Name of Him who loved us unless we are living in the holiest passion of adoring love. " My Jesus, my King, my Life, my All, I again dedicate my whole self to Thee," Livingstone wrote on his last birthday as we are reminded in the chapter, " The Holy Spirit and Missions."

If we are still desirous of mastering this most profound of all the lessons in prayer, that it is the name that secures the answer, let us open once again " The Ministry of Intercession " and read the Chapter XI, " Praying in the Name " and we shall marvel at the deep mystery.

" The name of God is meant to express His whole Divine Nature and Glory. And so the Name of Christ means His whole nature, His person and work, His disposition and Spirit. To ask in the name of Christ is to pray in union with Him.

As Christ's prayer-nature lives in us, His prayer-power becomes our's too. To pray in the Name of Christ we must pray as He prayed on earth ; as He taught us to pray, and in union with Him as He now prays in Heaven.

Christ Our Example.

" Christ knew," Dr. Murray writes in this connection,

" how the holiest service preaching and healing, can exhaust the spirit, how too much intercourse with men could cloud the fellowship with God, how time, full time is needed, if the spirit is to rest and root in Him, how no pressure of duty among men can free from the absolute need of much prayer." Let it be noted that the necessity for long hours of fellowship with God is here regarded as inherent in the spirit just as the need of rest after labour is rooted in the physical constitution of man, and Christ as the holiest of men, as well as the Eternal Son of God, set us this example of prayer. His life was full of service, preaching, healing, teaching, contraverting Pharisees, Scribes and Sadducees, but He made this no excuse. After the busiest day the next morning He was up a great while before day to get alone to pray. Before some special and important act He spent the whole night in prayer.

This is therefore the twofold lesson from Christ's prayer-life ; we need prayer as the preparation for service and after service prayer for the recuperation of our exhausted powers. Fletcher to be alone with God sat up two whole nights every week in the beginning of his ministry, and afterwards his habitual prayer was so intense that he stained the walls of his study with his vehement breath. Brainerd, though he did not, like his Lord and Example, sweat great drops of blood, yet he did sweat violently in the cold winds, praying in the wood for his benighted Red Indians. His diary reveals the secret of this intensity, where it records again and again, " *God enabled me to wrestle* ardently for immortal souls." Fletcher declares it is the grand device of Satan to keep us from vehement wrestling in prayer which a false quietism and mysticism would condemn as the energy of the flesh, and says, " It is still the law : The Kingdom of heaven suffereth violence and the violent take it by force : the imagery being taken from the siege of a fortified castle." To say nothing of mighty prayer warriors among the old Scotch Covenanters, there was a plain Methodist Minister of the Gospel of a hundred years ago, named John Smith, who never went to any circuit without having a double revival, first among saints and then among sinners, and the twofold secret God had taught him was that the Gospel though divinely meant for all could not be effective without the Holy Spirit, and that the Holy Spirit would not be given without believing and persevering prayer, and so, as well as preaching vehemently as God's ambassador, he gave himself to prayer and fasting for hours and hours oft times wetting his study floor with tears over sinners. A condensed account of his extraordinary life bears the expressive title, " Calloused Knees."

One sermon preached in Wales by a Robert Roberts led a hundred sinners to the Saviour and commenced a great spiritual awakening. A brother minister said to him, " Roberts where did you get that wonderful sermon." For answer he said, " Come with me into this parlour ; there it was that I spent the night in prayer, often lying on my face before God."

What a rebuke to those ministers of the Gospel referred to in the Prayer-Life who at their Synod meeting by show of hands, at the chairman's request, confessed that only one minister spent thirty minutes daily in prayer, one half only fifteen minutes and the rest five minutes. Are there not twelve hours in the day, *that is seven hundred and twenty minutes*, and out of this sum only five given to prayer by men who are set apart to " give themselves continually to prayer and the ministry of the Word." Five minutes for fellowship with God, seven hundred and fifteen for other things ! Is not Andrew Murray right, that whatever the ministry says about its dependence on the Holy Ghost, *it does not give the right proportion of time for securing this power.*

Christ Our Teacher.

When the mind is left to itself it devises its own theories of prayer, like a spider weaving its web from its own body. One favourite sophistry, as an excuse for vain and useless prayer is that its chief value consists in its reflex influence upon us. By prayer we are either calmed into peace or raised into ecstacy in the presence of the Father of our spirits. And if there is any place for direct supplication it is considered to be subordinate to the higher exercise of spiritual fellowship with God.

Once at a Ministers' Meeting in connection with a series of Conventions Dr. Murray was conducting, there was a young minister who strongly contended with him that this aspect of prayer, its subjective reflex influence on us, and not objectively on God was the true philosophy of prayer. But it need not be said, that it was conclusively proved by Scripture and argument and experience that this is not the Saviour's teaching. To quote from " The Ministry of Intercession," " If we carefully study all that our Lord spoke of prayer we shall see that this is not His teaching. Everywhere our Lord urges and encourages us to offer definite petitions, and to expect definite answers." To cite one instance given for the sixteenth day in the ' Secret of Intercession,' he reminds us of the China Inland Mission at one time needing more labourers for certain districts totally unprovided for. They therefore agreed to ask during the year for 100 additional labourers, and £10,000 to meet expenses. At the end of the time, the 100 suitable men and women had been found, with £11,000.

Christ as our Intercessor.

" We have gazed upon Christ in His prayers, we have listened to His teaching as to how we must pray, but to know fully what it is to pray in His Name we must know Him too in His heavenly intercession." When He was on earth we could see Him praying at the river Jordan when the Holy Ghost descended upon Him like a dove, and on the Mount of Transfiguration, when He prayed His face and raiment were transfigured with glory, and in the Garden when the angel strengthened Him and being in an agony, He prayed more earnestly, and at last on the Cross

interceding for those who crucified Him, but now He is
" within the veil " and His form is invisible and His voice
inaudible to us, but the Spirit of truth reveals His unceasing
ministry. " He ever liveth to make intercession." If a
man lives for any object, it means that it is the one purpose
that occupies his thought and engages all his energies.
Think of it ! He just lives to pray. " I will pray the
Father and He shall give. Just think what it means ; that
all His saving work wrought from heaven is still carried on
just as on earth, in unceasing communication with, and
direct intercession to the Father who worketh all in all,
who is All and All. Every act of grace in Christ has been
preceded by and owes its power to intercession. His
intercession is nothing but the fruit and glory of His
Atonement. Christ's intercession is the Father's glory,
His own glory, our glory. And now this intercessor is our
life, He is our Head, and we are His body. His spirit and
life breathe in us. As in Heaven so on earth, intercession
is God's chosen, God's only channel of blessing."

If Andrew Murray is right in this bold assertion, that
intercession is God's only channel of blessing, we are not
surprised that he should follow on with another chapter
entitled : " God Seeks Intercessors " and should give this
reason, among others, " He will not, He cannot, take the
work out of the hands of His Church," and this is why, in
one of his most eloquent passages, he reiterates : " God
wonders, God wonders, God wonders there is no intercessor ! There is a world with its perishing millions with
intercession as its only hope." It was because of this,
God looked throughout India and found a missionary,
John Hyde, who became, as his biographer says : " a
living example of one who actually lived with Christ in
the School of Prayer." But he had embarked for the
mission field, alas, like too many missionaries, without
the one supreme equipment, the fulness of the Holy
Ghost. Angry at first with a friend's letter who wrote in
a farewell message, " I shall never cease praying for you

until you are filled with the Spirit," he flung himself down on his cabin floor and cried mightily. God answered that prayer on the outward voyage, and for this is the divine equation, filled with the Spirit he was filled with prayer to such an extent that he became known as " Praying Hyde." What a singular commendation, what a sad reflection on others. The marvellous story must be read in the book, *A Present Day Challenge to Prayer*. It is two hundred years since Brainerd was born to become the most conspicuous example to the whole Church of a praying missionary, but here is a present-day illustration of one who seemed to have surpassed him in his agonised burden for souls, which expressed itself in impassioned prayer, " Give me souls or I die, Give me one a day, Lord," he cried, and God gave them. Next year, two, then three, and at length five for prayer is definite, and God granted his request. But what shall we say of his sleepless vigils, his long hours of prayer and fasting during Conventions and Missions, and of one notable instance in England, where he took upon himself the burden of a difficult Evangelistic Mission conducted by Dr. Chapman, and by prayer and fasting he helped to change everything. But read one chapter only, " Within the Veil," and it will be seen, that like his Master in the Holiest of all, he seemed to live only to pray.

> " Pray, always pray,
> The Holy Spirit pleads."

Chapter XXI

THE ATTAINABILITY OF HOLINESS

" Sanctify them by Thy Truth." *John* xvii. 17.

" A soul without holiness is like a diamond without lustre."
—*Charnock*

NEVER can the hearers who were present forget a striking incident during the Holiness Convention in Pietermaritzburg, which Andrew Murray was conducting. Taking for his text, " And ye know that He was manifested to take away our sins, and in Him is no sin," *I John* iii. 5, he suddenly lifted up his watch, and said : " This is designed and made as an instrument to tell the time. It may be beautiful as an ornament, valuable as a piece of metal, but if it does not tell me the time, it has failed altogether in the object for which it was manufactured and sold. In like manner the Son of God, eternal, co-equal with the Father, was manifested in time in a human form, and in that human form made a complete propitiation for sin, with the purpose of removing it. He may be beautiful in His immaculate character as our Example, and admirable in His miraculous deeds, and useful as a Teacher sent from God, but if He does not remove sin from us, He fails altogether in the One supreme, sovereign purpose for which He became incarnate and poured out His blood unto death."

After using this illustration, it was easy for him to point to the possibility and necessity of holiness from the Divine side, and consequently the attainability on our part. That the Divine intention was not only the removal of the guilt of sin, but its presence also, he had already shown the Christian Church in his first English volume, " Abide in Christ," which at once established him as a leading teacher in the deep things of God. The chief object of writing this manual was to establish the converts of the revival of 1860. There a whole chapter is devoted to shewing that St. John taught the actual subjective taking away of sin from the believer's life.

If, then, as we have seen in the preceding section, that it is " the effectual prayer of the *righteous* which availeth much " ; if as Andrew Murray says : " There is a life that can pray," our transition from considering the practise of prayer to seek the highway of holiness is most natural and necessary. And if we seek instruction we shall find that our author has already provided an abundance of books on this all-important theme. There is *Sanctification, The Spiritual Life, The Second Blessing, The Two Covenants, Wholly for God*, and in Dutch ; *Een Beter Leven* (the Better Life) ; *Het Godzalig Leven* (The Godly Life), and *De Kracht van Jezus Bloed* (The Power of Jesus' Blood). We select only five, *Holy in Christ, Be Perfect, The Holiest of All, The Power of Jesus' Blood*, and *Humility*. But even of these we can only make a superficial study, sufficient, however, to show that this sanctification is what the Lord our God doth require of all without distinction for " without holiness no man shall see the Lord."

Taking them in their chronological order, we begin with *Holy in Christ*, which was published soon after *With Christ in the School of Prayer*, and like it is divided into thirty-one chapters, to be read daily through the month. They are entitled : " Thoughts on the Calling of God's Children to be Holy as He is holy." They are not sweet mediations to please and to soothe the soul, which like so many Daily Portions leave the soul fed and comforted in its sloth and sin. They are thoughts which we have to ponder. They are truths by which we are urged to be sanctified. If we compare this book with the later one, *The Holiest of All*, we shall find resemblances and yet considerable differences. The same thoughts are in both, but in the latter they are expanded and matured. The chapter " The Way into the Holiest," for example,

seems to have supplied the germ of *The Holiest of All.*
The difference appears in the arrangement for in the
latter book we have one hundred and thirty short chapters,
instead of the daily portion. Then the style is quite
changed, here is the fervour of the preacher glowing in
the expositions of the teacher. Like the writer to the
Hebrews he says : " And I beseech you, brethren, suffer
the word of exhortation." There is the most passionate
intreaty to advance like Joshua saying : " Let us go up,
we are well able to possess the land." It is this passion
for the reader's sanctification that animates him with the
truest eloquence. Fenelon says in his *Dialogues concerning eloquence* : " In order to make a lasting impression
on people's minds, we support their attention by moving
their passions," and he quotes Plato as saying : " The
oration that moves the passions of the hearers is true
eloquence." Applying this test, it must be said that in
this book his ripest, richest, and most spiritual expositions
are enforced by the noblest of eloquence. Dr. Denny
highly commends the book as holding a unique place
among commentaries on the Epistle to the Hebrews, of
which it is an accurate exposition as well as a devotional
study. The analysis at the beginning is admirable and
most useful to the reader.

It was a saying of Richard Baxter's that : " Illumination
is the first step in sanctification." The value of the first
book, *Holy in Christ*, is this, that it illuminates the mind
on this profound subject of Holiness in God, and in man.
The Notes at the end show that what is really meant by
Holiness is not so easily comprehended. Many theological
writers are quoted, mostly Continental. One English
divine, Howe, author of *The Living Temple*, is referred to
as saying : " The Divine Holiness is the most perfect
pulchritude, the ineffable and immortal pulchritude, that
cannot be declared by words or seen by eyes. It is the
very lustre and glory of His other perfections." What,
then, must be the vitiated taste, the total depravity of

man, the creature, who can see no beauty that he should desire Him in this glorious Being, his Creator and Redeemer.

There is another Note which explains the meaning of the word " holy," in Hebrew and Greek. To refer only to the Greek, Cremer shows in his Lexicon of New Testament Greek, that the word *hagos* is an entirely Biblical idea, and that the Scriptural conception of God's holiness is diametrically opposed to all the Greek notions. The very word and thought of holiness we owe distinctly to revelation. " Is not this the reason that though God has so distinctly called His people holy ones, the word holy has so little entered into the daily language and life of the Christian Church ? "

It may seem something like a digression in the foregoing Notes to have enquired into the essential nature of Divine Holiness, but to repeat Baxter's aphorism, " illumination is the first step in sanctification," we must understand what the pattern is, before we can imitate it. " Be ye holy, for I am holy. Like as He who has called you is holy." " There is not one standard of holiness for God and another for man," writes Dr. Murray, " The nature of light is the same, whether in the sun or a candle, and so the nature of holiness remains unchanged, whether it be in God or man in whom it dwells."

The command as it issues from the throne of God : " Be ye holy," is as imperative as the law of Sinai : " Thou shalt not kill," and as unalterable as the nature of God. And the sinful soul would sink to the bottomless pit of despair if God who demands were not the God who provides. " Give what thou commandest," said Augustine, " and command what thou wilt." And if we pass to the second chapter, entitled : " God's provision for Holiness," we shall discover that the thing which is impossible to man is possible to God, who has found in Christ the ransom to save man from going down to the pit. To the very men of Corinth once so debased, Paul writes : " Ye are holy in Christ Jesus," and Andrew Murray says : " In these two expressions, ' Holy,' ' In Christ,' we have, perhaps the most wonderful words of the Bible." The expression " in Christ " implies two moral facts. First, the act of faith by which the soul lays hold of Christ, and secondly the community of life contracted by means of this faith. The limb has the same life as the Head, the branch as the Vine, and this, and nothing less than this, expresses our vital, intimate relation with Christ who is the life indeed. The chapter on " Holiness and Faith " brings out this truth, by showing how the believing soul is to appropriate in personal experience gradually and unceasingly for the need of each moment, all which is treasured up in Christ Jesus, so that the man is " rich in faith " as well as rich " in Christ," and is not like a man having wealth in a distant bank while living here like a pauper in utmost need.

In Christ we see that the path to perfect holiness is perfect obedience. " The Holiness of God is death to all that is in contact with sin." In Christ's Crucifixion He reveals the law of sanctification. Holiness is the full entrance of our will into God's will, or rather holiness is the entrance of God's will to be the death of our will. " Obedience is not holiness, which is something higher. But obedience is indispensible to holiness ; it cannot exist without it."

These detached extracts will show that the objective holiness must become subjective, and like righteousness must be imparted as well as imputed, and there are two chapters, one " Holiness and Redemption," and the other " Holiness and Blameless," which insist that the truth must be held in righteousness of life, or it becomes the veriest delusion, and the most fatal danger. " Only holiness brings the assurance and enjoyment of Redemption. If I am seeking to hold redemption on lower grounds, I may be deceived. If I become unwatchful or careless, I should tremble at the very thought of trusting to redemption apart from holiness as its object." " For I am the

Lord that bringeth you out of the land of Egypt to be your God : ye shall, therefore, be holy, for I am holy."

C. W. Burns, the great Scotch Preacher, whose apostolic mantle seems afterwards to have fallen on him, and whose Bible and cloak it was young Andrew's honour to carry to his wonderful meetings in Aberdeen, once exclaimed in his pulpit : " Ah, the soul that has washed its filthy garments in the stream of Calvary, is careful how the remedy is used." And let it be added the soul that seeks ardently to possess God's holiness will be careful to avoid the reproach cast upon frequenters at Holiness Conventions, that they are not careful to adorn the doctrine of God in all things. For this reason the chapter " Holiness and Blameless " is written, which shows that the very words to express the faultlessness of the Lamb of God are to be applied to His followers : " That ye may be blameless and harmless as the sons of God." Forgetting this, a man intent on discovering the secret of holiness from the Divine side, may be tolerating faults which all around can see. " There have been such saints, holy yet hard, holy but distant, holy but sharp in judgment of others, holy but men around said unliving and selfish. If this be true, it is not the teaching of Holy Scripture which is to blame." " Selfishness and holiness are irreconcilable." " To love God and man is to be holy. In the intercourse of daily life, holiness can have its simple and sweet beginnings and its exercise ; so, in its highest attainment, love is made perfect." A prayerful study of his book *Humility as the Beauty of Holiness*, should be made in this connection.

The Preface to this anointed booklet opens with this sentence : " There are three great motives that urge us to humility. It becomes me as a creature, as a sinner, as a saint." The twelve chapters which follow show how it must manifest itself in each of these three relations. First, humility is the glory of the creature as such, whether sinless seraph or unfallen man ; the second chapter, " Humility : the Secret of Redemption," traces our need to the first Adam who by sin corrupted the race at " its very root with that most terrible of all sins and curses the poison of Satan's own pride." As surely as pride came from the first, so the new life of humility which overmasters it must come from the Second Adam our Redeemer. " Humility is the only soil in which the graces grow." In the Redeemer Himself humility shines resplendent in His Incarnation, the death on the Cross, His Ascension, and even now as the Lamb on the throne.

In the seventh chapter, " Humility and Holiness," the writer uses words that probe the wound, and make the sincere soul wince with pain lest it is deceived, " The one infallible test of our holiness will be our humility before God and men which marks us. Humility is the bloom and beauty of holiness." On the other hand, " The chief mark of counterfeit holiness is its lack of humility. Every seeker after holiness needs to be on his guard, lest unconsciously what was begun in the spirit be perfected in the flesh, and pride creep in where its presence is least suspected."

John Fletcher, Vicar of Madeley, is, perhaps, the best purely human illustration that these two qualities, holiness and humility, can be perfectly joined together. His contemporaries spoke of him as " the most unblameable man seen in Europe," as " an eminent saint," " as unearthly a being as could tread the earth," as " perhaps the most holy man since the apostolic age " and Dr. Elder Cumming in his book *Holy Men of God*, concludes his sketch by saying : " Perhaps a holier man never stood in English pulpit," and yet acknowledges that eminent humility was the most conspicuous trait in his beautiful character.

" Let all teachers of holiness, whether in the pulpit or on the platform, and all seekers of holiness, whether in closet or convention, take warning. There is no pride so dangerous because none so subtle and insidious as the pride of holiness." And again, " O, brethren, let us beware, unless we make with each advance in what we think holiness, the increase of humility our study, we may find that we have been delighting in beautiful thoughts and feelings, in solemn acts of consecration and faith, while the only sure mark of the presence of God, the disappearance of self was all the time wanting. Come and let us flee to Jesus, and hide ourselves in Him until we be clothed upon with His humility. That alone is our holiness."

None can deny that at least this teacher of the Higher Life, this prominent leader of the Holiness Movement, although so conspicuous in the esteem of the Churches, was enabled by God's grace to escape the danger of which he warns us, and to exemplify in public and private life the grace of humility which he so highly extols. Indeed, audiences in Europe and America were as much impressed by his meek and lowly deportment as they were enthralled by his impassioned utterances. Even his severest critics admired his Christlike bearing in hearing and replying to their needless objections to this teaching.

As the tree that bears most fruit bends lowliest, and almost breaks under its own weight, so the holier he grew in advancing years, and the more famous he became, the humbler he appeared and the more his very face shone with the glory within. Here, for example, is a letter written at the advanced age of 86, the very last received only five months before his departure. In speaking of the new edition of his message, " The Full Blessing of Pentecost," he says : " I forget almost what I have written," adding, " I, too, have still much to learn."

We have been told that on the 80th Birthday, Andrew Murray, with all his fire unquenched and vigour unabated, preached from a most appropriate text : " Now also when I am old and grey-headed, O God, forsake me not, until I have shewed Thy strength unto this generation and Thy power to every one that is to come." *Psalm* lxxi. 18.

God has abundantly answered that prayer, and even before it was uttered, God had begun to answer it in the already written book *The Holiest of All*, in some respects perhaps the best of his writings, where all are excellent. The inception of it was due to a Ministerial Conference at Somerset West, 1891. Here he shows what is the divine strength for Christian weakness, and the cure of what looks like an incurable malady judging from its prevalence and permanence in the Christian Church. To deal with it in the Apostolic day, the Epistle to the Hebrews was written, and because there is the same tendency to-day to decline, to decay and to depart from the living God, its message is needed still. The particular truth unfolded here is God's own specific for this terrible heart-failure. The heavenly truth about the glory and ministry of our Great High Priest would make heavenly people. " Holy brethren, partakers of our heavenly calling, let us consider Jesus Christ the Apostle, and High Priest of our confession." Reminding us that the word " consider " originally meant the contemplation of the stars by the astronomer, he says : " Let our study of the glory of Christ in this Epistle, be in the spirit of worship, let all tend to make us fall down in adoring worship."

It is said that a young artist entered the Cathedral in Antwerp to study Rubens' masterpiece, *The Descent from the Cross*, and he stood before it absorbed, until the sun began to decline. There he was found by the verger, who told him it was time to depart. To which he naively replied : " Sir, I was only waiting until these holy men had finished taking His Body down from the Cross." Oh, if one can study so intently a work of art, a mere pictorial representation of the dead Christ, what ought to be our adoring and absorbing contemplation of the living exalted Son, who appears now in the presence of God as our High Priest wearing the garments of beauty and glory ; perfect humanity and perfect divinity.

" The insight," says Andrew Murray, " into the more abundant glory, the divine all-surpassing greatness of His salvation is what will compel me to give up all to buy the Pearl of great Price."

Let us turn to the booklet he wrote with the title *Be Perfect*, wherein he unfolds verse by verse the true Scriptural teaching from Genesis to the Epistle of John, showing undisputably that there is on earth what God calls the perfection of His child. Space will not allow as was intended to give a summary of that inspiring booklet which first appeared in the *South African Pioneer* as a series of meditations, and which should be read without prejudice and with meekness, enough here to quote words which may fittingly prepare us to study in the right attitude the Perfection—Truth, which this Epistle is designed to teach. " Let us go on to prefection." " Perfecting holiness in the fear of God."

" Until the Church is seen prostrate before God seeking this blessing (Christian Perfection) as her highest good, it will be no small wonder if the very word Perfection, instead of being an attraction and a joy, is a cause of apprehension and anxiety, of division and offence."

It is in this posture, and in no other, that of prostration and adoration while we chant our *Te Deum* : " Thou art the King of Glory O Christ, Thou art the Everlasting Son of the Father," that we can learn what Christ's Ministry within the veil is, and how He can lead us into the Holiest of all and keep us there !

Starting, then, with the Divinity of Christ as the rock on which we rest—for with this the Epistle opens, we are told by our Author : " It is in virtue of His Divinity that he effected a real cleansing and putting away of sin, that He can actually communicate the divine life in us, that He can enter into our inmost being and dwell there. If we would but believe that Christ the Son, is God, is Jehovah the Eeternal One, the Creator, how He would make our inner life the proof of His Almighty Power. The deeper our insight into the true Godhead of our Lord Jesus Christ, His perfect oneness with God, the more confident shall we be that He will, with a Divine power make us partakers of His work, His life, His indwelling." This is the great salvation which we dare not neglect lest we drift away.

" There are too many Christians," he says, " who see in Christ only the fulfilment of what Aaron typified. Christ's death and blood are very precious unto them. They do seek to rest their faith upon them. And yet they wonder that they have so little of the peace and joy of the purity and power which the Saviour gives, and which faith in Him ought to bring. The reason is simple, because Christ is only their Aaron, not their Melchizedek. They do believe indeed that He ascended to Heaven and sits upon the throne of God, but they have not seen the direct connection of this with their daily spiritual life. They do not count upon Jesus working in them in the power of the heavenly life. They do not know their heavenly calling with the all-sufficient provision for its fulfilment in them, secured in the heavenly life of their Priest-King. And as a consequence of this they do not see the need for giving up the world to have their life and walk in heaven."

" The Cross proclaims the pardon of sin ! The throne gives power over sin. The Cross with its blood sprinkling is deliverance from Egypt, the throne with its living Priest-King brings us into the rest of God with its victory. And therefore I cannot urge my reader too earnestly to enter fully into the *infinite difference* between the two orders of the ministries of Aaron and Melchizedek."

One characteristic difference of vast importance is indicated by the phrase, " The power of an endless life " an indissoluble life. Life is contrasted with law, the older system with the new. Generation after generation the Aaronic priests appeard and departed through death, having performed merely isolated acts of service at the altar, and all external to the worshipper. *" These precious words, endless life, are the key to the Higher Life.* They show how he breathes into us His own life, And He works in us in the power of an endless life, that is strong and healthy because it is His own life from Heaven. An endless

' *indissoluble* ' life that never needs a break or interruption, because it is the life of eternity, the life that is maintained in us by Him who is a *Priest* for *ever*, a Priest who abideth continually."

If the reader gazes upon this life as upon a lofty ideal, beautiful but unattainable, he will argue he is not morally bound to attempt it, for as Professor Upham shows in his *Interior Life*—a real classic in holiness literature—it is really unphilosophic to urge us to do in the Christian Life what is actually impossible. We are reminded by Dr. Murray that it is a divine obligation imposed upon all for he says :

" It is not a question of some higher privilege which you are free to accept or reject. It is not left to your choice, O believer, whether you will receive the fulness of blessing which the Holy Ghost offers." To quote also from the book *Be Perfect*, " In the Church of to-day it is to be feared that the great majority of believers have no conception of their calling to be perfect. They have not the slightest idea that it is not only their duty to be religious, but *to be as eminently religious*, as full of grace and holiness as it is possible for God to make them."

Why is this so ? it may be asked. To quote from Marshall's *Gospel Mystery of Sanctification*, which Dr. Murray translated into Dutch, " *Holiness in this life is absolutely necessary to salvation*, not only as a means to an end but by a noble necessity, as part of the end itself." For one answer at least we quote once more from *The Holiest of All*, as follows, " The necessity of daily sinning, the impossibility of living for one day without actual transgression, is such a deeply-rooted conviction, and there is such confidence that God's Word teaches it, that the mind cannot for a moment enter into what the Word has said of the radical difference between the old covenant and the new in this respect. The confounding of the freedom from any sinful tendency, and freedom, in the power of Christ's indwelling, from actual sinning, even with the sinful tendency still remaining, is so universal that every attempt to press home the promise of the law written in the heart, in its contrast to the Old Testament life, is regarded as dangerous. The wonderful promise is levelled down to the ordinary Christian life, and entrance through the rent veil into the Holiest of All is postponed to another world."

It is evident from these words that Andrew Murray still held what is considered the orthodox teaching of a remaining sinful tendency, but also he held as quite compatible with this a freedom from actual sinning. In Dr. Smellie's *Life of Evan Hopkins*, the Keswick leader, he tells us how Bishop Moule (then Canon Moule) assured a friend that since the higher life had come to him, he felt he could sincerely pray, with hope of answer, " Vouchsafe O Lord to keep us this day without sin."

It is when we come to study carefully what Andrew Murray says about the infinite energy and efficacy of the precious Blood—and here it seems his profoundest, most original teaching comes out—that we can understand how Christ can save unto the uttermost.

" If the blood be to us, what it is to God, the boldness which God meant it to give will fill our hearts. The more we honour the blood, in its infinite worth, the more will it prove its mighty energy and efficacy in opening heaven to us, *and in us*, giving us in divine power the real living experience of what entrance into the Holiest is."

If entrance into the Holiest is so inexpressibly desirable, it is of the first and utmost importance that we should understand clearly where the Holiest is and what is meant by entering and dwelling there. Briefly it is a spiritual state of uninterrupted fellowship with God rather than a place. It is a condition, a sphere where the sanctified soul dwells in closest communion and fellowship with God. It was in the Holy of Holies the Shekinah dwelt, and to enter it now the Veil is rent means according to St. John to dwell in God and God in us.

Andrew Murray's conception is that the threefold division of the Temple may in a sense represent three degrees of Christian experience. There are the Outer Court Christians, who see the blood of sacrifice ; there are those in the Holy Place who also serve, but there are a third class consisting of those, who aspiring after God's best, understand what that wonderful saint said, "The Lord shows me, and more than ever, *that I must be made holy before death.*" "After I had lived," says someone "for thirteen years in the Holy Place seeking to serve God there, it pleased Him who dwelleth between the cherubim to call me to pass through the veil and to enter the Holiest of all through the blood of Jesus."

Here are two things specified, "through the veil" and "through the Blood," and we dare not disjoin them nor confuse them. To speak first of the Veil, what is that ? "The Veil that separated man from God was the flesh, human nature under the power of sin. Christ came in the likeness of sinful flesh, and dwelt with us outside the veil. Through the rent veil of His flesh, His will and life as yielded up to God in death, He entered into the Holiest. And this is the way He dedicated for us." It is the same way for us, sacrifice and death. "Whosoever accepts His finished work, *accepted what constitutes its spirit and power*, it is for every man as His Master—to put away sin by the sacrifice of self." In the addresses delivered in America published under the title, *The Spiritual Life*, he speaks about a "Second Conviction" of carnality—the flesh, which conviction comes to every Christian earnestly seeking holiness just as the conviction of guilt comes to the soul crying out for salvation. *Absolute Surrender*, the title of Dr. Murray's Addresses delivered in England, *is still God's ultimatum to the soul*. But no amount of self-denial, no entire consecration, although both are essential, will bring the soul into the Holiest. These only make it possible for the Eternal Spirit to work in us even as He empowered the Blessed Son to offer Himself on the Cross ;

and He works in us through the blood, and we enter by it, as our Exalted Forerunner, and complete Sacrifice entered into heaven itself through His Own Blood. " It is the cleansing of *sin* God insists on ; in a desire so intense that He gave His Son to die for it ! " " To live in God's presence and fellowship, two things must be clear, the *thought of sin* must be put away out of God's heart and the *love of sin* out of our heart. This double work is done by the Blood. Let us seek to cultivate large thoughts of what the Blood has effected, and can effect. The strange fascination, the irresistible attraction that word has is not without reason. There is no word in Scripture, in which all theology is so easily summed up. In earth and heaven, in each moment of our life, in each thought and act of worship, this word reigns supreme. There can be no fellowship with God but in the blood in the death of His Blessed Son."

Well may the newborn soul sing in its rapture, the song which is but the echo of the " harpers harping with their harps."

> " Covered is my unrighteousness,
>   Nor spot of guilt remains in me,
> While Jesus' blood through earth and skies,
>   Mercy, free boundless mercy cries."

And nothing shall be said to dim the glory of that blood as the objective propitiation in the government of God, and as the sole and only substitute for the guilty sinner, but what must be said, and not to lessen but to magnify its surpassing efficacy is this, that it is necessary to see and to show that the pardoned soul needs to be purified, and that the Blood of the Everlasting Covenant has assured the threefold blessing, sin for ever put away, the law written on the heart, and fellowship with a holy God, the joy of His people. " And that blood," says Andrew Murray, " such is its efficacy, heavenly cleansing power, can keep the soul clean so that no sin can touch us whereby we lose our fellowship with the Father." And again, " When the Holy Ghost comes into the heart with power He applies the Blood in a power far beyond what we can think or understand."

" Never," said the saintly John Smith, " have I felt a greater need of the blood of Jesus than now, and never have I been enabled to make a greater use of it."

' Now the Holiest with boldness
  We may enter in ;
For the open fountain cleanseth
  From all sin."

It is perhaps well for us at this stage to review the lessons we have so far learned as a mountaineer will pause and measure the height he has reached and review the scenery he has passed through.

We have come then to understand that there is what may be termed, Perfection-truth, unfolded in this Epistle. That it all centres in the person and ministry of our great High Priest, our Melchizedek, in the Holiest of All. Three things are said of Him, that He entered *once for all* into the Holiest, that He entered *through His Blood*, and that *He continues to apply* His Blood by His Spirit to His holy bretheren. Our study of these deep truths is not to leave our hearts as unaffected as the study of the higher mathematics leaves the student's conscience and will unmoved by his sublime calculations. It is feared that many read their Bible without understanding that the end and issue of reading is to make us holy. " The knowledge of the mysteries of God, of the highest spiritual truth cannot profit us. We have no capacity for receiving them except as our inward life is given up to receive as our's the perfection with which Jesus was perfected. When this disposition is found, the Holy Spirit will reveal to us that Christ hath perfected for ever in the power of the endless life those who are sanctified." This quotation is taken from *Be Perfect*, and the meditation which deals with the charge to press on to perfection. It is, therefore, not deeper knowledge, but a higher life, the heavenly calling, the power of the indissoluble life, that we are to experience and to experience even while we are on earth.

This is the conclusion of the whole matter. The Holiest of all is not only a place where the Saviour has entered for us ; *it is a spiritual state*, which before death the sanctified can enter, and remain there until death. It is entered by the blood applied through specific faith, and it is entered by one definite marked and well-remembered crisis, which may be expressed as Entire Consecration, or the Baptism of the Spirit and fire, or the Fulness of faith. John Bunyan seems to have described it as the Delectable Mountains, although he made the mistake of deferring it too much towards the end of the Pilgrim's Progress to the Celestial City. God's plan is that soon after conversion, the sooner the better, we should enter in. Payson, that godly minister, declared that even in the midst of his excruciating bodily sufferings his soul was happy in God and that he could date his letter according to his spiritual experience from the Delectable Mountains and the land of Beulah. Dr. Murray tells us, in *Aids to Devotion*, of a lady who sought and found the fulness of blessing, and retained it, and who, when a minister said to her : " But you cannot always live on the mountain," replied : " Yes, you can, for I am always living there." Others have realised on earth the fulfilment of the promise : " Thy sun shall no more go down."

In a remarkable book which relates truthfully the " Deeper Experience of Famous Christians," such as Madame Guyon, Fenelon, George Foxe, Wesley, Whitfield, Fletcher, Christmas Evans, Bramwell, General Booth, Moody, Dr. Gordon, A. B. Earle, Havergal and others, it is made abundantly clear from their own testimony and the fruits that followed this experience that they, after their conversion sooner or later by a definite crisis, as marked as a birth, or a death, or a marriage, passed into

a new state and experience, a new relation to Christ and
the Holy Spirit, and a new apprehension and application
of the all-cleansing power of the Blood to cleanse and to
keep clean. From all these witnesses, so illustrious and
reliable, we call up one, whose name is a household word,
whose Sacred Songs have been sung in the Church of God
everywhere in rapturous strains. We mean Frances
Ridley Havergal. Her deeper experience is selected
because it furnishes a concrete example of the wondrous
power of the blood of the Lamb, which Andrew Murray
considers to be the special teaching of the Epistle to the
Hebrews : " How much more shall the blood of Christ
cleanse."

Before asking Frances Ridley Havergal to relate her
vivid experience of the purifying, transforming effect of
the Redeemer's blood on her heart, life and service, the
reader ought to be introduced to one more book by Andrew
Murray on the subject of Holiness, namely : *De Kracht
Van Jezus Bloed* (the Power of the Blood of Jesus) which
contains twenty addresses on this transporting theme.

As we learn from his introduction, it was on his voyage
to Europe, 1882, that he meditated much on the expression
" There is power in the blood," and his memory recalled
the popular hymn in which the words are repeated again
and again :

> " There is power in Jesus' blood
> It washes me white as snow."

The more he meditated, the more he enquired in the
spirit of prayer : What is this power, and why has it this
power ?   And the following year, on his return, he decided
to give the answer to the question in a series of fifteen
addresses delivered in the Dutch Church during the season
of preparation for Easter, corresponding to what is otherwise called Lent.   Five other addresses were subsequently
added, and the whole published in the *Kerkbode* the
Magazine of the Dutch Church.

Just think of the intellectual concentration and spiritual

illumination ; the richness of thought and freshness of language sustained to the very end of two hundred and eight pages on one truth only, that the spiritual experimental power of the blood is *absolutely necessary for the soul's conscious and joyous fellowship with God.*

The chapter on Redemption through blood deals with its necessity because of sin, which entails God's wrath on the sinner, and prevents his fellowship with a thrice-holy God.

Cleansing through the blood is the title of the fourth chapter. The initial grace of pardon prepares the soul for the sanctification (subjective) which God provides. In this chapter the language is most unequivocal, as to the marvellous efficacy of the blood on the surrendered heart and will.

For example take the following sentences kindly translated for this section : " The conscience purged by the blood witnesses to nothing less than an entire and full salvation. At the slightest stumbling the soul finds immediate restoration and cleasning. The heart can be kept each moment under the protection the cleansing and sanctifying power of the blood. Sinful lusts and desires are destroyed. The blood of Jesus Christ cleanseth from all sin. The blood works its spiritual heavenly power in the soul. Purity of heart must be the mark of each child of God because it is the indispensable condition of fellowship and the enjoyment of His salvation. Cleansing from sin is only the preparation for holiness which is the full blessing the blood brings in."

The seventh chapter, " The indwelling in the Holiest by the blood," may have been in the author's mind the anticipation and introduction to his later and greater work, *The Holiest of All*, with its profound theology and exalted spirituality. Two sentences from this chapter must suffice, " When the blood of Christ works with power there always follows death to self. The flesh must be offered up and given over to death."

These thoughts, as we have seen, are worked out more thoroughly and constantly in *The Holiest of All*, and it may be advisable to explain here to those who think it is too fanciful and transcendental to think of the life in the Holiest as a present earthly experience, that this same explanation is given by the author of *The Real Christian*, who has one chapter entitled the " Holiest of All." He says : " 'The Holiest of All ' was God's special place of abode. In real Christianity this abode is in the Holy Spirit transferred to the believer." He quotes with approval Andrew Murray's book, and Dean Alford's Commentary, which says : " Materially we are yet in the body : but in the spirit we are in heaven."

Before Miss Havergal passed into this deeper experience, she had had an unmistakable conversion, leading to a life of entire devotion to her Saviour and continual service for Him unchecked by any deviation from the path of righteousness, or backsliding into sloth, worldliness or sin. Still, she longed for a deeper, richer, fuller experience. In her *Gleams and Glimpses* she wrote " Oh to be filled with the Holy Ghost." Once she wrote : " Oh that He would indeed purify me, and make me white at any cost," and again : " I wait for the hour when He will reveal Himself to me more directly, according to *John* xiv. 21." And by a crisis, as distinct as her conversion, she passed into this second experience of grace, and her Journals and Letters, a rich heritage for the Church of God, show us what intimate communion she enjoyed with the Triune God, whom she adoringly loved, until her very body was overwhelmed with " that speechless awe which dares not move." At length the long looked for experience came, and lifted her whole life into perpetual sunshine. The " Sunless ravines " were for ever passed. She could now sing : " Like a river glorious is God's perfect peace." What was it brought this transformation ? It was a little booklet, setting forth the fulness in Jesus. She read its contents and the letter of her correspondent explaining the power of the Blood to cleanse from all sin. To this she sent a joyous reply : " *I see it all and I have the blessing.*" She saw it as a flash of electric light. She remembered the place, Winterdine, in the Midland Counties, and the day, December 2nd, 1873. She saw that there must be a full and true consecration before blessing. Absolute surrender as Andrew Murray insists. Then trust in the Blood to cleanse from all sin, all means and all power to keep clean because of the present tense " cleanseth." " It goes on cleansing, and I have no words to tell how my heart rejoiceth in it. Not a coming to be cleansed in the fountain only, but a remaining in the fountain, so that it may and can go on cleansing."

" One of the intensest moments of my life was when I saw the force of that word ' *cleanseth.*' The utterly unexpected and altogether unimagined sense of its fulfil-ment to me, on simply believing in its fulness, was just indescribable. *I expected nothing like it short of heaven.*"

What more shall we say, what further need have we of witnesses ? There is enough to confirm Andrew Murray's luminous exposition of this most glorious epistle, that one can enter into the Holiest now through the blood, " *and heaven comes down our souls to meet,*" even while we are on the way to heaven. Need we be surprised that when at length, after a life of holiness and still more fruitful service that when she came to die, suffering could not prevent her saying : " *God's will is delicious.* It is so beautiful to go. It is all perfect peace. I only wait for Jesus to take me in. When I am gone, let my favourite text be put on my tomb, ' the blood of Jesus Christ His Son cleanseth from all sin.' "

Oh, that like her, all the saints of God would seek to have the blood on the heart and to testify to its power. The danger is in thinking such an experience as her's and others like it are exceptional, and holiness is optional. But the possibility argues its necessity ; *that it is attainable shows it is indispensible.* But if there are allurements to incite us to progress heavenward, there are temptations to turn back, and in the Epistle five solemn warnings are sounded to prevent our going back to perdition.   Holiness is our only safety, " To be sure of being kept from wilful sin, let us keep from all sin.   The only sure sign that *the perseverance of the saints will be ours is perseverance in sainthood*, in sanctification and obedience."

Chapter XXII

THE NECESSITY OF THE PENTECOSTAL SPIRIT

FOR LIFE AND SERVICE

" Ye shall receive power, the Holy Ghost coming upon you."
Acts i. 8.

" Oh, my friends, let us wrestle for a more abundant outpouring of the Spirit."—*John Fletcher*

In the preface to *Holy in Christ*, there occurs this sentence : " *There is such a thing as a Pentecost still.*" This assurance is the connecting link between this present section and the preceding. There is not only a logical connection in thought, but a vital relation between Holiness and the Spirit who is called holy, not because He is more holy than the Father or the Son, but because as the Executive of Godhead, *He* undertakes to communicate the holiness of Christ to us. The vital truth of the New Testament, the Christian is Holy in Christ, needs as its correlative; the Holy One is in the Christian. And the outcome of personal holiness must be active service for Christ in saving men. " The single aim of the Blessing of Pentecost is to reveal Jesus as a Saviour so that He may exhibit His power to redeem souls in us and by us, here in this world." And again : " We have said more than once, that the Spirit comes as power for work. How can anyone ever dream of having the Spirit of Christ otherwise than as a Spirit who aims at the work of God in the salvation of souls. It is an impossibility." So we read in *The Full Blessing of Pentecost*.

In a remarkable book entitled *Holiness and Power*, the inseparable connection betwixt the two experiences is asserted and abundantly illustrated, the writer says : " It was the power of the Holy Ghost upon the heart and life of Andrew Murray that has caused his spiritual influence to be felt throughout Christendom, and his books about Christ and the Spiritual Life are like a spice-laden breeze carrying refreshment to the whole Christian world ! "

The principal works dealing with the Person and offices of the Holy Ghost are *The Spirit of Christ, The Full Blessing of Pentecost, Back to Pentecost, The Divine Indwelling,* and *The Power of the Spirit* (consisting of extracts from William Law) and several books in Dutch.

It was *Abide in Christ* that first introduced the writer to this new author, and it was *The Spirit of Christ* that revealed a master-mind in dealing luminously and authoritatively with the deep things of God's Spirit as they affect the human spirit. One became convinced for the first time that the Spirit of God must have absolute supremacy in study, in devotion, in public worship and preaching, and consequently the evil power most to be dreaded was the carnal mind, self, the soulish nature in its intrusion into out holiest hours and our most earnest efforts to serve God. It was at this time that one became acquainted with Pember's writings and with a saintly lady, deeply taught of God, who subsequently went as missionary to China, and they both confirmed Andrew Murray's profound teaching as to the supreme exhalation of the Divine Spirit in illuminating and ruling man's spirit, and the consequent subordination of everything to Him who proceedeth from the Father and the Son. This principle runs like a golden thread through all his books. He never tires in insisting upon it, and it is a marvel that he never wearies the reader in inculcating this underlying principle of the spiritual life. One sentence of his explains both system and method, " Accept this as the secret of the life of Christ in you, the Holy Spirit is dwelling in the hidden recesses of your spirit." This principle is undoubtedly the secret of Andrew Murray's perennial power and world-wide popularity in books that have no attraction or style. Doubtless he could be eloquent if he wished, but he would not write with enticing words but only and always in the demonstration of the Spirit and of power. And the following incident explains the reason of his simple style.

In Cape Town a friend once showed him a very eloquent and rhetorical book on Missions. " Do you think," said Andrew Murray, " that a man full of the Holy Ghost would make such a studied display of his own brilliant talents ? " It is remarkable that this writer received a fresh infilling of the Spirit, and his style of writing was soon manifestly changed.

Turning first to the book *The Divine Indwelling*, let us mark these searching words in the Preface. " We think that we know what is meant by the words, the Holy Spirit being sent into our hearts. Christ dwelling in our hearts. God being the God of our life and working all in us, while the Divine Magnificence of these conceptions neither overwhelms, nor attracts us."

(1) *The Place of the Indwelling.*

If we are to know what it means, it is of the first importance to understand what is the place of the indwelling, and the Note C. at the end of *The Spirit of Christ* gives an exhaustive explanation. To condense it briefly. According to Biblical psychology, man's nature is tripartite, threefold, consisting of spirit, soul and body. The soul is the seat and organ of man's human personality ; by it man is linked to the visible world through the body, and on the other side through the spirit to the unseen and divine. God's plan was for the soul to follow the lead of the spirit, and in Eden man was left voluntarily to decide whether the soul would yield to the spirit and be carried up to God, or yield to the solicitations of the body and be dragged down to the dust. Man made his fatal choice, and in the Fall the soul became the slave of the body and became flesh. The spirit lost its crown, threw away its sceptre and its kingdom was given to another.

The spirit now stands in opposition to the flesh, the Scriptural name given to the life of the soul and body together in their subjection to sin.

To gather up what has been said. The spirit is the organ of the God-consciousness; the soul of the self-consciousness; the body of the world-consciousness. In the spirit God dwells, in the soul self, in the body sense. By the fall the right relation was subverted, and the soul, self, selfishness, became the ruling principle.

Climbing once the Welsh mountains, the traveller accidentally let fall his aneroid which recorded the height he was ascending, as well as changes in the atmosphere. From that moment it lost its power to do either, and it never recovered it. So terrible is the effect of the Fall of Adam that our faculties are now unable to perform their original functions. The Fall is twofold, not only from our original righteousness, but also from the God-given wisdom. Even in the regenerate unless one is filled and dominated always by the Holy Spirit, the subordinate powers will try to be supreme. " And now so subtle and mighty is this spirit of self that not only in sinning against God, but even when the soul learns to serve God it still asserts its powers and refuses to let the spirit alone lead, and in its efforts to be religious is still the great enemy that ever hinders the operations of the Spirit." As William Law insists : " The inward work of God is hindered by bad men, through their obedience to earthly passions ; by good men through their striving to be good in their own way, by their natural strength and a multiplicity of seemingly holy labours and contrivances."

Just as Ithuriel, by his spear piercing the toad squatting close by the ear of innocent Eve discovered Satan in Paradise, so Andrew Murray reveals to us Satan appearing in our holiest service for God, using his crafty device to keep souls in bondage by inciting to a religion in the flesh. He knows how, in due time, the flesh that has gained supremacy over the spirit in service for God, will assert and maintain that same supremacy in the service of sin. " And," says he, " if I am to deny self in intercourse with men and to conquer selfishness and temper and want of love, I must first learn to deny self in intercourse with God. *There* the soul, the seat of self, must learn to bow to the spirit where God dwells." As Mrs. Penn-Lewis says in her new book *Soul and Spirit*, " Only that which comes from the Holy Ghost through your spirit has its origin in God."

" Believers need to be reminded," Dr. Murray adds, " that deeper than mind, and feeling and will, deeper than the soul itself where these have their seat, in the depths of the spirit, that comes from God, there comes the Holy Spirit to dwell."

" The Lord is in His holy temple, let all the earth keep silence before Him."

In a Russian-poem of rare excellence, printed, it is said, in letters of gold, the poet is made to say : " Yes, in my spirit, does Thy Spirit shine, as shines the sunbeam in a drop of dew," but how different in this poetical conception from the profound spiritual significance of the Saviour's parting promise : " For He dwelleth with you and shall be IN you." This is the theme dealt with in Andrew Murray's sixth chapter, " The Divine Indwelling," which he explains thus : " The eternal life was to become the very life of man hiding itself within the very being and consciousness, and clothing itself in the form of a human will and life." " He is to be one with us in the absoluteness of a Divine immanence dwelling in us, even as the Father in the Son and the Son in the Father." " Out of the hidden depths His power will move to take possession of mind and will, and the indwelling in the hidden recesses of the heart will grow into a being filled with His fulness."

It is evident from this overwhelming and awe-inspiring conception of the Divine Indwelling, that it cannot be a mere mechanical filling, like water poured into a cup, it is vital because spiritual, and capable of expansion, as Godet puts it, " Man is a vessel destined to receive God. A vessel which must be enlarged in proportion as it is filled, and filled in proportion as it is enlarged," and, therefore, it can be spoken of as an experience that will grow.

At the Last Supper, the departing Lord promised wonderful and unprecedented things as the result of the Advent of the Other Paraclete—power to witness to the facts of Redemption ; power to convince of sin a world about to reject its only Saviour ; power to apprehend spiritual truth ; power to see the surpassing glory of the rejected Man of Sorrows, but as we are told, " Before all this, as its own condition and only source " (the realisation of these magnificent prospects) " Christ places the promise : " *The Spirit shall be in you.*"   It avails little that we know all that the Spirit can do for us, or that we confess our entire dependence upon Him, unless we clearly realise, and place first what the Master gave the first place to, that is, that it is as the Indwelling Spirit alone that He can be our Teacher and strength."

Continual failure comes from neglect of this fundamental truth and blessing can only come from an intelligent devout recognition of it as an essential condition for the reception of the Baptism of power.

In the chapter entitled, " The Temple of the Holy Spirit," one of the most devout in the book, where the analogy of the three-fold division of Solomon's temple is worked out suggestively as indicating the threefold way of the divine approach to man as well as man's approach to God, he says with reverential awe :   " I will meditate and be still, until something of the overwhelming glory of the truth fall upon me, and faith begin to realise it :   I am His Temple and in the secret place He sits upon the throne."   Then at the close this prayer rises like incense : " I do now tremblingly accept the blessed truth :   God the Spirit, the Holy Spirit, who is God Almighty dwells in me. O, my Father, reveal within me what it means lest I sin against Thee by saying it and not living it."

If the believer is to be what Moule describes as a " living water course, a living secondary cause in others of faith, though not an original fountain, for only Christ is that," it can only be because the prospect of Pentecost is realised. " This "—the influence flowing out like rivers of living water—" spake He of the Spirit." The second chapter explains and applies the promise of Christ's forerunner, " He shall baptise you with the Holy Ghost." The note to this chapter should be carefully studied where the two rival theories of the Spirit's Baptism, the one advocated by Asa Mahan and the other by Ernest Boys, are discussed but not without this word of rebuke : " This surely is a proof of how much we are lacking its full experience. Where the Spirit is in great power He will bring His own evidence that we have the Baptism and what it includes."

(2) *The Promise of the Father.*

Let us read his explanation of what the Promise of the Father means. " The Baptism of the Holy Ghost," he says, " is the crown and glory of Jesus' work, and we need it, and must know that we have it if we are to live the true Christian life. It is more than the Spirit's work in regeneration. It is the personal Spirit of Christ making Him present with us, always abiding in the heart in the power of His glorified nature. It is the Spirit of the life of Christ Jesus making us free from the law of sin and death, and bringing us as a personal experience into the liberty from sin, to which Christ redeemed us, but which to so many regenerate is only a blessing registered on their behalf, but not possessed or enjoyed. It is the induement with power to fill us with boldness in the presence of every danger, and give the victory over every enemy. Whether we look upon this Baptism as something we already have, or something we must receive in this all agree it is only in the fellowship of Jesus, in faithful attachment and obedience to Him, that a baptised life can be received or maintained or renewed." "Ye shall receive power, the Holy Ghost coming upon you."

If we accept this as a Scriptural definition or description of what it is, and how it is received, let us devoutly kneel and join with our author in his petition at the close of this chapter.

"My Holy Lord! I bless Thee that the Holy Spirit is in me too. But Oh! I beseech Thee give me yet the full, the overflowing measure Thou hast promised. O my Lord Jesus! Baptise me, fill me with the Holy Spirit. Amen."

If this prayer is to be answered something must be done on our part. In Goodwin's great work on the Holy Spirit, he says we must use means which have a kind of sacramental efficacy to secure the blessing. Trying to obtain this priceless gift is not he says like seeking a prize in a lottery when you may receive only a blank. Christ's promise is twofold, and cannot fail. "I will pray the Father, and He shall give." "He that asketh receiveth."

Will it help us if we suggest that the first requisite is understanding, the second believing, and the third waiting. "Wait! Tarry! The one final condition imposed by the ascending Lord for the fulfilment of the promise."

(1) *We put understanding first* and not prayer, for this order was Christ's method with the Woman at the Well. "If thou knewest the gift of God and Who it is, that asketh of thee, thou wouldest ask of Him and He would give." But, do we know Him as the Baptiser imparting the Holy Ghost or only as the Atoner, the Lamb of God taking away the sin of the world. And yet John's message was a double one, "the same is He who baptiseth as well as atoneth" like the king's ministers, holding the two-fold office of Premier and Chancellor. And if Frances Ridley Havergal, as we have seen, received such blessing through the new apprehension of the present tense "*cleanseth*" shall we ignore the same tense "*baptiseth*" as applied to

the bestowal of that supreme gift, which was purchased by the precious Blood of Redemption. If we know Him not as the Baptiser, how can we know His peculiar Pentecostal gift. We must distinguish things that differ and perhaps there is no more luminous distinction than that made by Bishop Westcott, the Paschal and Pentecostal Spirit. First, the Paschal reception when on the glorious Easter, the Risen Lord breathed into them and said : " Receive ye the Holy Ghost " ; and the Pentecostal, when the now exalted Lord poured down in unmeasured floods what He had just as the reward of His redeeming work received from the Father : " Therefore God hath anointed thee with the oil of gladness above Thy fellows." ." Thou hast ascended up on high and received gifts for men." " Having received of the Father He hath poured forth this."

The chapter on " The Outpouring of the Spirit " will explain why there was an entirely new manifestation of the Eternal Spirit on the Day of Pentecost. We only refer to it to quote the opening sentence : " In the outpouring of the Holy Spirit, the work of Christ culminates." We notice how everything which preceded it, the Incarnation, Crucifixion, Resurrection, Ascension, were only preliminary stages, but their goal and their crown was the coming down of the Holy Spirit. But not only the glory of if, it is the mystery of it which shines in the following words of rare beauty and energy, " But that the same Spirit (who came to the Saviour's immaculate body at Bethlehem) should now come and dwell in the bodies of sinful men, that in them, the Father should take up His abode, this is a mystery of grace that passeth all understanding. But this, glory be to God, is *the blessing Pentecost brings and secures.*"

No wonder with this exalted conception of Christ's purpose to actually restore the lost Indwelling, Dr. Murray should write in his preface to William Law's teaching on this transcendent theme such words as these : " This blessing is so wonderful, so spiritual, so altogether super-natural, that so few seek after it or receive it in its Divine fulness." And it was to arouse people to think about it that with intense fervour surpassing anything in any other of his writings, he wrote *The Full Blessing of Pentecost* in order to urge them to lay aside everything to obtain it. In the introduction he says : "The message which this little book brings is simple, but most solemn, *It is to the effect that the one thing needful for the Church, and the thing which, above all others, men ought everywhere to seek for with one accord and with their whole heart, is to be filled with the Spirit of God.*"

A missionary home on furlough was the guest, in a city where he was speaking on behalf of missions, of an enthusiastic admirer of Andrew Murray as evidenced by the walls of two rooms being adorned with his portrait. His host shewed him a large collection of his writings, with the remark : " I have read most of Andrew Murray's books, and I owe everything in my spiritual life to him." The visitor enquired if he had read *The Full Blessing of Pentecost*. He replied that he had never seen it, but would at once purchase it. Reader ! Go thou and do likewise ! It was not long before a letter was received from him, saying : " I am reading for the second time *The Full Blessing of Pentecost*. It is priceless, and I think I can say that I have received the filling to some extent. The study of this book has, I think, been the explanation of the blessing here." He refers to the immediate success God gave him in winning many souls, first in a Military Camp during the Great War, and then in conducting special missions.

The following sentences, which are taken at random, will give some idea of the sublime magnificence of the gift.

" The unheard-of wonder, the mystery of ages was to be their portion " (on the day of Pentecost). " They were to know that they were in Him, and He in them. What is promised us is a wonderful work of Divine Omnipotence and love. The gift of the Holy Ghost is the most personal act of the Godhead. It is the goodness of God alone that must give it. It is His Omnipotence that must work it in us. The blessing of Pentecost is a supernatural gift, a wonderful act of God in the soul. My brethren! it is an unspeakably holy and glorious thing that a man can be filled with the Spirit of God."

In the second chapter entitled " How glorious it is " it is set forth as a sevenfold blessing :

(1) The abiding presence of Jesus, " This was the source of all the other things that came at Pentecost."

(2) The life and power of sanctification. " This in very truth is still the only way of a real sanctification, a life that actually overcomes sin."

(3) A heart overflowing with love. " The Spirit, the disposition, the wonderful love of Jesus, filled them because He himself had come into them."

(4) Weakness changed into strength. " It is the joy of the blessing of Pentecost that gives courage and power to speak for Jesus, because by it the whole heart is filled with Him."

(5) The Scriptures were illuminated from heaven. " The whole of their ancient Scriptures opened up before them ; the light of the Holy Spirit in them illumined the Word."

(6) The blessing blessed others. " Alike in preaching and in the daily life of a servant of Christ, the full blessing of Pentecost is the sure way of becoming a blessing to others."

(7) Pentecost makes the Church what it ought to be " The power of Jewish prejudice, and of pagan hardness of heart was overcome, and the Church of Christ won glorious triumphs. This grand result was achieved simply and only because the first Christian Church was filled with the Spirit. He dwelt in them and wrought in them all His wondrous deeds. It is to this same experience that the Church of Christ in our age must come back. This is the only thing that will help her in the conflict with mere

civilisation or paganism, with sin or the world. *She must be filled with the Spirit."*

As a contrast to the ideal Church of Pentecost, the following chapter : " How little it is enjoyed," sets forth in sombre colours the actual state of the Church of to-day. And this not because of some natural inability or infirmity, but because of inexcusable guilt in not seeking and securing the proferred grace. For in the chapter " How the Blessing is Hindered " it is stated that it is not some insuperable external obstacle, but the internal, unchangeable self ; the infernal poison of price that exalts itself. " To the minutest details always and in everything, you must deny that self-life ; otherwise the life of God, cannot possibly fill you." In his book on Humility, Dr. Murray does not scruple to call self " the poison of Satan's own pride," as we have already seen.

Bodily suffering may really be sin if it is caused by knowingly indulging in food unsuitable, as Christians indulge in unwholesome literature ; or in neglecting fresh air and exercise as Christians omit secret prayer and service, therefore the lamented powerlessness of the Church must be branded as guilt because it rejects the all-sufficient might, and neglects the means to obtain it. The conviction must be brought home that people are not living the life of Pentecost, and then they must confess the guiltiness of this condition. " They ought to see that if they have not yet rendered obedience to the command ' Be filled with the Spirit,' this defect is to be ascribed to sluggishness and self-satisfaction and unbelief."

In this connection, the sinfulness of this deficiency may appear by quoting Finney's estimation of the threefold guilt of not being filled, words that can never to any serious mind lose their awful solemnity how often repeated. " Our guilt is measured (1) By the paramount authority of Him who commands us to be filled ; (2), By the evil which we have done by not being filled ; (3) By all the good which we might have done if we had been filled."

These searching and crushing words are inserted here after having read afresh Mahan's Baptism of the Holy Ghost and especially the chapters by Finney on the Enduement of Power attached to it. It seems impossible that anyone can read these arguments and copious illustrations and personal testimonies and not rise up with the burning conviction there *is* such a divine bestowment of power promised in the Scripture ; and then overwhelmed with a sense of utter and absolute need, fall down with strong crying tears to implore this indispensable gift. "This enduement " writes Finney, " is nothing or it is *everything* in the sense of being wholly indispensable for success."

To quote again from *The Full Blessing of Pentecost*, only one paragraph—and it would be spoiled if not given in full —we shall see that Dr. Murray agrees with Finney that it is indispensable. " *I must have the blessing at any cost.* To get possession of the pearl of great price the merchant man had to sell *all that he had*. The full blessing of Pentecost is to be obtained at no smaller price. He that would have it must sell all, must forsake all sin to its smallest item, the love of the world in its most innocent forms, self-will in its simplest and most natural expressions, every faculty of our nature, every moment of our life, every pleasure that feeds our self-complacency, every exercise of our body, soul and spirit—all must be surrendered in the power of the Spirit of God. In nothing can independent control or independent force have a place : everything—everything I say—must be under the leading of the spirit. One must indeed say, ' Cost what it may I am determined to have this blessing.' "

Will the reader on bended knee repeat these words to his Redeemer and Lord, " *Cost what it may, I am determined to have this blessing,*" or will he turn away with a sigh as a minister did in a Cape Town book-room, who having purchased the book and looked at its contents said, " *Ah, Mr. Murray puts the price too high.*" But no that were impossible, for Mr. Murray has already said, " Count nothing too precious or too costly to give as an exchange for this pearl of great price." As Job says of wisdom, " It cannot be valued with the gold of Ophir, with the precious onyx or sapphire."

In his book, " Back to Pentecost " with its rousing trumpet blast to a sleeping Church, he says of the early disciples, and their giving up of their all, " It was this complete surrender of the whole heart and life which was accepted by Christ as the preparation that made them capable of receiving the fulness of the Spirit." It is true, true to Scripture and experience, that we receive the Promise of the Spirit through faith, but it is forgotten that faith itself demands its own condition, and that is nothing short of a deliberate, entire and irrecoverable dedication of all our powers to the Redeemer's Kingdom. " I will place no value on anything I possess " said Livingstone " except in relation to the Redeemer's Kingdom." When this is done, the soul like a bird with wings capable of flying is able to believe, but without this consecration man is morally incapable of believing for it.

(2) *There must be believing* as well as understanding. " When once you have made this choice cleave firmly to what is the chief element in it—namely, the faith that expects this blessing as a miracle of divine omnipotence. Contemplate yourself in faith as a man betwixt whom and God a firm compact has been made that you must receive the full blessing. You may take it for granted it will surely come." This is what Professor Upham calls " The Faith of Acceptance." Andrew Murray's Chapter in *The Spirit of Christ* entitled " The Spirit through Faith," should be consulted at this critical juncture lest the soul should be deceived with a dead faith, the mere semblance of this vital reality and God-given energy. We learn there in that chapter that faith is not an independent act of the will apart from the man's life, or God's truth ; nor is it passive, but receptive in the conscious presence of God and His Word. It deals with the Promiser first as well as the promise. Abraham is the father of the faithful

and the pattern of faith. Abraham standing in His presence and hearing His living voice believed God. Exercising faith as an organ of the spirit, as a spiritual sense, the soul hears the living voice of the Almighty saying, " So shall thy seed be, so shall thy Pentecostal power be " ; and it sees the invisible and finds it easy to believe in the improbable. " Out of Him shall flow *rivers* of living water."

" To read, to think, to long and to pray, to concentrate ourselves and grasp the promises, to hold fast the blessed truth, the Spirit dwells within us ; all this is good in its place, *but does not bring the blessing.* The one thing needful is to have the heart filled with faith in the living God, and in that faith to abide in living contact with Him ; in that faith, to wait, and worship and work as in His holy presence. In such fellowship with God the Holy Spirit fills the heart."

> " Obedient faith that waits on Thee,
> Thou never wilt reprove,
> But Thou wilt form, Thy Son in me,
> And perfect me in love."

(3) *Then waiting upon God* is the third and supreme condition following the two former directions of under-standing and believing. But the objection is at once raised by many, " Why should we Christians of the Twentieth Century wait ? " For them of the first age Pentecost was an anticipation, to us it is a commemoration. For them it was a promise, for us it is an accomplished fact, and a feast. True indeed, but as miracle becomes parable, history prophecy, this experience of the first disciples has set the pattern for all time. " See that thou make all things after the pattern shown on the Mount." " Pentecost is the glorious sunrise of that day, the first of those days of which the prophets and our Lord had so often spoken. Let the Church return to Pentecost, and Pentecost will return to her. The Spirit of God cannot take possession of believers beyond their capacity of receiving Him." Thus we read in the chapter on " The outpouring of the Spirit," and

turning to the other chapter where the charge to wait for the Promise of the Father is specially dealt with, he shows, *that the ten days' waiting is meant to be for all time the posture before the throne*, which secures in continuity the Pentecostal blessing. And all this asking, paradoxical as it may seem, is shown to be in perfect harmony with our first reception of the Holy Ghost. " The Father has indeed given us the Spirit ; but He is still, and only works as the Spirit of the Father. He is indeed our's, *but our's as God.*" " When God gives His Spirit He gives His inmost self." " The fulness of the Spirit, and our waiting are inseparably and for ever linked together." If we turn to the little book so richly blessed of God entitled *Waiting on God*, we find one whole chapter given to this command to wait for the promise of the Father. One sentence will suffice, " Each moment the same Spirit that is in us is in God too, *and he who is most full of the Spirit will be the first to wait on God most earnestly*, further to fulfil His promise and still strengthen him mightily by His Spirit in the inner man." In giving His Spirit God does not part with Him as we give away our money to a beggar.

But if this is necessary for him who is " most full," what of him who is empty, who has never experienced its power ? " If they do these things in a green tree what will they do in a dry ? " His answer to the anxious question as to why those who are really burdened with the felt want of this blessing, and who to relieve their want have tried to believe and tried to lay hold and tried to be filled and yet have failed, is this, " *They have never known what it was with it all to wait.*"

For their sakes it may be helpful to ask, How then shall we wait ? The answer is that it must be in devout worship, " The Holy Ghost is given *in* worship and *for* worship." Prior to Pentecost they were continually in the temple praising God, and as God is a blessed Trinity, we must worship Father, Son and Holy Ghost.

" If we believe " says Goodwin quoted approvingly by

Dr. Murray, " that the Holy Ghost is a person in the Trinity let us treat with Him as a Person, apply ourselves to Him, glorify Him in our hearts as a Person."

" Hail ! Holy Ghost, Jehovah, Third
In order of the Three ;
Sprung from the Father and the Word
From all eternity."

" God's image, which our sins destroy,
Thy grace restores below ;
And truth, and holiness, and joy,
From Thee their fountain flow."

It is sometimes tremblingly asked " *Is it right to pray to the Holy Ghost ?* " as if so doing it were defrauding the Father and the Son of their divine rights. Handley Moule in his *Veni Creator* reverently discusses this question and firmly answers affirmatively and gives his reasons for so doing and says, " We are to pray *to* as well as *in* the Holy Ghost." There can be only one answer if we really believe He is essentially God, and, as Augustine shows, His Deity is manifest in that we are not called to build a temple of stone to Him but we are ourselves to be one. " The Holy Ghost does not present Himself for our articulate adoration."

" Thy Deity the saints adore,
Thy offices of mercy bless,
Thy help in utmost need implore,
Thy all-sufficiency confess.
Without Thee wretched poor and blind,
Health, wisdom, joy in Thee they find."

There is still another question raised and that is, *Is it necessary to pray for the Holy Ghost* since He has already come ?

Dr. Murray quotes with approval the words of Bowen who says " The Greek is wonderfully felicitous in that it does not represent the Spirit of God as coming once for all, but as persistently coming. He comes as the rain from heaven, that must still come and come again. We are not to look back for our Pentecost." And it will be remembered how again he says in his Note about the Baptism of the Spirit dealing with the opinion that we may not ask since Pentecost is past, " It would be indeed sad if a believer having once received the Spirit, were to feel that Christ's precious word, ' How much more shall your Heavenly Father give the Holy Spirit to them that ask Him ' was something he had now out-grown, and that this chief of blessings he need now no longer ask." This promise in Luke has been beautifully called *The Dawn of Pentecost*, and in Chapter X, " The full blessing of Pentecost, is shown the Father's infinite willingness to fulfil it.

In his last book—for the others are booklets—*Back to Pentecost*, published after his death, the trumpet gives no uncertain sound, that not only is prayer permissible, *but positively indispensable*. Oh that the Church would listen to his words that seem indeed to speak from Heaven, for it was published after his death, " As essential as the promise of the Father was the prayer of His children ; the one as indispensable as the other. As inconceivably glorious as was the promise, was the glory and the power of the prayer by which the gift was to be brought down. That prayer of the first disciples is an example throughout the ages and a pledge of how much prayer can avail. We have in very deed the office and the right to ask in the name of Christ, and in answer to our prayer the Father will give the Spirit to the souls around us."

Brief as these extracts are from an altogether wonderful yet beautifully simple book, they suffice to show the supreme importance that he to the very last attached to united persistent prayer as the only way to bring back Pentecost to the Church, and he has left this charge to us as Elijah left his mantle to Elisha. " Knowest thou not that the Lord will take away thy master from thy head to-day."

The very last word he spoke on earth was the tender " Good-night my child " as his daughter kissed him on his forehead the night before his translation. But his final message for the Church of Christ was given four days previously. Suddenly being inspired to write down some fresh thoughts stirring his mind he called for pad and pencil, but being unable to write, his devoted daughter who for years had acted as his faithful amanuensis, wrote at his dictation the following pre-eminently solemn sentences.

(1)   Everything in us must be like God.

(2)   Everything can only be like God by partaking of His nature.

(3)   Everything must have the nature of God.

(4)   Nothing can be like God but God Himself.

Oh, that this dying message from the saint of God might be broadcasted from Africa to the Church of God throughout the world. And now that the living voice is hushed in death, it is not too much to anticipate that his printed words will speak to coming generations, and his inspiring writings take their place with the Classics of the Devout Life, which great saints such as Augustine, Guyon, Tauler, Thomas à Kempis, Jeremy Taylor, Rutherford and William Law have left as a lasting heritage to the Church.

It would be a most serious omission in giving an account of his works if in conclusion no reference were made to one of his most important books, *The Key to the Missionary Problem*, which shows the quiet mystic as the fiery enthusiast burning with unquenchable ardour to spread the Gospel to all the tribes of the Earth. Other parts of this book will record his doings as the missionary statesman, it is sufficient here to refer to him as thinker and author urging God's people to undertake without delay the very task for which the Pentecostal Spirit was given.

(3)   *The Purpose of Pentecost.*

When this book was published Bishop Moule wrote, " I commend this volume to the perusal, the thought and the prayers of all ministers of Christ and His flock. Dr. Alexander Maclaren, hoped that this heart-searching book would be widely read and prayerfully pondered, saying, " It is the Key to the Missionary Problem indeed, but it is also the Key to the most of our problems." Dr. Horton considered it the most inspiring and inspired book written in 1901, the true note of a New Century." Dr. F. B. Meyer was enthusiastic in declaring, " Of all the books that I have ever read of the call of our Lord to the evangelisation of the world this appeal by the beloved Andrew Murray must stand in the front rank if not first. I believe (if read) it would lead to one of the greatest revivals of missionary enthusiasm that the world has ever known."

The object in writing the book was to explain why he could not accept the urgent request to speak at the Ecumenical Missionary Conference at New York 1901, and to review its published report which to his mind revealed one great lack, that the real root cause of so little interest in Missions was not noticed, namely lack of spiritual life through the lack of the Pentecostal Power of the Holy Ghost in ministers and Church members.

Commenting on the statement so frequently made at the Conference that *if* the Church were this, *if* the members gave so much, *if* the leaders had done this, with the sad confession, " the Church is not what she ought to be, and is not prepared to do her duty," he says, " *The charge is unutterably solemn and simply awful.* Whatever be the cause here is the solemn fact—a Church purchased by the blood of the Son of God to be His messenger to a dying world, for the greater part failing entirely in understanding or fulfilling its duty. It needs the same Spirit—the Spirit by which God gave His Son for the world—to revive His Church to win the world for His Son."

This is followed by references first to the Moravian Church and the Renewal which came to it after a solemn Covenant had been made to live in love. This was soon succeeded by its Baptism with the Holy Spirit and its consequent dedication to the evangelisation of the heathen. The Church Missionary Society is next referred to and the revival of its missionary zeal through the " Cambridge Seven," and the Keswick Movement, showing as the writer of *After Pentecost What?* has said that, " The spiritualisation of the Church is necessary for the evangelisation of the world." The China Inland Mission is cited to show what God can do with one man like Hudson Taylor who had the " incubus of heathendom " so heavily upon him that he could hardly bear it, and through him with the China Inland Mission, with its spiritual methods and devoted members.

But it is when Andrew Murray comes to his chapter, " The Church of Pentecost and the Holy Spirit " that he speaks out with all the pent-up fiery energy of his life-long conviction that it is the Pentecostal Baptism which the Church of this age must have, as at the first, " To know what Pentecost means, to have its faith and its spirit is the only power to evangelise the world in this generation. The Pentecostal commission can only be carried out by a Pentecostal Church in Pentecostal Power.

" It is vain to think of this generation accomplishing the Pentecostal commission without a return to the Pentecostal state." But how, he enquires, is this to be done, and to get the leaders to take up the watchword, " Back to Pentecost for without this the work cannot be done." He answers the question by saying, " Prayer must be preached as the first and last duty of the Church that hopes to have the power of God seen in its work." And when speaking of the China Inland Mission in the earlier part of the book, he cites Hudson Taylor as saying at the Ecumenical Conference, " To-day the Holy Ghost is as truly available and as mighty in power as He was on the day of Pentecost. But as the whole Church ever since the days before Pentecost put aside every other work and waited for Him for ten days that the power might be manifested. Has there not been a source of failure here? We have given too much attention to methods and to machinery and to resources and too little to the Source of Power—the filling with the Holy Ghost. If we are not filled we are living in disobedience and sin."

As the correlative of this truth—the command to tarry until endued with power. Hudson Taylor spoke on another occasion when preaching before the Missionary Conference in China of the corresponding imperative to preach the Gospel to every creature now, as if he would harmonise these two principles like the centripetal and centrifugal forces in the starry sphere.

" If," he urged, " as an organised conference we were to give ourselves to obey the command of our Lord to the full we should have such an outpouring of the Spirit, such a Pentecost as the world has not seen since the Holy Ghost was outpoured in Jerusalem. God gives His Spirit *not* to those who long for Him, not to those who pray for Him, not to those who desire to be filled always—but He *does* give His Holy Spirit to them that obey Him."

To Hudson Taylor his biographer tells us, " The command ' Preach the Gospel to every creature,' came with all the urgency of a royal mandate that brooks no delay." To Andrew Murray, the Church's disobedience to the King's Commandment is a sin so heinous and appalling that he feels compelled to issue a Call to Prayer and Humiliation (see chapter IX) for prayer alone will not suffice. " We speak of the need of a Pentecostal era : it will have to be preceded by a great putting away and turning from sin. It is the contrite heart that God makes alive. It is to the humble soul He gives more grace."

This preaching of humiliation on account of our lack of obedience to Christ's great command will be no easy thing. " We shall need men," he assures us " who will give themselves, in study and prayer and love, to take in all the terrible meaning of the words we utter so easily— that the Church is disobedient to her Lord's last command. As they yield themselves to the awful truth of thirty millions a year dying in hopeless darkness, BECAUSE GOD'S PEOPLE DO NOT CARE ; of Christ's love seeking in vain to find a channel through them to save the perishing ones, because they refuse to place themselves at His disposal ; of their resting perfectly content with a selfish religion, that hopes for heaven with a Christ whose Cross it refuses to bear upon Earth—these men will begin to feel they are dealing with a power of darkness in God's children which nothing can penetrate or remove but God's Almighty Power.''

In estimating the results of Foreign Missions we are warned to avoid the error of optimism on the one hand and pessimism on the other. The only safe course is to deal with '' Things as they are.''

'' When once,'' to take up again the *Key to the Problem,* '' we are brought face to face with this truth : Millions are perishing to-day without the knowledge of Christ, *and will go on perishing simply because the Church is not doing* the work for which she was redeemed and endowed with the Spirit of Christ, our hearts will immediately cry out in humiliation and shame and make confession of sin. The sin of bloodguiltiness, the sin of disobedience—these sins will become a burden greater than we can bear until we have laid them at our Lord's feet and had them removed by Him.''

If, besides having them removed we are to prevent a recurrence of them it can only be by the Church seeking and finding the indispensable and invincible grace promised by our Lord specially for the work of preaching among the Gentiles the unsearchable riches of Christ. For Dr. Gordon in his inspiring book, *The Holy Spirit in Missions,* proves conclusively, '' That a fresh effusion of the Spirit has invariably prompted to missionary zeal.'' And Dr. Murray insists as the converse to this, '' That no one can expect to have the Holy Ghost unless he is prepared to be used for missions. Missions are the mission of the Holy Ghost.''

How then shall we explain this flagrant delinquency ? Is it because the Church thinks the love of God is not universal or being universal, the world's evangelisation is not possible, and if possible, the Church is not responsible for it ?

Let the chapter entitled, " Every believer a soul-winner " be read to condemn this vain excuse. At the outset the calculation is referred to that by the law of arithmetical progression. If there were only one Christian in the world, and he in a year won a friend to Christ, and each convert won another and so on continually, in thirty-one years the whole world would be won for Christ. The truth underlying this calculation is " that every believer has been saved with the express purpose that he should make the saving of other souls the main, the supreme end of his existence in the world."

The Apostles and first disciples accepted the responsibility commenced the task, and expected to appear at the judgment seat. " So every one of us must give an account of himself to God." " We must all appear before the judgment seat of Christ." It is to be deplored that a section of the Church of Christ misunderstanding in our day as in the past generations the meaning and purpose of Divine grace, have tried to lessen the solemn significance of the Judgment of believers. The Bema truly is not the same as the Great White Throne, with its terrors for the wicked dead. But it is still a *judgment seat* and not the umpire's chair to distribute prizes. Pilate to give judgment sat upon a Bema placed on the Pavement. Julius Ceasar carried about with him his marble Pavement on which to place his judgment seat. " If we believe in the judgment," wrote Andrew Murray, " we shall honour the blood ; and if we believe in the blood we shall fear the judgment."

That he believed in the reality of judgment is evident from the heart-searching words recurring in the last chapter of *Be Perfect*, as follows, " The day of judgment !

What a day that will be! Many have no fear of that day because they trust they have been justified. They imagine that the same grace which justified the ungodly will give them a passage to heaven. This is not what Scripture teaches. The reality of our having obtained forgiveness will be tested by our having bestowed forgiveness on others. Our fitness for entering the Kingdom is by the way in which we have served Jesus in the ministry of love to the sick and the hungry." And let it be added to the sick and hungry heathen who are perishing for lack of that which we possess in abundance.

Possibly this sterner aspect of his teaching, which cannot be overlooked in a full consideration of his writings, may surprise many and anger some, but he confidently asserts it is Scriptural. It is also supported by a great host of illustrious divines, such as Rutherford, Flovel, Owen, Richard Baxter, Jonathan Edwards, Dr. Chalmers and the seraphic Fletcher. And in our own day the foremost missionary advocates such as Dr. Pierson, A. B. Simpson and Hudson Taylor have made their most impressive appeal for missions by referring to our moral responsibility, our present opportunity, and our future accountability to God.

For example Hudson Taylor made his most impressive appeal at the Perth Conference by his use of the verse in Proverbs, *"If thou forbear to deliver."* The incident he told of the Chinese fisherman forbearing delaying to deliver the drowning man until it was too late sent a thrill of indignation through the whole assembly. The application was obvious and terrible, to the sin of the Church in forbearing neglecting to deliver the heathen in China who are drawn to eternal death. " Have we forgotten " he cried with impassioned energy, " that we must all appear before the judgment seat of Christ, that every one may receive the deeds done in the body. Oh, remember, pray for labour for the unevangelised millions of China, or you will sin against your own soul ! "

The effect of those words was so thrilling that the meeting broke up almost in silence under the realisation of coming judgment on the house of God ; like the stillness before the gathering storm. We too should feel the powerful pressure of this motive. " *And so much the more as ye see the day approaching.*" Commenting on these words in *The Holiest of All*, as applicable first to the day of Judgment on Jerusalem, and then to the world at the end, Dr. Murray says, " Christians need to be reminded of the terrible doom hanging over the world and of all the solemn eternal realities connected with our Lord's Coming in their bearing upon our daily life."

A fuller reference by him to the Second Advent can be read in the chapter wholly devoted to it in his booklet, *Waiting on God*. If Andrew Murray does not write much about this Advent truth, what he does say is intensely spiritual and practical. And this also is the aim of that eminent authority on Prophecy, Dr. Gratton Guinness in his noble book, *The Approaching End of the Age*, with its elaborate calculations based on the Divine arithmetic as put into the Scriptures of Truth by that " Wonderful Numberer " referred to in the margin of *Daniel* viii. 13. That those calculations about Christ's Coming have been abundantly verified none can doubt by the startling events of the present years 1917-1923 as seen in the Jewish race and the Ottoman Empire, bring in the end of the Times of the Gentiles. They are only thus briefly referred to here to accentuate the truth *that the end is rapidly approaching and the time is short in which to do our appointed task.*

" That the end of this Christian age—that end so bright with the glow of coming glory to the true Church, so lurid with the fires of approaching judgment to apostate Christendom, so big with blessing to Israel, so full of hope for the nations of the earth—Is close at hand, seems for those who accept the testimony of Scripture beyond all reasonable question."

Holding this conclusion not as a curious speculation, but

as a vital conviction Dr. Guinness asks earnestly how shall we best employ the remaining moments : now the harvest is red with the glow of setting sun. He answers, as Andrew Murray would if he were with us still, " Let us reap while the light lasts. Bring in these golden sheaves. Now or never, *bring them in !* "